This World and
Nearer Ones

Brian W. Aldiss

This World and Nearer Ones

Essays exploring the familiar

The Kent State University Press

For Will and Genevieve
and the exotic evenings
of Fullerton

Library of Congress Cataloging in Publication Data
Aldiss, Brian Wilson, 1925 —
    This world and nearer ones.

    Includes index.
    I. Title.
PR6051.L3T46   1981   824'.914   81-8179
ISBN 0-87338-261-7   AACR2

To complain of the age we live in, to murmur at the present possessors of power, to lament the past, to conceive extravagant hopes of the future, are the common dispositions of the greatest part of mankind.

Edmund Burke, *Thoughts on the Present Discontents*, 1770

Contents

Illustrations

Introduction and Acknowledgements

Did dinosaurs dream? Was there, in those tiny saurian brains, room for night-visions which related obliquely, flickeringly, to the daylight Mesozoic world? Looking at a triceratops skull, where the chamber designed for the brain forms a dungeon in a great Chillon of boney armament, I find it impossible to think that consciousness, however dim, would not have wanted the emergency exit of dreams from such confinement.

And later. Those scampering tarsiers who were our remote ancestors – they must have experienced dreams of such towering paranoid ambition as to wake them twitching in their treetop nests – or whatever sort of nocturnal arrangements tarsiers prefer – only to find themselves unable to cry, or even to know they were unable to cry, 'Today a eucalyptus tree, tomorrow the world!'

Dreams must have preceded thought and intention. They are the argument with reason omitted. The essays in this volume concern themselves with dreams, or applied dreams, or reason; the applied dreams of art and science contain both elements.

In these idle things, dreams, the unity of everything is an underlying assumption. Scientists have always needed artists to broaden their imaginations; artists have needed scientists to sharpen theirs. When William Blake wrote, 'To see a world in a grain of sand ...', he was not referring only to a visionary experience, as is customarily supposed when the lines are quoted; but also to the strictly practical business of looking through the microscopes of Robert Hooke and Antony van Leeuwenhoek.

However important dreams may be, they are far from being our whole story. For the human species, reason must take precedence, for reason is a human monopoly. Animals have reasoning ability; we have reason. Twelve million years ago the great physical world, this world, was different in no important way from the world of today. But the living world was greatly different: there was no reason, no pair of eyes to take a cool look at what was going on over the left shoulder or after the next meal. There were no human beings. Only tarsier dreams.

This prosaic reflection has been acceptable coinage for only two hundred years, if that. The great divide in the history of thought under which we all live, even the least philosophical of us, is brought about by the theory of evolution: that theory heard as a mutter in the seventeenth century, rising to a prolonged murmur in the eighteenth, and finally becoming articulate last century. Evolution has sharpened our ideas of time; the world of living things, previously frozen into immobility like a stop-action movie shot, has burst into action in our understanding, filling us with fresh understandings of change.

Darwin, Wallace, and the many men of vision whose work went towards formulating evolutionary theory − not least Captain Fitzroy of the *Beagle* who remained a lifelong opponent of Darwin's ideas − altered our way of viewing both the world and ourselves. Possibly it is just a coincidence that during the eighteen fifties, when *The Origin of Species* was published, photography was all the rage. In particular, the stereoscope, without which no good Victorian family was complete, was familiarising people with ancient civilisations and the beauties of other countries and times. A new way of seeing was in the air.

Photography combines art and science in an ideal way. It is now so much a part of our lives that we hardly notice its all-pervasive nature. Yet it has not persuaded us to regard art and science as the complex unity I believe they are.

In their modest way, these essays represent my lifelong interest in working in this ambiguous area. They could also be said to trace the path through the last two centuries which can be seen leading us towards a fruitful concept of the present; for our present is just someone else's discarded future. We tread in the ruins of futures as well as of the past.

As for the essays themselves, they are also ruins in their way. They are salvaged from years of work I have done whilst not plying my trade as novelist and short story writer, expended in reviews and articles, mainly trying to educate myself. Everything has been revised or rewritten – or thrown out in disgust.

Although not every essay concerns itself with science fiction, this volume is being published in connection with a science fictional event, the Thirty-Seventh World Science Fiction Convention, Seacon, being held in Brighton, England, during August 1979, at which I am British Guest of Honour (the American Guest of Honour being Fritz Leiber).

Whilst the ordinary novel slumbers, paralysed perhaps by the gibbous awfulness of the twentieth century, sf makes its cislunar excursions. Year by year, its progeny grow. Science fiction now accounts for between ten and twelve percent of fiction sales. Yet it is very little discussed. When reviewed by newspapers and literary journals, it is either 'done' in a special issue, as a mad annual diversion, or else confined to small cemeteries on the fringes of a book page – semi-hallowed ground, the sort of spot where suicides are buried, its titles lying athwart one another like uprooted gravestones.

Other special purgatories are reserved for science fiction authors. They are invited to appear on BBC television with people like Uri Geller, Bruce Bellamy, or Dr Magnus Pyke. They are introduced at literary luncheons with jokes about their not having two heads or green skins (less of that lately, thank goodness). They have to endure conversations with people who assume automatically that they believe, as do their interrogators, in Flying Saucers and telepathy and Atlantis and the Bermuda Triangle and God as Cosmonaut and acupuncture and macrobiotic foods and pyramids that sharpen razor blades. They are scrutinised closely by their neighbours for traces of android-like behaviour.

At festivals of literature, they are regarded askance by chairmen of panels, who may make jocular interjections if they chance to refer to either E.E.Smith on the one hand or Dr Johnson on the other. More orthodox writers present suspect them of earning far more money than they do, or far less. (Both are true, by the way.)

All this may suggest that I have reasons to dislike being labelled an sf author. I have my reasons; but I do not dislike being an sf author. On the contrary. Although my first loyalty is to literature, I owe a great deal to a field to which I have been able to contribute something.

I am regarded as a difficult author, because I write non-fiction as well as fiction, ordinary fiction as well as science fiction, and occasionally what is considered a difficult book; but in my experience the readership of sf, on its more informed level, is remarkably patient, and will always endeavour to comprehend what they at first find incomprehensible.

Let me name two additional advantages in being a writer of science fiction, apart from becoming pampered Guest of Honour at a Convention, since they are germane to these essays.

Firstly, over the last twenty years, the span of my writing career, science fiction has developed remarkably all round the world, the toothed peak of its progress rising like a population graph. Playing a role in that process has been tremendously rewarding.

Despite all the expansion, readers and writers have managed to remain closely in communication, as this Convention indicates. This may be in part because of the indifference of people beyond the field, and the condemnation of critics armed only with the antique weaponry of standard lit. crit.; but it more probably springs from an inner mystery – the attempted complex unity of art and science – in sf itself. Because of that mystery, which every writer tries to interpret in an individual way, and because of the indifference from outside, we have been forced to form our own body of criticism, our own canons of taste; we have established our own editors, reviewers, scholars, booksellers and publishers, in a remarkable burst of creativity for which I can think of no parallel. We have done it all ourselves and given the world a new literature, whether the world wants it or not.

Secondly, that close community of interest, that fascination with the mystery, is global, and not confined to Western Europe or the United States. Largely thanks to friendly connections overseas, I have been able to travel about the world a good deal in the last decade, as some of the contents indicate, and have wandered as far afield as Iceland, Scandinavia, the Soviet Union, Japan, Brazil, Sicily, Mexico, Australia, Sumatra, and now Brighton. (Some of the trips were made by good old private enterprise, such as the Mexico and Sumatran ventures, but I should perhaps add that the Soviet visit was laid on by the Arts Council of Great Britain and the GB/USSR Association, to whom I wish to express my thanks.) Even the most casual traveller abroad must notice the way in which the whole world is caught up in a scramble of change.

In England at least, reviewing is very much part of a writing career, a valuable part; low pay and the general education give one a feel for the somewhat marginal job of authorship. As well as reviewing for the *Oxford Mail*, for which I worked for many years, I have written articles for a spectrum of journals, among them the *Times Literary Supplement*, *Nature*, *Punch*, *Penthouse*, and the *Guardian*. To the latter, I contributed an irregular series on art, which I wish I had found time to continue. I have reviewed films for this paper and that, and for the BBC. I have read for publishers and for the Arts Council. I have contributed to countless fanzines. Millions of words, wind into the wind.

From all that material, I could have bundled together enough wordage to fill several volumes. But a book is a book is a book, and rarely a collection of old journalism. I have tried to reshape everything in order to make a new book. Only in the section entitled 'Rough Justices', where I appear primarily as reviewer, is the material almost as originally published.

'Ever Since the Enlightenment' is based on a speech given in Canberra, thanks to Colin Steele. The James Blish article is a development of an interview I made with Blish; earlier stages of the article appeared in *Foundation* and a critical volume for Queensland University Press edited by Kirpal Singh and Michael Tolley (to both of which gentlemen my thanks for aid beyond the scope of literature). 'Dick's Maledictory Web' appeared first in *Science Fiction Studies* and then as an introduction to an edition of Dick's *Martian Time-Slip*. 'Why They Left Zirn Unguarded' is based on a review which appeared in *Vector*. The Nesvadba article appeared as an introduction to an edition of Nesvadba's *In the Footsteps of the Abominable Snowman*. The Vonnegut article is based on one which appeared in Andrew Mylett's *Summary*. The 'Barefoot' article is based on an introduction for a Swedish translation of *Barefoot in the Head* which, despite gallant efforts by John Henri Holmberg and Sam Lundwall, never got published. 'The Gulf and the Forest' is based on an article with the same title which appeared in the *Magazine of Fantasy and Science Fiction*.

'Looking Forward to 2001' is based on a speech delivered to the Oxford Union, with apologies to Arthur C.Clarke.

'The Hiroshima Man' is an extended version of a review which appeared in Michael Moorcock's *New Worlds*. 'The Hashish Club' appeared as an introduction to a book of the same name, published by Peter Owen. '1951' appeared in slightly different form in Mary Banham and Bevis Hillier's *A Tonic to the Nation*.

'The Sower of the Systems' is based on a review of a Watts exhibition published in the *Guardian*. 'The Fireby-Wireby Book' appeared in a fanzine, *Cidereal Times*. 'The Film Tarkovsky Made' was first published in *Foundation*. 'Kissingers Have Long Ears' is based on an article written for *Art and Story*. 'Spielberg' began life as a lecture delivered at the ICA.

'Sleazo Inputs I Have Known' was published in *Foundation*. 'It Catechised from Outer Space' was published in *New Review*. 'The Flight into Tomorrow' appeared as an introduction to an edition of Harness's *The Paradox Men*. The Burroughs article appeared in *Punch*. 'Yes, well, but ...' appeared in *Science Fiction Studies*. 'The Universe as Coal-Scuttle' was developed from two reviews which appeared in the *New Statesman*.

'California' is based on an article in the *Guardian*. 'Modest Atmosphere' was broadcast in the BBC Third Programme, with George Macbeth and me playing all twelve voices, and later appeared in *Encounter*. Passages from 'Cultural Totems' appeared in *New Review*.

Two awards for criticism have been bestowed upon me. I am first holder of the James Blish Award for Excellence in Science Fiction Criticism (1977), presented for services to sf, with particular reference to my book *Science Fiction Art* (a revised version of the text of which is included here), and the introduction to Philip K.Dick's *Martian Time-Slip* (which is included here). In 1978, the SFRA presented me with a Pilgrim Award in recognition of distinguished contributions to the study of science fiction, with particular reference to *Billion Year Spree*, and my anthologies.

To both these bodies, the British and the American, I offer my thanks for such encouragement. Come, gentlemen, what more fascinating subject for study is there?

Oxford   Brian W. Aldiss
December 1978

Writing

Ever Since the Enlightenment

There is no finality in the current state of the world. The present power blocs within which we pass our lives in this posture or that will be gone in two hundred years as surely as the Holy Roman Empire or Byzantium.

Europe's security was threatened by Islam in the sixteenth and seventeenth centuries. The removal of that threat in the late seventeenth and early eighteenth centuries paved the way for a comparatively halcyon period for Europe (already prospering from its scientific discoveries and its ventures in the New World or round the globe) which we call the Enlightenment and the Age of Reason.

The Ottoman Empire was once as mighty as China. In July 1683, Ottoman armies stood at the gates of Vienna, and Christendom itself was besieged. After sustained fighting, the Turks retreated, leaving behind colossal hordes of treasure, as well as piles of coffee which, disseminated through coffee houses, helped to make Europe a more civilised place. From this battle dates the rise to power of the Habsburg Empire.

A distinguished part in the battle for Vienna was taken by Prince Eugène of Savoy, a great general who was later to play a larger and more decisive role in the fight for the integrity of Europe.

If you sail down the Danube from Vienna, you come eventually to a place where the river flows round a dramatic outcrop of rock. Standing on top of this rock is a great fortress with green roofs. You can enter the fortress nowadays and eat an excellent meal in its chambers. This is Petrovaradin; before the country became Jugoslavia, these lands belonged to Austria, and the fortress was Peterwardein, but *wienerschnitzel* has given way to *razniči* and *hajdučki čevap*. Here, in 1716, Eugéne and his army defeated a great Turkish force, killing six thousand of them. The spoils were enormous, and enriched the European imagination as well as the pockets of Eugène's men. Eugène himself retained the Grand Vizier's tent, which was sumptuously decorated in gold and contained many apartments; it was so large that five hundred men were required to pitch it.

Sail a little farther down the Danube. Where it meets its tributary, the Sava, Belgrade stands, set in a great curve of the river, now a modern capital, once an Ottoman fortress. There, almost exactly a year after his victory at Peterwardein, Eugène of Savoy inflicted another defeat on the Ottoman Power.

There is never security without arms. Following the Turkish defeat, Belgrade itself, Hungary, sections of Bosnia and Serbia became part of the Habsburg domains, and the menace to western Europe was dispersed. Over the mounds of corpses and coffee, the way for the enormous progress of the eighteenth century was open – though of course the European states still squabbled amongst themselves.

The Enlightenment and the Age of Reason sought for balance, the kind of balance enshrined in the great houses of the period, with East wing balanced against West, in the rapid advance of justice and civil order, in the antitheses of Johnsonian prose, as well as in the paradoxes and heroic couplets of Pope's poetry. Humanism progressed, science progressed, all arts elaborated themselves – not least in music, where the pale counterpoint of Domenico Scarlatti was transformed into the complex statements of Haydn, Mozart and Beethoven. And the industrial revolution gathered in a tide which still floods round the remotest shores of the world.

There now appears something slightly one-dimensional about the world of the Enlightenment, so greatly has social modification worked since then. In its peaceableness, its reasonableness, the Enlightenment lacks our painful perspectives on human nature. We can no more resurrect its values than read the poems of Ossian. Captain Cook was allowed to sail where he would in time of war, unmolested by his enemies, who recognised the value of his scientific research. G.B.Tiepolo painted the Queen of the Nile in High Renaissance costume, being concerned not with anachronism but with what looked best. In the eighteenth century you dressed up for science, as you did to have your portrait painted.

It is less with Tiepolo than Cook that we are concerned, although art and scientific discovery are closely linked during this period.

Tiepolo, luminary of a maritime republic, like Turkey in eclipse, died at virtually the same time as Cook was setting up his observatory in Tahiti to observe the transit of Venus. The old painter's day was done, his style superceded by the classicism of Mengs. James Cook also represented a new style. His painters, under Sir Joshua Banks, had no truck with queens or goddesses; they were trained to scientific observation. Cook himself was an excellent cartographer, and carried on his voyages new-style theodolites and accurate chronometers to chart his way.

Nor was it only in instrumentation, in the gadgetry, that things were changing. Other mariners, such as Samuel Wallis, had sailed the Pacific before Cook, and sought the mysterious Southern Continent; but they had been too ill on reaching those far waters to carry out their proper duties. Scurvy and dysentery claimed their crews. Cook observed proper diet, proper hygiene, and his crews stayed fit.

The South Seas acted as counterbalance to what enlightened Europeans experienced as the smallness of Christendom. Eighteenth-century security bred boredom. A new world was needed. In fact, what was eventually discovered was unsought: new dimensions of time, evolution, Romanticism and the complex of ideas which dominate our own times, whether we realise it or not.

We have a sense of the future very clear in our age, but all ages have their infancies in previous ones. Romanticism, evolutionary theories, speculations on time, were none of them new to the nineteenth or even the eighteenth century. While the bells of Rome and every other European capital were ringing for the relief of Vienna and the defeat of the Turks, Thomas Burnet in Cambridge was translating into English his *Telluris Theoria Sacra*; it was published in 1684 as *The Sacred Theory of the Earth*. In a sonorous style which imitates Sir Thomas Browne, Burnet reveals his cosmological theory, which states that, before Creation, Earth was perfectly smooth like an egg until such time as it hatched and released a universal Flood. Burnet remarks, in a striking phrase, that we 'have still the broken materials of that first world, and walk upon its ruins'.

Despite his egg theory, Burnet was no fool, and believed that since we had been endowed with Reason, we should exercise it to discover and understand the world in which we found ourselves. This is the doctrine of the Age of Reason.

Burnet continues, 'The greatest objects in Nature are, methinks, the most pleasing to behold ... Whatsoever hath but the shadow and appearance of INFINITE, as all things have that are too big for our comprehension, they fill and overbear the mind with their Excess, and cast it into a pleasing kind of stupor and admiration.' Perfect Romantic doctrine, looking forward to Burke – and back to Lord Bacon: 'There is no excellent beauty that hath not some strangeness in the proportion.'

The great philosophers of the time, Berkeley in particular, were more effectively working changes in perception. But new philosophies filter only slowly through the general populace; it was the voyages of men like Cook in undiscovered places which immediately caught the public imagination.

The motives behind the exploration of those distant regions were mixed, as man's motives generally are, as the motives for the Apollo flights to the Moon in the sixties were. Unlike the discovery and opening up of the North American continent, the story of the South Seas must remind us of our own generation's experience of space travel – not least in a remark Cook makes in one of his letters; in his reference to his 'ambition not only to go farther than any man had ever been before, but as far as it was possible for man to go', even the phraseology forges an unsought parallel between the *Endeavour* and the starship *Enterprise*.

To an eighteenth-century man, that distant part of the globe was the equivalent of a new planet, a watery planet like Perelandra. In some respects very like Perelandra; for, as in C.S.Lewis's novel the inhabitants of Venus act out a religious drama, an allegory, so the inhabitants of the South Pacific served to act out some of the preoccupations of eighteenth-century man. Were they models of what the Ancient Greeks had been, enlightened people in a state of grace with nature; were they corrupt savages in need of a missionary; or were they sinless, Adams and Eves before the Fall, inhabitants of multitudinous Edens?

More than one construction can generally be made from one set of facts. Just as sf writers become accustomed to hearing from uninformed reviewers that they are 'new Wellses' or 'latter-day Vernes', so Europeans, striving to focus on the essential qualities of newly discovered races, claimed that they were 'what the ancient Britons were before civilisation', while the Australian aborigines were compared with Gaelic bards. Not analogies only but morals were to be drawn. As William Cowper put it, in the first book of his poem, *The Task*:

> E'en the favoured isles,
> So lately found, although the constant sun
> Cheer all their seasons with a grateful smile,
> Can boast but little virtue; and, inert
> Through plenty, lose in morals what they gain
> In manners – victims of luxurious ease.

It is a Protestant viewpoint not entirely dead today.

From the discoveries, from the debates, new sciences sprang. 'Geography is a science of fact,' said Bougainville, knowing he challenged an older and contradictory point of view. The depressing story of Tasmania – its history of the slaughter of the indigenous population boding ill for the inhabitants of any possible future planet any possible future space-travellers might come across – is lightened only by the French expedition there in 1802, when François Péron made the first anthropological record. Péron established amiable relations with the Tasmanians, and brought back to Europe 100,000 animal specimens, of which 2500 were of unknown species. Numerous meetings with the inhabitants were faithfully recorded.

All such findings were closely linked to the continuing search for the nature of man. Péron himself, addressing the French authorities, declared, 'No doubt it is wonderful to gather the inert moss which grows on the eternal ice of the Poles, or to pursue into the burning heart of the Sahara those hideous reptiles which Nature seems to have exiled in order to protect us from their fury; but – let us have the courage to say it – would it be less wonderful, less useful to society, to send with the naturalists on this mission some young doctors specially trained in the study of man himself, to record everything of interest in both moral and physical matters which diverse peoples may have to reveal – their habitat, their traditions, their customs, their maladies both internal and external, and the cures which they use?'

The study of man himself. It was a sensible and enlightened goal. Yet, only a year after the French expedition to Tasmania, the British established a penal colony there. The wretched Tasmanians were then hunted to death, suffering alike at the hands of criminals and philanthropists. All became extinct within thirty years. The unfittest had not survived. Neither the most enlightened statesmen, nor all the rococo in all the churches in Europe could stem a general extermination.

Ideas or ideologies always arise which cushion us from clear perceptions of our own cruelty; the Victorians took refuge in a popular view of Darwinism, garbled in a loose phrase, 'the survival of the fittest'; the Nazis believed they were ridding the German race of impurity by massacring six million Jews; Stalinists justified the Great Purge by their sterile belief in the entrails of Marx and Lenin; and the West turned a blind eye to the killing of perhaps a million Chinese in Indonesia in 1965 and 1966 because the victims were labelled Communist.

Despite the slaughters, the findings brought back by British and French three-masters stimulated a debate on the nature of man and his place in the universe which still continues. The slow, creaking three-masters have been replaced by speedy surrealist kitchen utensils cutting up the sky. The findings of Mariner spacecraft, with their startling crop of pictures, the harvest from Pioneers, Vikings and Voyagers, give impetus to the quest for extraterrestrial life. But our modern findings are undoubtedly less corporeal: eighteenth-century sailors copulated on warm sands with the dusky ladies of the South Seas in exchange for nails. The rewards of technology were never better or more immediately demonstrated.

The more efficiently the early engines could be seen to work, the faster they multiplied. The faster they multiplied, the more dominant they became. It was like a re-run of the story of pre-historic reptiles. Samuel Butler observed this phenomenon clearly and, in *Erewhon* (1872), gives one of his scribes this ominous sentence: 'The present machines are to the future as the early Saurians are to man.' The argument goes on, 'I would repeat that I fear none of the existing machines; what I fear is the extraordinary rapidity with which they are becoming something very different to what they are at present.'

Butler's fear was not a particularly common one, judging by the success of technology. When Cook was killed in 1779, Britain was rapidly becoming covered with a network of canals – the first modern transport system, the biggest thing since Roman roads. Soon no major city lay farther than fifteen miles from a busy water link. In another generation, the new roads had arrived; 1600 Road Acts went through Parliament between 1751 and 1790. On new roads, new light coaches – a new thing; all classes could afford to travel. And in a further generation, at the moment when coaching had reached its zenith of speed and organisation, in came the men from the North with their railways, and swept into darkness with a vast exhalation of coal smoke, the slow moving past.

When the painter J.M.W.Turner, born as the American War of Independence began, died in 1851, the Western world had undergone one of its greatest periods of transition – and was undergoing another.

New landscapes required new perceptions. The interpretation by trained artists of those exotic panoramas first sighted over the taffrail of the *Endeavour* or the *Bounty* led to the overthrow of a classical generalised style of art in favour of the art of the closely studied and the particular. This is what Ruskin means when he says in *Modern Painters*, apropos of Turner, that, 'For the better comfort of the non-imaginative painter, be it observed, that it is not possible to find a landscape, which if painted precisely as it is, will not make an impressive picture.' So Zoffany and Reynolds give place to Constable and Ward, and early Turner to late.

The earthworks thrown up all over England to accommodate the railway line left their mark in the minds of men. When

Brunel built his Great Western Railway from Paddington to Bristol, the comparative feebleness of his steam-power meant that the track had to run level to within 1/12,000th of an inch for the whole hundred-mile journey. One can see Brunel's cuttings still, guarding the line up the Thames valley to Oxford. There lie the chalk strata, put down millions of years ago by minute creatures, brought back to the grimy light of day a century ago by sturdy Victorian navvies.

A cardinal perception dawned: that the rocks of old Earth, or the coral islands of the new oceans, were petrified Time. It was almost but not quite what Burnet meant when he said: 'We have still the broken materials of that first world, and walk upon its ruins.' Embalmed in gritty streets lay secrets of past history just as urgent as a journey from Birmingham to Liverpool. Understanding lent a window on epochs long past and on times to come.

Geology was in many ways the giant, the Prometheus, of nineteenth-century science, bursting open the other doors of the cultural gallery. It is a curious linkage of the physical and the metaphysical to think of the poor stonemason, Hugh Miller, chopping away in the dust of the red sandstones of Scotland, and thereby helping to sketch that teeming pageant of organic life we now accept without blinking: that pageant which belongs with amino acids in a nameless ocean, and the first single-celled creatures, and which swells in grandeur and colour and possibly hideousness through the ages of amphibians and rampant trees and great dinosaurs that walked like men, on to the dodo and to Us, going about our archaic rituals. That pageant is among the most permanent to emerge from the permanent ways of the Railway Age.

Almost all that we can learn or imagine is inherited, the produce of the labours of others. So it always was. Aided by the work of Miller, and of Lyell and James Hutton and Wallace and others, Charles Darwin pieced together the jigsaw of facts which form evolutionary theory. Darwin's researches took him many years; they began when Captain Fitzroy, a godfearing sailor, had the misfortune to take Darwin aboard the *Beagle*.

The voyage of the *Beagle* was almost as momentous as that of the *Endeavour*; its findings concluded part of the debate opened up by Cook. No longer 'in doubt to deem himself a God or Beast', man now saw himself ranged with the animals rather than the angels. Theology was never to be as popular again; but zoology won many adherents.

The early geologists learnt to distinguish between rocks of a sedimentary character and rocks formed by what Darwin calls plutonian processes. One wonders how far this dramatic inorganic model of rock-formation influenced that other great iconoclast of last century's thought, Sigmund Freud, when formulating his theories of conscious and unconscious, from which latter well up the raw lavas of the personality's core.

Whilst new cosmologies were discovered in the heavens – the first star photographs were taken in the 1850s – the earth yielded immense troves of dinosaur bones, notably in North America, like strange stations on the route of the railroad. Students of both Earth and sky helped roll back the carpet of the globe's prehistory. The consequent development of scientific understanding, which takes in first one discipline and then another, creating channels of fresh thought like a flood inundating a parched land, has structured our mental frontiers; we abandon its watchtowers for superstitious faiths at our peril. Yet ours is an age easily tempted towards the mysticism of drugs and the bending of spoons by telepathy – not least because last century's advances opened the doors of lunatic asylums as the complex nature of human mentality was unlocked, leaving us heir to a lessened fear of madness.

Whichever way we go, we see strange panoramas. As far as we can know, our vision is unique in the universe. And mankind is at present only at the beginning of its corporate lifetime.

Decade by decade, more time was needed in which to contain scientific findings related to the age of the Earth, and to cosmology. The good Bishop Ussher's estimate that God created the world one morning in 4004 BC was laughable by Lyell's time – the iguanodon upset that tea party. Just as men looked back to a truer perspective, other findings encouraged them to look forward. That was a new thing, too.

Not all that was new was of a sort to induce optimism. Though evolution could be made to stand as a justification for

ruthless economic oppression or empire-building, it does not, on a proper evaluation, encourage any permanent feeling of security. The same might be said of Lord Kelvin's reformulation of the second Law of Thermodynamics, which carried with it intimations of the heat death of the universe. Utilitarianism was a bleak enough creed for men; how much worse to find it written in the stars themselves.

As for a work designed to counterbalance the optimism of the Enlightenment, Malthus's influential *Essay on Population*, its message that poverty and starvation, and more poverty and starvation, was mankind's lot, added little to the gaiety of nations. Fortunately, in the New World, the wide prairies of the Mid-West seemed to give the lie to Malthus; in many ways, the United States could escape from the gloomy prognostications of Europe.

In Europe, the century culminated in a general pessimism (brought on, it must be added, by a series of dire events, revolutions and wars, as much as by depressing books). Great inventions, too, brought inventive whispers of mortality. I mentioned photography in my introduction. Photography brings us news of distant places; it sometimes appears, through the medium of the cinema screen, to bring us light itself, clothed in images of majestic beauty. Yet its primary use – at least among ordinary people – is to record ourselves and our families, and thus to expose as never before the ageing process, the heat death of the individual, to the very generations who have lost belief in the consolations of the Hereafter.

Photography is comfortless (Susan Sontag has recently made perceptive remarks on this score). It gives a twist to the Enlightenment philosopher Berkeley's new theory of vision. 'The objects of sense exist only when they are perceived,' said Berkeley. Now we have become so enslaved by our cameras that we hardly exist unless we have been perceived by the lens; I have known functions to be called off because the television cameras were not coming – therefore the event was not important enough, even in the eyes of its participants, and ceased to exist.

In the nineteenth century, as now, the sketchy frameworks of possibility expanded at exhilarating speed. Yet the new light fell only on the old darkness of the human condition. The physical laws of the universe were disclosed as conveying less warmth than a kindly Providence.

In the autocratic societies of Enlightenment Europe, it mattered not what the common people thought. They had their own hand-down folk culture; new things were for the learned, the élite, whose opinions both had influence and could be influenced. After the American and French revolutions, that situation changed. Nineteenth-century Europe seethed with populist movements. In democratic societies, the people have influence, and so must be influenced. It was necessary to disseminate the grand gloomy ideas which had originated through science (science itself had suddenly become democratic, not to mention riddled with socialists). The people must learn to rule as well as being ruled.

Means of dissemination of ideas were provided by technological developments. All things conspired to the swifter propagation of information, from mechanical inventions such as the development of the rotary press, to repeals of newspaper tax and the abolition of excise duty on paper, to the establishment of municipal libraries and public museums. The Victorian Age spawned penny encyclopaedias and many factual publications, whilst nourishing the growth of the novel which – in England at least – had appeared defunct in the decade when Queen Victoria came to the throne.

Grand gloomy ideas do not necessarily make headway in a period of euphoric advancement such as the early Victorians enjoyed. 'We are on the side of Progress,' said Macaulay. The novelists, chasing other goals than philosophy, established the novel as a great social force and as a social form. The forte of the novel was the portrayal of character striving with character within society. Balzac or Zola, Mrs Gaskell or Trollope, Dostoevsky or Turgenev, this was the novelist's territory. And this, by the way, was the territory on which the newly arrived literary critics based their activities.

Complacency is always on the side of Progress. William Morris, near the end of the century, talks of 'the Whig frame of mind, natural to the modern prosperous middle-class men, who, in fact, so far as mechanical progress is concerned, have nothing to ask for'. The first novelists to attempt evolutionary themes and essay the grand gloomy ideas were three autodidacts, Samuel Butler, Thomas Hardy and H.G.Wells.

To call Butler an autodidact is to exaggerate. He was of the prosperous middle class, his father being a canon of Lincoln, and he was educated at Shrewsbury and Cambridge. But he repudiated his father's religion and influence, becoming virtually a different man by leaving home for New Zealand, where he farmed sheep. In New Zealand, he began his literary career, the fruits of which are noted for their anti-Christian and unorthodox flavour – foremost among them being *Erewhon* (1872).

One can see that *Erewhon* is not science fiction; one can also see how in many ways it resembles science fiction. An imaginary journey, the crossing of some mysterious barrier (in this case mountains), and the discovery of another society with attendant marvels – these are the common stock alike of the medieval romance and of modern science fiction. *Erewhon* also has negative attributes which distance it from the ordinary novel. The central figure is solitary, a corollary of which is that there is no great emotional depth in the story; and human psychology is not a strong element of the design, which focuses instead on what is new, unknown. What is new and unknown is embodied in a series of brilliant ideas, brilliantly handled in a satirical way which reminds us somewhat of Peacock or, to look forward, Aldous Huxley. These ideas stem in the main from Darwinism, a subject to which Butler devoted several books.

Thomas Hardy attended Darwin's funeral. His sombre imagination was fired by the misty stretches of landscape revealed by evolutionary thought.

We do not read Hardy for his ideas, thought they are present – the ideas of a dreamer more than an intellectual; we may read him as the novelist of countryside now largely vanished, though Hardy could scarcely distinguish one flower from another. In fact, what is most compelling in the Wessex novels is the struggle at all levels between traditional and disruptive new ways of thought. More directly, an evolutionary emphasis is present from the early novels to – and climaxing in – *The Dynasts* (1903), Hardy's great para-historical drama with an evolving Immanent Will.

The case of H.G.Wells, who was taught by Darwin's friend

and ally, Thomas Huxley, is too familiar to need examination
here. Like Hardy, Wells got his education where he could, and
taught himself by teaching. His brilliant entry into the literary
field marks the congruence of two grand gloomy ideas, evolution
crossed by the Second Law of Thermodynamics: *The Time
Machine* (1895). *The Time Machine* is distinctively science
fiction in the way that *The Dynasts* distinctively is not. Indeed, it
is science fiction in a way that much later science fiction is not –
not only does it contain new ideas, but it combines them in a
new way. Small wonder that it has been the exemplar of much
that followed.

   The Island of Dr Moreau, published the year after *The Time
Machine*, shows Wells again worrying the bone of evolution.
Wells himself pointed to its similarities with Mary Shelley's
Frankenstein. And he says, 'I have never been able to get away
from life in the mass and life in general as distinguished from life
in the individual experience, in any book I have ever written.'
This viewpoint of Man as Statistic, typical of many an sf writer,
is encouraged by Malthusian thought. Wells and Hardy and
Butler, being outside the swim of middle-class society, had little
to lose by a new approach; it came naturally to them to express
what was not received wisdom, and to propagate the unpopular.
With the unpopular, Wells caught the popular ear.

   These distinguished English writers were preceded by considerable writers from across the Channel. France was the first
country of the Enlightenment; in Paris in 1771 was published a
book which is in every way a product of its age – except that it is
recognisably kin to science fiction.

   While Cook was busy discovering Botany Bay, Boston was
holding its Tea Party, and the first iron bridge was being built,
Sebastien Mercier published his predictive work, *L'An Deux
Mille Quatre Cent Quarante*. Mercier visualised a time, seven
centuries ahead, when society had improved and perfected itself.
The actual and the metaphorical Bastilles have vanished. This
futuristic utopian fiction was translated and published in other
European countries and eventually in the newly independent
America.

   How was it that the English by contrast took, even then, a
much less sanguine view of the future? I cannot resist contrast-

ing Mercier's dream of the future as a place of fountains and fine buildings with the typically British preoccupation with disaster. Take for instance, an anonymous squib by one 'Antonius' published in *Lloyd's Evening Post* for 25-28 November, 1771 (and never noticed again until now). It looks two centuries ahead to a ruinous Britain overcome by an American Empire.

Two Americans are guided round London by a poor Briton. The latter provides a running commentary as follows:

'Yonder is a field of turnips, there stood the Palace of Whitehall; as to St James's there are no traces of that left, it stood somewhere near that pond. Here stood that venerable pile of antiquity, Westminster Abbey, which was founded in the year 796; at the west end was the famous Chapel of Henry the Seventh, in which were interred most of our English Kings. That on the right is the remains of Queen Elizabeth's tomb; that on the left, those of King William the Third; all the rest are swept away by time.

'The whole church had been ornamented with monuments of Admirals, Generals, Poets, Philosophers, and others, two of which only we found legible, that of Locke and Newton, some being quite defaced, and others we could not come at on account of the ruins fallen in upon them. – What a melancholy sight, we exclaimed, that this venerable dome, dedicated to God, should be now converted into a stable!'

And so on. South Sea House is a mere jakes, its infamy well known. India House was destroyed one hundred and sixty years earlier, 'for the blood they shed in India called for vengeance, and they were expelled the Country'.

Why this dark vision? Only a generation after Antonius, a girl of eighteen was writing the melancholy and perverse *Frankenstein* – an English girl of eighteen. Perhaps our national lack of hope has preserved the country from some of the excesses inflicted on the rest of the world in the last two centuries.

In the erudite and naive patchwork of creations we call science fiction, there is no other figure like Jules Verne; even his fellow-countrymen have not come to terms with him. Beyond

pointing out that his immense *Voyages Extraordinaires* stands
like an Enlightenment fortress which slowly crumbles into the
darkness of the twentieth century, I prefer to mention two of his
honourable predecessors who also precede H.G.Wells.

Restif de la Bretonne's *La Decouverte Australe par un
Homme-Volant*, was published in 1781. It is a major speculative
work describing flying machines, airborne fleets, and a civilisation in the wilds of Australia (something no living Australian
would dare postulate). In a later work, *Les Posthumes* (1802),
Bretonne describes other planets and extra-terrestrial beings.

But in 1854, in Paris, a much more intensely science-fictional
work was published: more science-fictional because it uses for
its structure those grand gloomy ideas I have already mentioned.
Charles Ischir Defontenay's novel *Star ou Psi de Cassio-
pée* combines symbolism and science fiction; the result is rather
like a painting by Gustave Moreau. *Star* is a sophisticated
story concerning a remote solar system of which Star, oddly
enough, is not the sun but the planet, the sole planetary body
of a system containing three suns and some satellites.

The humanoid races living on Star exhibit the features of
various conflicting evolutionary theories. The Savelces result
from miscegenation between a god and a small worm; the
Ponarbates derive from animal species which occasionally give
birth to superior types; the Nemsedes are the fruit of a kind of
spontaneous generation 'born from the sour lime of the soil
heated by electric air', and so on. One of Defontenay's tribes is
hermaphrodite, anticipating similiar themes by Theodore Sturgeon and Ursula Le Guin by a century or more.

Defontenay's tone might be described as religious but cheerful, which possibly explains why his remarkable book was
forgotten for so long.

By the end of the nineteenth century, pessimism was coming
back into fashion. *The Oxford English Dictionary* lists as one of
the meanings of the word Future, 'A condition in times to come
different (esp. in a favourable sense) from the present.' Significantly, the usage quoted comes from 1852. The optimism of
that favourable sense of the word had evaporated forty years
later, when Wells's first novels appeared. But gone forever was
the eighteenth-century attitude expressed by Pope, 'Oh,

blindness to the future, Kindly given.' Nineteenth-century findings rendered it both necessary and possible to speculate on the future; knowing the worst was a new tool in the intellectual armoury.

It may be that part of the stigma still attaching to science fiction lay originally in the fact that the men who helped create it as a form of expression were themselves outsiders, or regarded themselves as outsiders; examination of, say, one hundred typical texts would probably reinforce the theme of isolation (prominent for instance in *Frankenstein*). Even in over-population novels, which proliferated in the sixties of this century, the solitary individual occurs, almost in defiance of his context.

Isolation is manifestly one of the problems liable to crop up on a newly discovered planet, where you can find yourself alone except for a computer, a captain who has got religion, and the ship's cat. It was particularly to the concept of new planets that American sf writers turned when they entered the science fiction lists with the launching of the pulp magazines. This phenomenon is generally explained as the Quest for the Last Frontier. It is less glib to consider imaginary planets as evidence of the fear and attraction of isolation.

Just as Hollywood on the West Coast of the USA was largely run by émigrés – Hungarians and the like – so was the pulp industry, peddling dreams and traumas on the East Coast. The émigrés came from the over-populated cities of Europe to another over-populated American city. Many sf writers, editors, and publishers were strangers in a strange land, autodidacts like Hardy and Wells. Isaac Asimov is a case in point. Born in a suburb of Smolensk in Russia, he was brought over to the United States at the age of three. His family settled in Brooklyn; his father ran a candy store. By the age of nine, Asimov Jnr was reading sf and educating himself by it; since when, with great single-mindedness, he has been trying to educate the rest of us. There can be few sciences which have not escaped his net. (The abrupt uprooting in early childhood sets him in a class with Mary Shelley, Nerval, Wells, Stapledon, Ballard, Aldiss, and many others).

Although we can point to the new science-fictional planets as logical extensions of such fictitious lands as Laputa and Butler's *Erewhon*, we should bear in mind scientific considerations as well as literary ones. True, as the terrestrial globe shrinks, it is increasingly difficult to convince readers of the probability of finding even a satirical utopia in some undiscovered nook. Arthur Conan Doyle's siting of the *Lost World* in the Amazon was plausible in 1912 (Professor Challenger's 'journey to verify some conclusions of Wallace and Bates,' and his discovery of scientifically accurate and astonishing water-colours, designedly remind us of Cook's and Darwin's expeditions to undiscovered regions). After World War I, the increasing range of flying machines made similar caches of evolutionary anachronisms less and less likely. Science, a creative part of man's mind, banishes literature, another creative part. One could chart the banishment of Doyle's dinosaurs down the scale of fiction, down the scale of likelihood, to the boys' magazines of the thirties, to the comics of the forties and fifties, to the Hanna Barbera cartoons of the sixties, and from the Matto Grosso to inside Everest, and from Atlantis back to – for in the most desperate fantasies credulity is neither here nor there – South America.

As the imagination needed new planets for its proper exercise, the new tools of theoretical science could supply them. This is revealed in the chief literary use to which new planets were put in early science fiction. Satire and utopianism, favourite ploys of the eighteenth century or earlier, were no more. The new planets did not form stages on which man could enact his social problems; instead, they were themselves the centre of the action, working models of scientific thought.

For to imagine out the full implications of evolution, geology, Malthusianism, and the famous Second Law, one needs to construct either a time machine, as Wells did, or a planet that represents Earth in an earlier or later stage of its life history. Even existent planets were converted for this purpose. By common consent, Mars became a dried up senescent version of Earth, and Venus a model of earlier terrestrial history, hot and steamy, sweltering under a Jurassic dream. Both models totally ignored astronomical fact, but fulfilled the need to act out in imagination current scientific theories.

The other element that assisted in the model-making was Infinite Lay Time. That also was a nineteenth-century invention. All time machines are ILT vehicles. Before their invention by sceptical theoretical scientists and mathematicians, anyone venturing back in time to 4004 BC would have banged his head on solid rock. The new speculative element, which rendered time immense, allowed the time traveller to go back far beyond page one of Genesis or forward beyond Armageddon to the ultimate heat death of the universe. Sf writers had the job of making both accessible to the lay imagination. No-one else would touch the taunting task.

The connections between our world of today and the Enlightenment are now faint, erased by the horrors of our century, two world wars and the long-planned, long-term massacres of millions of people by Hitler and Stalin and their willing agents. Yet there are echoes. Europe has shrunk again, and is threatened by a new kind of Turk, though we are hardly likely to finance a new Prince Eugène.

Science fiction is here to stay, or will stay as long as we can at least speak of progress and dare to look at the future. In the West sf writers are still not mouthpieces of the state; one can see for them a unique function as disseminators of philosophical and scientific thought. Writers like Wells and Huxley excelled in that role, as did Olaf Stapledon, with his imaginative transformations of combined evolutionary and cosmological theory.

But the great commercial success of science fiction in the seventies diminishes the possibility that it will be treated even by its practitioners with proper seriousness. Money is not the enemy, but the greed for money. Sf has become a sort of cultural reflex like the mother-in-law joke, used to sell cars and biscuits. Every time it is so used, it is drained of challenging ideas. Eventually it may become so trivial, so light, that it will sink below the intellectual horizon.

Paradoxically, this new commercial success comes at a time when its prime base – the grand gloomy ideas I have described – has worn thin, as genre material always does. As it becomes or tends to become less a literary genre, so – paradoxically again – it is being greatly taken up by universities, especially in the States, and the first international congress of sf critics has been held in Palermo (for sf is now an international pursuit, endowed by UNESCO).

But, science fiction has always been contradictory, and its best creators of a sturdily independent kind. This is perhaps the time of greatest potential for them and for the genre.

Even in a popular film like *Star Wars*, admittedly a mammoth with the brains of a gnat, one perceives at least latent thought. Although *Star Wars* was widely condemned by sf writers for its triviality, one can see how easily the idea of the Force as a *spiritual* weapon, rather than Robin Hood's stave, could have been developed and deepened. The rebels would then have been fighting against the evil of the Empire with values on their side with which a general public would readily have identified; it could have entered scenes upon which, instead, it merely gazed.

The Force is a sort of corrupt version of the Samurai code. To have inserted the true thing with all its ritual of fasting and self-discipline and chivalric intent into the film would have increased immensely the film's significance without spoiling the pace. Admittedly, Luke Skywalker would then have become less of a Disney kid; it is not sufficient to have togged him up with a shorty Roman toga instead of giving him a character.

Star Wars was pretty, but underestimated its audience's intelligence. One of the lessons of the Enlightenment is that people are, on the whole, glad to learn and take pleasure in knowledge. Criticism should never be too prescriptive, but my hope is that science fiction will retain its old magic, and its sturdy if gloomy philosophical basic.

James Blish and the Mathematics of Knowledge

*We did not have the time to learn
everything that we wanted to know*

Retma's epitaph for Man in *A Clash of Cymbals*

The science fiction of James Blish presents us with a number of pleasurable dichotomies. Under the cloak of technological activity, he is a visionary of an old-fashioned kind, able, like Blake, to hold infinity in his hand. Such visionaries usually speak out against technology; but Blish saw in technology a chance to bring us nearer to the seat of knowledge, which – I hope to show – he equated with wisdom. Technology and the advance of science, in Blish's view, bring us nearer to the ends and beginnings of things which loom so largely in Blishian cosmologies.

Windows on eternity open in all his novels. I knew Blish well for several years before his death in 1975 and he often spoke fondly of his early novel, *Fallen Star* (*The Frozen Year*, US title). A window on eternity opens early in that novel:

'My post gave me a direct view of the magnificent photograph, about four by six, which was hanging over Ellen's desk. It looked like a star caught in the act of blowing up – as, in miniature, it was; the photo was an enlargement from a cosmic-ray emulsion-trace, showing a heavy primary nucleus hitting a carbon atom in the emulsion and knocking it to bits, producing a star of fragment-traces and a shower of more than two hundred mesons.

Nobody with any sense of the drama implicit in a photograph like that – a record of the undoing of one of the basic building blocks of the universe, by a bullet that had travelled unknowable millions of years and miles to effect the catastrophe – could have resisted asking for a closer look.'

In asking for a closer look at the photograph, Julian Cole becomes involved as a journalist on the International Geophysical Year expedition to the Arctic. A member of the expedition, Joseph Wentz, dies, and a short oration is made over his dead body by Farnsworth, the leader of the expedition. The oration includes these words: 'If You [God] . . . exist, and if You are still thinking about men, think of Joe Wentz. He admired Your fine workmanship in the stars, and never reproached You for spoiling him.'

Another member of the expedition responds angrily, 'It is proven: He never punishes crime; He cares nothing for stars; why should He care about man?' Much of Blish's work is devoted to answering this question. Is there a God? Does he care? Can we achieve answers to these vital questions by pushing science (knowledge) to its extremes?

Juxtaposed, these questions form a central riddle, the nature of which changes slightly throughout Blish's long career. Blish never satisfactorily answers the riddle himself. This may imply a failure as a theoretical novelist, but the riddle is often embodied in an image of great power; this is his success as a poet. The riddle is given form in *Fallen Star*, for instance, by the little pebble which Farnsworth embeds in an ordinary ice cube.

The pebble is a tektite fallen to Earth from the region of the asteroid belt, and consists of *sedimentary rock*. The implications of this find are tremendous. An asteroidal protoplanet once existed which supported oceans for a long period. So its climate must have been warmer than Mars; it must have had an atmosphere. A later discovery carries these theories further. There was life on the planet. And it was destroyed by the Martians within the period of Man's span on Earth. There has been War in Heaven. As Farnsworth says – 'Cosmic history in an ice cube!'

These and similar preoccupations explain why Blish felt such admiration for C.S.Lewis, to whose memory *Black Easter* is dedicated. Yet Blish is of what we may term the Campbell Generation; his work bears at least superficial resemblances to the other writing forged on John W.Campbell's anvil. The Okie series, for example, gathered into book form as *Cities in Flight*, ran in serial form over a number of years in Campbell's

Astounding. Beneath the galactic gallivantings, however, lies
something more hard-headed than anything in Heinlein, more
intellectual than anything in Asimov, and more immense than
anything in Van Vogt. Moreover, that something has little in
common with the two sf writers Blish most admired, Henry
Kuttner and Cyril Kornbluth, for he rarely attempts the
romantic and satiric modes in which Kuttner and Kornbluth are
most successful.

In their spirit of enquiry, Blish's novels are centrally science
fictional. It is in the direction of that enquiry that Blish's
originality lies. We can only hope that some critic will come
along and investigate his whole considerable *oeuvre* for us,
revealing Blish's true stature. I hope to point to a few lines of
enquiry in this essay.

One main topic in the *Astounding* to which Blish contributed
his early stories may be summed up in that striking phrase of
Winston Churchill's: 'The Stone Age may return on the gleaming wings of science.' Campbell's writers, whatever they might
profess on the surface, were ambivalent regarding the virtues of
the future world to which they saw themselves progressing as
the outriders of culture. Time and time again, their stories
dramatise experiments which — like those of Wernher von
Braun in real life – metaphorically aim for the stars but hit
London. Only in the stories of Isaac Asimov do we glimpse
some kind of ordered and rational future. Yet, in the most
popular of all sagas to emerge from Campbell's forge, Asimov's
Foundation, (the title of that civilisation which Hari Seldon must
preserve against the forces of decline) culture has nothing to do
with the arts and humanities: it signifies merely an extrapolated
twentieth-century technology which encases Trantor in metal,
opposed by a barbarism which rides in spaceships.

Blish's conception of culture and of science is more profound:
he sees beneath them to their warring source. He perceived how
every civilisation is dominated by a few major ideas and how
these ideas become gradually outmoded, dooming the culture
concerned; the fate of the Martians in *Fallen Star* is not that
their planet has lost its atmosphere, but that they 'have gone
frozen in the brains'. Blish appreciated the seminal value of the
pre-Classical culture in Greece, and dismissed out of hand

Campbell's assertion that 'Homer was a barbarian'. Ideas
infused from other sources can regenerate older cultures, as is
demonstrated in *Dr Mirabilis*, the biography of the 'miraculous
doctor', Roger Bacon, over which Blish laboured so long. The
same seminal thought moved Blish to yoke four totally distinct
books, *A Case of Conscience, Black Easter, The Day After
Judgement*, and *Mirabilis*, together as an uncomfortable
tetralogy entitled *After Such Knowledge*. His obsession with the
true scientific nature of cultures is dramatised in *The Seedling
Stars* which owes much to Olaf Stapledon. There an Adapted
Man is not so much a man as an Idea from Earth, inserted into
an alien environment to regenerate it (the reverse of the situation
in *Fallen Star*).

The Seedling Stars is ultimately crude because the grand
experiment of seeding stars takes little account of the feelings of
the living beings forced to participate in the experiment, despite
the moralising about the venture which goes on. Blish was
interested in morality as a consciousness structure, while
singularly lacking conventional moral tone. Individual lives
rarely moved him. What concerned him was connecting together
incompatible structures; he had come to believe, through
Oswald Spengler, that there were no eternal verities, not even in
the mathematics which is the basis of culture; hence his preoccupation with eschatology.

A passage in Spengler's *Decline of the West* must have
attracted Blish's attention, and certainly is relevant to the
present day.

> 'The modern mathematic, though "true" only for the
> Western spirit, is undeniably a master-work of that spirit; and
> yet to Plato it would have seemed a ridiculous and painful
> aberration from the path leading to the "true" – to wit, the
> Classical – mathematic. And so with ourselves. Plainly, we
> have almost no notion of the multitude of great ideas
> belonging to other Cultures that we have suffered to lapse
> because *our* thought with its limitations has not permitted
> us to assimilate them, or (which comes to the same thing) has
> led us to reject them as false, superfluous, and non-
> sensical.'

Our culture, sensing that the numbers in the Renaissance hour-glass are running out, is now trying belatedly to derive notations from other cultures previously ignored. Hence such manifestations as Tao Physics – and possibly sf itself.

Throughout Blish's writing, we find two predominant pre-occupations: that some culture or phase of culture is coming to an end (generally with a new beginning implied in that end) and that fresh ideas transfigure culture. Both these preoccupations find resolution in concepts of number. What excites him is not the individual – how could it, given those preoccupations – but the alembic of mathematics.

So his books conclude with cryptic sentences, the like of which never was on land or sea.

'Earth isn't a place. It's an idea.'
God is dead.
'And so, by winning all, all have I lost.'
Creation began.
Then he, too, was gone, and the world was ready to begin.

This last is the final line of one of Blish's less appreciated novels, *A Torrent of Faces*, written with Norman L.Knight and, like *Dr Mirabilis*, a slow growth. It concerns – so the author tells us – a utopia of over-population. Blish did not regard this as a contradiction in terms. Again, numbers exercised their appeal. He says, 'Our future world requires one hundred thousand cities with an average population of ten million people each. This means that there would have to be seven such cities in an area as small as Puerto Rico, about twelve to sixteen miles apart, if the cities are spread evenly all over the world in a checkerboard pattern.' This culture survives only because a large portion of mankind lives under the oceans.

A Torrent of Faces is a cascade of figures. Every conversation seems to flow with them. As Kim and Jothen fly towards the mountain range of Chicago, she tells him, 'Somewhere inside is the headquarters of the Civic Medical Services. I was born there. Every day approximately fifteen thousand babies are born there. The nine outlying regional centres produce about the same number daily . . .' And so on. It is all rather like the scene at the end of *A Clash of Cymbals* where, heading for the collapse of the universe at the metagalactic centre of the universe, Hazelton borrows Amalfi's slide-rule to do a few setting-up exercises.

This is not just a ploy to baffle us with prestidigitation; the power of numbers is a real thing for Blish. In *A Clash of Cymbals*, it creates a new universe. Amalfi, the hero of the Okie saga, becomes the godhead, the very substance of the new universe ('the elements of which he and the suit were composed flash into pleasure . . .'). Never was life everlasting achieved on such a scale.

This apocalyptic idea of one state of being leading to another is fundamental to a number of Blish's novels and stories: one system of thought similarly supersedes another. Poor scientific Roger Bacon, arriving at Westminster, occupies a room foul with marsh gas from the sewer below; when he ignites it and blows himself up, he believes it to have been a visitation by the devil.

Blish's work as a whole is remarkable for the visitations it numbers from both devils and angels. They were perhaps his way of injecting a conflicting irrational idea into the rationalism of Campbellian sf. Such creatures earn themselves a book title – *The Night Shapes*. This is not one of Blish's best novels; perhaps Darkest Africa, with uneasy references to Rider Haggard – though E.R.Burroughs is nearer to the mark – suited the Blishian temperament less well than the Arctic. A terrible valley, likened to Eden, 'burns out' (and so becomes Hell?), releasing the night shapes. 'The night shapes aren't animals, or men, or demons, even to begin with. They're the ideas of evil for which those real things only stand. The real things are temporary. They can be hunted. But the shapes are inside us. They've always lived there. They always will.'

The context does not support the premise. But the premise of such night shapes often supported Blish.

Not only did he see them as convenient shorthand for an alien system of thought intruding itself on the cartesian universe, he had a markedly individual belief in Good and Evil. Through his windows on eternity he watched the Fall re-enacted. His purest version of the Fall is played out on Lithia, the planet in *A Case of Conscience*, the first volume of *After Such Knowledge*. That

ponderous title, *After Such Knowledge*, is a quotation from
T.S.Eliot: 'After such knowledge, what forgiveness?' Nobody
earns forgiveness in Blish's worlds; the math is against it.
Religion's no help. Even the Devil has to suffer by taking up the
burdens of God at the end of *The Day After Judgement*.

Not that Blish believes in or asks us to believe in actual devils.
But he has an interest in them which some might find excessive.
He likes to hold the proposition open, if only as one of 'the multitude of great ideas belonging to other cultures' (devils being far
from a Christian prerogative); perhaps he teased himself by the
quotation from C.S.Lewis's *The Screwtape Letters* used in
Black Easter: 'There are two equal and opposite errors into
which our race can fall about the devils. One is to disbelieve in
their existence. The other is to believe, and to feel an excessive or
unhealthy interest in them.'

The night shapes in the African valley soon found more
sophisticated embodiment. When devils materialise in Death
Valley (in *The Day After Judgement*), the whole world is under
threat. Language is used as a defence against them, as language
has conjured them. US military intelligence protects the troops
from the dreadful knowledge of demons by use of typical
military double-talk:

'Enemy troops are equipped with individual body armour.
In accordance with ancient Oriental custom, this armour has
been designed and decorated in various grotesque shapes, in
the hope of frightening the opposition. It is expected that the
American soldier will simply laugh at this primitive device.'

Earth has become a hinterland of Hell. This is the Blishian
law: close to home, devils appear. Farther away from Earth,
apparitions become more celestial. Not only is Mother Earth
inescapably soiled by her fecundity; Blish shares the belief,
common to many American sf writers of his generation, that for
Man to remain on Earth is to invite stagnation (as if the Chinese
show any signs of stagnation by remaining in China).

Lithia, only forty light-years away from Earth, may or may
not be the province of the devil. But far away, far from home in
the centre of the galaxy, in the light, in the Heart Stars, there we

find angels. 'Inside that vast dust cloud called the Greater Coal Sack, the Angels orbited and danced in their thousands, creatures older than the planets, older than the suns, many of them as old as the universe itself.'

What, we may well wonder, lies behind the fantastic notion of a localised evil, and of a heaven accessible to star-travellers? Are we to regard this as just another mad sci-fi idea, or take it seriously, perhaps as an extended version of John Donne's lovely paradox:

> At the round earths imagin'd corners, blow
> Your trumpets, Angells, and arise, arise
> From death?

Deploying this vision through several books, Blish demands we take serious notice of it if we are to take him seriously.

So what are all these angels and devils doing, flitting so anachronistically through modern science fiction? The answers are complex, and spring from the complex nature of James Blish, who contained in himself much of the crabbed knowledge and temperament of his star, Roger Bacon. Sometimes, we are meant to take the devils literally, as in *Black Easter* and *The Day After Judgement*; sometimes, they are deployed more metaphorically. As for the vast distance wherein we are purified, where we may meet with angels, they also represent passages of time, during which knowledge and judgement can be achieved. Several Blishian heroes make at least part of the journey, and acquire part-purification.

One who makes it all the way is Mayor John Amalfi. He becomes more than angel, God (a reversal of the way in which the Devil becomes God by visiting Earth in *Day After Judgement* – here the factors of the equation are transposed). For it is Amalfi, of all Blish's human characters, who travels farthest; and the anti-agathics which make him nearly immortal ensure that he can travel almost forever. So in Blishian terms he has to head away from Earth. At the end of *Clash of Cymbals*, he reaches metagalactic centre, where a new universe is coming into being. Amalfi virtually creates that new universe, in one orgasmic burst of parthenogenesis.

This climax is Blish's most daring reach for balance, for a treaty between good and evil, armistice between love and death. But the longing for treaty, for balance, is continually expressed, often in metaphor. There is a wish to see standard religion take its place beside a rigorous science (typically, in *A Case of Conscience*); then demons will become mere humans in armour and humans angels without armour.

The contradictions between antipathetic systems are ones Blish is constantly driven to bridge. In a memorable story entitled 'Bridge' (later incorporated into the tetralogy *Cities in Flight*, as part of the novel *They Shall Have Stars*), he dramatises the journey of a man across a perilous ice bridge on Jupiter, a bridge which represents the joining of two incompatible systems, since the man is not on Jupiter in actuality but illusion. An actual crossing of the ice bridge can never be achieved. Oppositions admit of no real bridges, or not under any math at present accessible to us.

It was towards such a bridge that Blish worked. His writing slowly becomes more concentrated towards the problems of knowledge and evil (that is, if we exclude the volumes of *Star Trek* which Blish turned out − for money but also, presumably, for relief from his pursuit of his dark quarry). The devils become thicker, the angels fewer.

In two renowned stories, Blish subsumes the symbolic angels and devils into mathematical functions.

In 'Common Time', Garrard is the pilot of an experimental inter-stellar vessel, capable of accelerating to near-light velocities. He finds himself undergoing extreme time-dilation.

'During a single day of ship-time, Garrard could get in more thinking than any philosopher on Earth could have managed during an entire lifetime. Garrard could, if he disciplined himself sufficiently, devote his mind for a century to running down the consequences of a single thought, down to the last detail, and still have millenia left to go on to the next thought. What panoplies of pure reason could he not have assembled by the time 6,000 years had gone by? With sufficient concentration, he might come up with a solution to the Problem of Evil between breakfast and dinner of a single

ship's day, and in a ship's month might put his finger on the
First Cause!'

The passage carries a reminder of Sir Thomas Browne,
physician of Norwich whose writings Blish enjoyed ('Julius
Scaliger, who in a sleepless fit of the gout could make two
hundred verses in a night, would have but five plain words upon
his tomb . . .'). The quotation from 'Common Time' gains vigour
from deployment of similar antitheses. It is the mark of a
genuine writer that, in the fibres of one characteristic sentence,
he delivers a minute image of his whole thought, much as
physicists once believed the whole solar system was modelled in
the atom.

Without being aware of any contradiction, Garrard leaps
between sentences from dreaming of 'panoplies of pure reason'
to solving the Problem of Evil, as if he (or rather Blish) believes
Evil could be resolved by Reason; the two questions are presented not as oppositions but complementaries. 'Common Time'
was published in 1953, in the same year as first publication of *A
Case of Conscience*. In *A Case of Conscience* also, Evil seems
curiously to be something only discernible by tortuous reason.
How fortunate, then, that Ruiz-Sanchez happens to combine the
function of scientist and priest.

One of the tokens of Lithian evil is the mystery surrounding
mating and birth on the planet. Chtexa, a Lithian with whom
Ruiz-Sanchez talks, explains that he is living alone because no
female has chosen him to fecundate her eggs that season. The
priest asks, 'And how is the choice determined? Is it by emotion,
or by reason alone?'

'The two are in the long run the same,' replies Chtexa.

If emotion and reason are the same 'in the long run', then so it
seems are religion and science. 'Clouds and clouds' of angels
follow the Ariadne back to Earth, riding the same Standing
Wave as the ship (but the Standing Wave was in a field which
'relatively rejected the universe'). In that same novel, *The Star
Dwellers*, the children have a tiny transistorised transceiver
often unusually employed; as young Sylvia says, 'Dad uses it to
talk to Lucifer.' (Similarly, the characters in *Black Easter* listen
to Armageddon taking place over Radio Luxembourg. We have

to assume that Blish thought such feats possible if there are wholly new ideas of number yet to be revealed.)

Such formulae are passing strange. Therein lies their attraction; they force us to recall the intimate connection between mathematics and reality. Blish's vision encompasses remote equations where the sedimentary strata of reason are indistinguishable from the igneous deposits of emotion.

He works towards a universe Milton accepted with one that Dirac envisioned, to justify the esoteric problem of evil with the recondite spin of the electron. This is not a problem one meets with regularly in science fiction, yet many people confront it daily. There is always a demand for a New Jerusalem among our dark satanic mills.

As Blake saw eternity in an hour, so the great Mary Somerville, translator of Laplace, saw a proof of the unity of the Deity in Differential Calculus. The American Edward Everett declared, a bit more gushingly, 'In the pure mathematics we contemplate absolute truths which existed in the divine mind before the morning stars sang together.' Perhaps Leslie A.White came nearer to Blish's position – and to Spengler's – when he remarked that 'Mathematics is a form of behaviour.'

So could belief in a Dirac transmitter, like absolute trust in God, free us from sin? Such seems to be Blish's assumption in his justly renowned story, 'Beep', published the year after *A Case of Conscience* and 'Common Time'. 'Beep' builds a remarkable bridge between love and judgment.

In 'Beep' we have with a vengeance a culture coming to an end and a fresh idea transforming culture, wrapped up in numerology. The peculiar structure of the story is designed to exhibit these transformations to best effect. (I refer to the original novella, not the slightly revised version published under the Browneian title, *The Quincunx of Time*.)

One of the pleasing ingenuities of 'Beep' lies curled up within its title; like a Samuel Palmer chestnut tree alert within the confines of a conker, so a forest of implications unpacks from the title's meaningless seed of noise. Here we encounter 'Common Time' Garrard's dream come true: the 'panoplies of pure reason' can be unravelled in less than 'a single day of ship-time' through the Dirac computer. This achievement results in a universe of rigid causal laws; the banishment of Chaos, the imposition of an Order more rigorous than anything we could achieve today with our inferior math.

'Beep' contains a central image, which, being a numerological incantation, banishes all devils:

> 'I've heard the commander of a world-line cruiser, [says one of the characters] travelling from 8873 to 8704 along the world-line of the planet Hathshepa, which circles a star on the rim of NGC 4725, calling for help across eleven million light years − but what kind of help he was calling for, or will be calling for, is beyond my comprehension.'

Communication, however, mysterious at first, is achieved; help is forthcoming.

Communication begets communion. 'Beep' concerns one of the central problems of a galactic civilisation, how to overcome those immense lines of communication stretching across space and time. Blish's Dirac transmitter provides a remarkable solution to the problem. For not only does it in part abolish space and time (bringing the metagalactic centre to our doorsteps, so to speak) but it proves to be, in effect, a machine which abolishes the Problem of Evil, root and branch. Heisenberg-Born-Dirac wield more clout than the Holy Trinity.

The story goes on to demonstrate what good effects follow − including having one of the characters married almost forcibly to a transvestite lady of mixed ancestry (to his great benefit).

Unravelling the skeins of this strange tale, Blish posits that if free-will could be removed from human affairs there would be no sin (a contrary assumption, if I have my theology correct, to the ones in *A Case of Conscience* − and, par example, Anthony Burgess's *A Clockwork Orange*).

Determinism shapes all activity: human consciousness is 'just along for the ride', or 'helpless'. An embodiment of this is the Richard Strauss persona, resurrected to create a masterpiece, in 'A Work of Art'. Again, events rule. Blish manages to make this hellish proposition sound utopian. The world of 'Beep' is the happiest one in the Blishian canon; as one of the characters remarks, 'The news is always good.'

This connection between instant communication and freedom from sin is bold – yet we commonly equate non-communication (secrecy) with wickedness. Blish makes the situation real by showing what tender care is taken by the Service to see that lovers always meet as planned, thus maintaining future events in their predestinate grooves. Never before did Secret Service so closely resemble Marriage Bureau.

Most sf writers, slaves to catastrophes, portray instant communication as something which can be seized upon and perverted to further the aims of the conqueror. In 'Beep', it is seized upon to bring further peace. Is Blish trying to equate instant communication with perfect communion? There seems no other way to explain why his all-powerful Service is so incorruptible. The Event Police have become veritable Angels on Earth.

Other riddles attend us. We puzzle at the way Blish has planted two people in disguise – one in the inner, one in the outer story. They assume their disguises for devious purposes, yet neither meets with so much as mild disapproval when they are discovered.

Perhaps deception carries no penalties in a utopia. The deceit is maintained for benevolent ends (though theologians, not least Ruiz-Sanchez, would look askance at that). But, in this utopia, deceit cannot be feared, since there is no aggression. If you remove reasons for aggression, will aggression vanish? Does the wish to throw stones disappear on a perfectly sandy beach? Useless to ask such questions about the world of 'Beep', since the Dirac transmitter makes cause and effect inoperative by rendering the whole universe totally open to scrutiny. After such knowledge, there is no room for Judgment Day.

If you grant that 'Beep' is of a utopian disposition, then you have to grant that it is a rare sort of story indeed, even among Blish's cabinet of curiosities. I know of no other galactic empire which could be remotely regarded as utopian; in general, the sewers of these glittering Trantors are clogged with the dismembered bodies of the oppressed. Yet, given angelic guidance, even Trantor could be made to blossom.

James Blish, in his wisdom, did a lot of strange things. He was a thinker, a maker, until the day of his death. Unlike so many science fiction writers – enslaved by editors, formulae and prospect of riches – he did not grow less interesting as he grew older, as he engaged in a daily fight with death and the night shapes. One of the themes that 'Common Time', 'Beep', and *A Case of Conscience* have in common is immortality: immortality of thought, immortality of material things, immortality of evil. When the city of Dis makes its dreadful apparition in the seared lands of America which Blish had by then vacated, we feel it as an eruption of a dreadful cancer – largely forgotten, yet ever-living.

In the volumes of the *Cities in Flight* series, along with the spin-dizzies go the anti-death drugs that confer extreme longevity on all. In the years when Blish was writing of Mayor Amalfi and the cities, he was carefree enough to use the idea as no more than a plot-device. But the evil days would come, and what was merely thought would be entirely felt. Reason and emotion would unite.

Like Mayor Amalfi, James Blish has made the perilous crossing into another state of being, where perhaps little survives but mathematics. In the words of Browne, he is 'by this time no Puny among the mighty Nations of the Dead; for tho' he left this World not many Days past, yet every Hour you know largely addeth unto that dark Society; and considering the incessant Mortality of Mankind, you cannot conceive that there dieth in the whole Earth so few as a thousand an Hour.'

As for the works Blish left behind, there were, as we might anticipate, several that will remain incomplete and uncompleted; for those that are complete we must be grateful. At their best, the cadences of his prose are spare, capable of keeping us alive to the unsparing intellect behind them. His originality, his unquenchable thirst for knowledge, must always ensure that we remember his name when the rolls of leading science fiction writers are called; but he would seek no finer epitaph than that which one of his characters bestowed on mankind: 'We did not have the time to learn everything that we wanted to know.'

Dick's Maledictory Web

'The trail levelled out and became wider. And all was in shadow; cold and damp hung over everything, as if they were treading within a great tomb. The vegetation that grew thin and noxious along the surface of rocks had a dead quality to it, as if something had poisoned it in its act of growing. Ahead lay a dead bird on the path, a rotten corpse that might have been there for weeks; he could not tell.'

Arnie Kott is on his way back into a schizoid variant of the recent past. Philip K.Dick is in the middle of one of his most magical novels, *Martian Time-Slip*.*

The setting is Mars, which is now partly colonised. Colonists live along the water system, where conditions of near-fertility exist.

This web of civilisation is stretched thin over utter desolation. There is no guaranteeing that it can be maintained. Its stability is threatened by the Great Powers back on Earth. For years, they have neglected Mars, concentrating dollars and man-hours on further exploration elsewhere in the system; now they may interfere actively with the balance of the colony.

Behind this web exists another, even more tenuous: the web of human relationships. Men and women, children, old men, bleekmen – the autochthonous but non-indigenous natives of Mars – all depend, however reluctantly, on one another. When poor Norbert Steiner commits suicide, the effects of the event are felt by everyone.

Behind these two webs lies a third, revealed only indirectly. This is the web connecting all the good and bad things in the

* *Martian Time-Slip*, by Philip K.Dick, NEL, 1976. This edition marks its first English publication, belated but perhaps – in view of Dick's growing reputation as a master of science fiction – not untimely.

universe. The despised bleekmen, who tremble on the edge of greater knowledge than humanity, are acutely aware of this web and occasionally succeed in twitching a strand here and there, to their advantage; but they are as much in its toils as anybody else.

These three webs integrate at various coordinate points, the most remarkable point being AM-WEB, a complex structure which the UN may build some time in the future in the FDR Mountains. The structure is visible to Steiner's autistic son, Manfred, who sees it in an advanced stage of decay.

Its function in the novel is to provide a symbol for the aspirations and failures of mankind. The structure will be a considerable achievement when completed; which is not to say that it is not ultimately doomed; and part of that doom may be decreed by the miserable political and financial manoeuvrings which form one of the minor themes of this intricately designed novel.

Martian Time-Slip comes from the middle of one of Dick's most creative periods. *The Man in the High Castle* was published in 1962. In 1963 came *The Game-Players of Titan* and then, in 1964, *The Simulacra*, *The Penultimate Truth*, *Clans of the Alphane Moon*, and the present volume. Although Dick is a prolific author, with some thirty novels appearing in fifteen years, his production rate is modest when compared with many other writers in the prodigal field of science fiction.

One of the attractions of Dick's novels is that they all have points at which they inter-relate, although Dick never re-introduces characters from previous books. The relationship is more subtle – more web-like – than that. There is a web in *Clans of the Alphane Moon*, made by 'the world-spider as it spins its web of destruction for all life'. The way in which Mars in the present novel is parcelled up between various nationalities is reminiscent of the parcelling up of Earth into great estates in *The Penultimate Truth*, and *The Game-Players of Titan*. The horrifying corrupt world of Manfred's schizophrenia, the realm of Gubble, reminds us of the tomb world into which John Isidore falls in *Do Androids Dream of Electric Sheep?* or of one of the ghastly fake universes of Palmer Eldritch in *The Three Stigmata of Palmer Eldritch*. When Jack Bohlen, in the first few pages of the novel, awaits the arrival of his father from Earth, change is about to creep in; and change is often paradoxically embodied in someone or something old, like the Edwin N.Stanton lying wrapped up in newspaper in the back of Maury Rock's Jaguar, in the opening pages of *We Can Build You*. And so on.

Such building blocks are by no means interchangeable from book to book; Dick's kaleidoscope is always being shaken, new sinister colours and patterns continually emerge. The power in the Dickian universe resides in these blocks, rather than in his characters; even when one of the characters has a special power (like Jones's ability to foresee the future in *The World Jones Made*) it rarely does him any personal good.

If we look at two of the most important of these building blocks and observe how they depend on each other for greatest effect, we come close to understanding one aspect of Dickian thought. These blocks are the concern-with-reality and the involvement-with-the-past.

Most of the characteristic themes of science fiction are materialist ones; only the concern-with-reality theme involves a quasimetaphysical speculation, and this theme Dick has made peculiarly his own. Among his earliest published stories is 'Impostor' (1953), in which a robot believes himself to be a man; the faking is so good that even he cannot detect the truth until the bomb within him is triggered by a phrase he himself speaks. Later, Dickian characters are frequently to find themselves trapped in hallucinations or fake worlds of various kinds, often without knowing it or, if knowing it, without being able to do anything about it. In *The Man in the High Castle*, the world we know – in which the Allies won World War II and the Axis Powers lost – is itself reduced to a hypothetical world existing only in a novel called *The Grasshopper Lies Heavy*, which the victorious Japanese and Germans have banned.

And it is not only worlds that are fake. Objects, animals, people, may also be unreal in various ways. Dick's novels are littered with fakes, from the reproduction guns buried in rock in *The Penultimate Truth* which later are used, and so became genuine fakes, to the toad which can hardly be told from real in *Do Androids Dream of Electric Sheep?*, to the androids masquerading as human in the same novel. Things are always talking back to humans. Doors argue, medicine bags patronise, the cab at the end of *Now Wait for Next Year* advises Dr Eric Sweetscent to stay with his ailing wife. All sorts of drugs are available which lead to entirely imaginary universes, like the evil Can-D and Chew-Z used by the colonists on Mars in *Palmer Eldritch*, or the JJ-180 which is banned on Earth in *Now Wait for Next Year*.

The colonists on the Mars of this present novel use only the drugs available to us, though those are generally at hand – in the very opening scene we come across Silvia Bohlen doped up on phenobarbitone. Here the concern-with-reality theme is worked out through the timeslip of the title, and through the autistic boy, Manfred.

Manfred falls into the power of Arnie Kott, boss of the plumbing union which, because water is so scarce, has something of a stranglehold on Mars (a typical piece of wild Dickian ingenuity). Arnie worries a lot. He asks his bleekman servant, Helio, if he has ever been psychoanalysed.

'No, Mister. Entire psychoanalysis is a vainglorious foolishness.'

'Howzat, Helio?'

'Question they never deal with is, what to remold sick person like. There is no what Mister.'

'I don't get you, Helio.'

'Purpose of life is unknown, and hence way to be is hidden from the eyes of living critters. Who can say if perhaps the schizophrenics are not correct? Mister, they take a brave journey. They turn away from mere things, which one may handle and turn to practical use; they turn inward to meaning. There, the black night-without-bottom lies, the pit . . .'

Of course, there are many ways of falling into the pit, one of which is to have too much involvement-with-the-past. Dick admits a fascination with the past, quoting lines of Henry Vaughan:

> Some men a forward motion love
> But I by backward steps would move . . .

Whilst saying how much he enjoys the junk of the past, Dick adds, 'But I'm equally aware of the ominous possibilities. Ray Bradbury goes for the Thirties, too, and I think he falsifies and glamourises them ...' (*Daily Telegraph Magazine*, 19 July 1974). The casual remark reveals much; Dick perceives fiction as a quest, not a refuge.

Arnie Kott has an innocent fascination with objects of the past – he possesses the only spinet on Mars. In the same way, Robert Childan's trading Mickey Mouse watches and scarce copies of *Tip Top Comics* to the victorious Japanese (in *The Man in the High Castle*) is represented as entirely innocuous. Trouble comes when the interest with the past and all its artifacts builds into an obsession, like Virgil Ackerman's Wash-55 a vast regressive babyland which features in *Now Wait for Last Year*.

And this is indeed where Dick parts company with Ray Bradbury, and with many another writer, in or out of the science fiction field. If he sees little safety in the future, the past is even more insidiously corrupting. So dreadful is Manfred's past that you can die in it. The past is seen as regressive; one of the most striking Dickian concepts is the 'regression of forms' which takes place in *Ubik*, that magnificent but flawed novel in which the characters try to make headway through a world becoming ever more primitive, so that the airliner devolves into a Ford trimotor into a Curtis biplane, while Joe's multiplex FM tuner will regress into a cylinder phonograph playing a shouted recitation of the Lord's Prayer.

In *Martian Time-Slip*, the involvement-with-the-past is general, as well as being particularised in Manfred's illness. Mars itself is regarded by Earth as a has-been, and is patterned with has-been communities based on earlier versions of terrestrial history. Here it is especially difficult to escape damnation.

With the past so corrupting, the present so uncertain, and the future so threatening, we might wonder if there can be any escape. The secret of survival in Dick's universe is not to attempt escape into any alternate version of reality but to see things through as best you can; in that way, you may succeed if not actually triumphing. The favoured character in *Martian*

Time-Slip is Jack Bohlen, whom we last see reunited with his
wife, out in the dark garden, flashing a torch and looking for
someone. His voice is business-like, competent, and patient;
these are high ranking virtues in the Dickian theology. It is significant that Jack is a repairman ('an idiot who can fix things,'
says Kott), a survival job, since it helps maintain the status quo.
Similar survivors in other novels are pot-healers, traders,
doctors, musical instrument makers, and android-shooters (since
androids threaten the status quo).

The characters who survive are generally aided by some
system of knowledge involving faith; the system is rarely a
scientific one; it is more likely to be ancient. In *Martian Time-
Slip*, it is the never-formulated paranormal understanding
of the bleekmen; Bohlen respects this vague eschatological
faith without comprehending it, just as Kott despises it. The
I Ching, or Book of Changes, the four thousand year old
Chinese work of divination, performs a similar function in the
The Man in the High Castle, whilst in *Counter-Clock World*
Lotta Hermes randomly consults the Bible, which predicts
the future with an alarming accuracy. In both Dick's two
early masterpieces, *Time-Slip* and *High Castle*, this religious
element – presented as something crumbling, unreliable, to be
figured out with pain – is well-integrated into the texture of the
novel.

Dick's next great book, *The Three Stigmata of Palmer
Eldritch*, was written very soon after *Martian Time-Slip*, and
the two are closely related, not only because Mars is in both
cases used as a setting. To my view, *Eldritch* is a flawed work,
over-complicated, and finally disappearing into a cloud of quasi-
theology; whereas *Martian Time-Slip* has a calm and lucidity
about it. But in *Eldritch* we also find an ancient and unreliable
metastructure of faith, in this case embodied in the ferocious
alien entity which fuses with Eldritch's being.

'Our opponent, something admittedly ugly and foreign that
entered one of our race like an ailment during the long voyage
between Terra and Prox ... and yet it knew much more than
I did about the meaning of our finite lives, here; it saw in
perspective. From its centuries of vacant drifting as it

waited for some kind of life form to pass by which it could grab and become ... maybe that's the source of the knowledge: not experience but unending solitary brooding.'

So muses Barney Mayerson. Jack Bohlen desperately needs a transcendental act of fusion; he is estranged from his wife, sold by his first employer, threatened by his second, invaded by the schizophrenia of the boy he befriends. He sees in this mental illness, so frighteningly depicted in the book, the ultimate enemy. From this ultimate enemy comes the time-slip of the title and that startling paragraph which seems to condense much of the feeling of the book — and, indeed, of Dick's work in general, when Bohlen works out what Manfred's mental illness means: 'It is the stopping of time. The end of experience, of anything new. Once the person becomes psychotic, nothing ever happens to him again.'

This is the maledictory circle within which Dick's beings move and from which they have to escape: although almost any change is for the worse, stasis means death, spiritual if not actual.

Any discussion of Dick's work makes it sound a grim and appalling world. So, on the surface, it may be; yet it must also be said that Dick is amazingly funny. The terror and the humour are fused. It is this rare quality which marks Dick out. This is why critics, in seeking to convey his essential flavour, bring forth the names of Dickens and Kafka, earlier masters of Ghastly Comedy.

Martian Time-Slip is full of delightful comic effects, not least in the way in which Steiner and the lecherous Otto Zitte ship illegal gourmet food items from Earth in unmanned Swiss rockets. Dick's fondness for oddball entities and titles is much in evidence, notably in the surrealist public school, where the Emperor Tiberius, Sir Francis Drake, Mark Twain, and various other dignitaries talk to the boys. Below this easy-going humour lies a darker stream of wit. Arnie Kott's terrible and fatal mistake of believing that reality is merely another version of the schizoid past is also part of the comedy of mistakes to which Dick's characters always dance.

There is a deeper resemblance to the work of Dickens and Kafka. Dick, like Dickens, enjoys a multi-plotted novel. As the legal metaphor is to *Bleak House*, the world-as-prison to *Little Dorrit*, the dust-heap in *Our Mutual Friend*, the tainted wealth to *Great Expectations*, so is Mars to *Martian Time-Slip*. It is exactly and vividly drawn; it is neither the Mars as adventure-playground of Edgar Rice Burroughs nor the Mars as parallel of Pristine America of Ray Bradbury; this is Mars used in elegant and expert fashion as metaphor of spiritual poverty. In functioning as a dreamscape, it has much in common with the semi-allegorical, semi-surrealist locations used by Kafka to heighten his Ghastly Comedy of bafflement. (Staring at his house standing in the meagre Martian desert, Bohlen smiles and says, 'This is the dream of a million years, to stand here and see this.')

Dick's alliance, if one may call it that, with writers such as Dickens and Kafka makes him immediately congenial to English and European readers. It may be this quality which has brought him reputation and respect on this side of the Atlantic before his virtues are fully recognised in his own country.

Perhaps I may be allowed to add that I feel particularly delighted to see this novel added to the growing list of titles in the Master Series. I read it over a decade ago in the American Ballantine edition, admired it greatly, and recommended it over the next few years to several British publishers. Some seemed to feel that it was too 'advanced' for the English market; also there were contractual difficulties. One admirer of the book was Mr Ronald Whiting, who was establishing his own publishing firm, but he was defeated by various unlucky circumstances; his firm closed down before it could publish *Martian Time-Slip*.

Since then, *Martian Time-Slip* had been floating round in a limbo of its own, in a tombworld of non-publication, with nothing ever happening to it again.

Why They Left Zirn Unguarded: The Stories of Robert Sheckley

The early and mid-fifties formed a period of great richness for sf (although we did not notice at the time). Magazines sprouted and proliferated as never before, in a last glory before the onslaught of paperbacks – in much the same way, I imagine, that all the crack stage-coach runs in this country were at their peak in the very years the railways were making them obsolete.

Smith's bookstalls were flooded with covers celebrating marvels of astronomy and space-engineering, much as they now sport anatomy and the freaky electronics of pop. Then it was that one bought one's first *Galaxy*s, *F&SF*s, *Thrilling Wonder*s, *IF*s, *Space*s, *Fantastic*s, and the lesser but delectable breeds, all of which seemed to be edited by Robert Lowndes: *Future*, *Original*, and *Dynamic*. These magazines were not imports but British reprints.

Among the clever new names, one searched particularly for those of Richard Matheson, William Tenn, Ray Bradbury, Philip K. Dick, Walter Miller, and – if one was smart enough – J. G. Ballard. They were all short-story writers; the sf magazines were the ideal medium; and none of them was as much fun as Robert Sheckley.

The typical Sheckley appearance was in *Galaxy*, edited by the celebrated madman H. L. Gold, where he appeared beside other celebrated madmen like Alfred Bester and Theodore Sturgeon. Madmen are essential to sf. We still have madmen today, but often the madness gets into the style rather than the story, as with Harlan Ellison and some of the layabouts in *New Worlds Quarterly*. Sheckley kept his madness honed to a fine point by writing clear English about utterly convincing impossibilities. After all the sobersides in *Astounding*, it was marvellous to read a man whose characters never scored victories (though they rarely suffered utter defeat), whose planets were lunatic and draughty, whose aliens pursued totally inane rituals (like the Dance of the Reciprocal Trade Agreement), whose technologies were generally dedicated to perfecting robots which lurched and squeaked, and whose spaceships were never airtight.

That whole epoch, and the entire Sheckley *thing*, comes back very clearly as one reads this omnibus* – which is possibly an adverse criticism, for we have a somewhat one-dimensional view of Sheckley here. All the stories hail from the fifties, when Sheckley was young and clever. Now he's old and clever, experience has had him by the lapels like one of his malfunctioning robots, and it would have been valuable to have been offered a few later fruits from his tree.

Those later fruits have a taste of acid to them, a fragrance of corruption, and a feel of loss, which makes the best of them more memorable than the earlier ingenuities which Conquest rightly celebrates.

For instance, in a 1972 short story, 'The Mnemone':

'But these are futile gestures. The truth is, we have lost Xanadu irretrievably, lost Cicero, lost Zoroaster. And what else have we lost, what great battles were fought, cities built, jungles conquered? What songs were sung, what dreams were dreamed? We see it now, too late, that our intelligence is a plant which must be rooted in the rich fields of the past.'

There's a note he never sounded in the fifties. Sheckley had roots only in the future. Nor could he write such a funny-poignant tale as his 'Zirn Left Unguarded, the Jenghik Palace in Flames, Jon Westerly Dead', (published in *Nova 2*, edited by Harry Harrison, 1972), in which Sheckley tenderly mocks the romantic-savage-analytical mode of science-fantasy of which he always had such easy mastery. And in *Nova 3*, there's his 'Welcome to the Standard Nightmare', which is all that Sheckley ever was: the old ingenuity is still there, and a whole planet surrenders to one Earthman; but the mood is darker, the etching done with acid that bites deeper into the copper than once it did.

* *The Robert Sheckley Omnibus*, edited & introduced by Robert Conquest, Gollancz, 1973.

The story ends with the words: 'For the Lorians were an advanced and intelligent people. And what is the purpose of being really intelligent if not to have the substance of what you want without mistaking it for the shadow?' In the fifties, Sheckley's characters were travelling too fast to worry about what was substance, what shadow.

My disagreement, then, is with editor Robert Conquest, not with Sheckley. He could have given us a more dimensional study of Sheckley. That has not been his intention. He admires Sheckley's skill in telling an ingenious story, and he includes those stories which seem to him to exemplify this rare ability.

The result is a portly volume containing one Sheckley novel, *Immortality Inc.,* and a dozen short stories, among them several well-known and beloved by the sf fraternity, such as 'Pilgrimage to Earth', 'A Ticket to Tranai', 'The Prize of Peril', and 'The Store of the Worlds'. Not a bad story among them.

Many of these stories use as their material the basic Shecklian preoccupations: the awfulness of institutions and corporations, the craziness of trying to establish a relationship with anyone, the arbitrariness of society's mores, the difficulties one can get into with women, the sheer down-at-heel ghastliness of the galaxy. These, you might say, are almost anyone's preoccupations; no disagreements or surprises there. The nice, the odd, thing about Sheckley's preoccupations is that they are all counterbalanced by their very opposites. The television company that exploits you to the point of death is scrupulous to a pernickety degree; the girl genuinely loved you, but it was just a financial deal; it's as efficient to hold citizens up in the street and rob them as to collect income tax, terrestrial fashion; your wife is perfectly nice, but when you find her in her lover's arms, it's because you refused to keep her in stasis; uncomfortable though we may find most worlds, there are races who are worse off, and leap from sun to sun complaining of the cold. In effect, Sheckley's madness is presented with a disarming reasonableness. At least his future's no worse than the present; and if you think the galaxy's hell, try staying at home. He's telling you a story, not presenting a case.

Of course Sheckley does have a case. His importance as a writer lies in his entertaining embodiment of the underdog's

viewpoint; his AAA Ace Agency stories in *Galaxy* represent a
way in which human beings are forced to exploit each other
under a capitalist system; indeed, they go beyond that – for this
is science fiction, and Sheckley shows how human beings, even
given great powers, will always exploit each other under any
system. It is this understanding, paradoxically exhilarating and
so much more to be prized than any cheap ideological identity
tag, which powers his fiction and at the same time prevents more
generous general acknowledgement of his strengths.

The madness is Blakeian, and so always unwelcome to the
fearful. But for Sheckley it is a necessity that human
relationships should continually break down, that Zirn should
perpetually be left unguarded.

Somewhere in the Sheckley hierarchy is another preoccupation. It would be too much to call it a hope. But ever and
anon comes the thought that there might be a system of non-
material things when circumstances fall out less laughably than
in our world. Conquest introduces us to several stories of this
nature. *Immortality Inc.* is Sheckley's version of the Afterlife –
several Afterlives, in fact. But the Afterlife is no more
satisfactory than this life – Sheckley is no Bradbury or Finney,
dreaming forever of a bright childhood world; he's too much of
a realist for that.

When a somewhat Asimovian machine is invented by a super-
race which can provide answers to all the most baffling philosophical questions of the universe, there is nobody around to
phrase the questions properly; the God is useless. Even the
Almighty makes an almighty hash of things in one of these
stories, calling all the robots up to Heaven on the day of the final
Judgement, and leaving mankind below on the battlefield.
Sheckley's is a universe of makeshift lives – Kingsley Amis
coined the perfect term for it: a comic inferno.

The story here I find most touching (I once anthologised it
myself) is 'The Store of the Worlds'. The protagonist finds
happiness. He gets a whole year of it, and it costs him everything he has. Admittedly, the year includes a maid who
drinks, trouble at the office, a panic on the stockmarket, and
a fire in the guestroom; but it is a year of ordinary family
life, containing, in Sheckley's phrase, desire and fulfillment.

Nobody's on the run, nothing shoots at anything, everyone is comprehensible.

Like Orwell, Sheckley is a utopianist. Unlike all other utopianists, Sheckley's and Orwell's ambitions are almost dauntingly humble – just to be left alone, to have a girl, a drink, a stroll in the park, a room to yourselves. Only one fancies that more fun would go on in Sheckley's shack than Orwell's. (An eccentric parenthesis: I've always suspected that Orwell wrote *1984* after reading Van Vogt; maybe he wrote *Animal Farm* after reading Sheckley.)

Robert Conquest hopes to introduce the civilised pleasures of Sheckley to a readership beyond the sf audience; in his introduction he likens himself to Belloc introducing Ernest Bramah, or E.C.Bentley introducing Damon Runyon. Bramah is a good touch, for there is something of a Kai Lung about Sheckley. He reminds me too of another excellent story-teller, 'Saki', H.H.Munro.

Unless I am mistaken, Conquest also addresses himself to the sf readers. First he warms their hearts by telling them what they long suspected (but are reassured to hear from anyone with credentials as imposing as Conquest's), that H.G.Wells is every bit as much the artist as Henry James; then he slips it to us that James is 'a model of unpretentious clarity compared with many more recent phenomena'. Here, one experiences three or four bodings, in anticipation of yet another Conquest–Amis tract on the worthlessness of anything in sf written since Mike Moorcock attained the age of puberty. Fortunately, the crisis is avoided; Conquest is too adroit to attempt praise of Sheckley by dispraise of lesser breeds.

However, this volume is a great success, a product of Conquest's dedication to the art as well as a celebration of Sheckley's skills. Many a writer would wish as distinguished an anthologist – most of us have to patch our own stories together.

Nesvadba: In the Footsteps of the Admirable Čapek

Josef Nesvadba and I are about the same age. We have met twice, once when he was travelling through London, and, many years later, when I was travelling through Prague, where he lives. This seems entirely appropriate, since Nesvadba's fictions are often filled with long and complex journeys. He is that compelling kind of writer who reminds us that our lives are really somewhat ramshackle fictions, full of unlikely coincidences and people who do not always behave in character.

The perfidious plot-lines of our lives first brought us together in 1965, when something Nesvadba said made a striking impression.

He was talking about his stories, and how he was attempting a sort of psycho-fiction, as he called it. We were agreeing, I seem to recall, that authors who called themselves science fiction writers should not regard science fiction as simply realistic simulation of an hypothecated future; we saw it more as a contemporary form of celebration of the mysteries that pervade human life. We admitted ruefully that the other kind was more commercially popular and, at this point, I underwent the experience of hearing Nesvadba say that a collection of his psycho-fiction stories had been published in Prague in a paper bag.

Prague is a magnificent city where High Baroque and Art Nouveau styles in architecture meet. At the entrance to Nesvadba's flat in the centre of the city, two voluptuous caryatids, less demure than Artemis would have allowed, guard the door he passed through daily. In the celebrated Golem Restaurant, I bought a packet of Apollo-Soyuz cigarettes and smoked them, though I normally detest cigarettes. I stood in the apartment building where Franz Kafka was born, looking up the winding stairwell; by a lugubrious turn of fate, the building has now been taken over by one pseudopod or other of Communist officialdom. Sometimes I have nightmares, dreaming I am Kafka. So I was scarcely bowled over, or only slightly bowled, to hear that publishers in Kafka's city should have issued Josef Nesvadba's work in this unorthodox manner.

The more I considered, the more it seemed appropriate that his kind of fiction should receive such treatment, the more easily I could visualise readers dipping into the bag, bringing out a tale like a pastrami sandwich, and munching thoughtfully on it in one of the little cafés in the shade of Hradćany Castle.

As are many Czechs, Nesvadba is a cosmopolitan, as familiar with Hollywood as with Paris. He speaks several languages, and his English is good. However, on this occasion I had mis-heard him. His paper bag was in actuality the less unusual paperback. I'm sorry about that. I still feel that his food for thought, and his story-telling techniques, are remarkable enough to be singled out for special treatment. The present publishers have voted against the paper bag format also, but it remains a privilege to be introducing Czechoslovakia's most distinguished science fiction writer to paperback readers in this country.

These stories* are set in the narrow alleyways of the mind. Black humour is scarcely dispersed by low-wattage electric bulbs. Whole life-cycles of ghastliness are displayed with gusto in very few lines.

'The dragoons had been the pride of our town. They had ruuined my marriage. Two years after the wedding my wife ran away with Captain Imre Kovacs to Salgotaryan. Perhaps that's what turned me against soldiers. Especially dragoons. I gave up my flat and never left my basement laboratory after that. I sleep there and a waitress brings me my meals from the restaurant. I have few demands on life.'

Although the dragoons are shot – every one of them – and Kovacs is humiliated, the central character can hardly be said to triumph; indeed, we leave him in some doubt about his life. The drama is one of erosion and corrosion, as if we were reading a Gothic Tale by a more sardonic Karen Blixen.

* *In the Footsteps of the Abominable Snowman*, by Josef Nesvadba, New English Library, 1979.

Nesvadba depicts normal sane sensual life as being surrounded by thickets of conspiracy and threatened by jungles of
doctrinaire belief. A favourite conspiracy is the one between
politics and science, the ganging up of one power bloc with
another to create a bigger totalitarianism. Scientists get jobs in
institutes by marrying directors' daughters, rather than by
qualifications; it follows that great scientific advances are made
by accident, or lost as easily. In 'Expedition in the Opposite
Direction', the connections between physics and politics are
made in a story involving a subterranean time-machine invented
by the Nazis and since forgotten. The time-machine represents a
technological hope for liberty, which of course does not work as
expected. Technology does not help people. New developments
in surgery can give you a new face, but the new face emphasises
only the insubstantiality of the character we previously set such
store by.

Surgery and transformation play considerable roles in these
stories. We are after all not far from the Golem and the dark
side of European literature, though the manner of narration is
more in the style of Karel Čapek. Nesvadba has written several
screen plays, one of the most successful of which is *Slecna
Golem* (Miss Golem), a feature film made in Czechoslovakia in
the early seventies, directed by Jaroslav Balik, with the delightful
Jana Breichova playing the dual role of the nice girl and the
naughty duplicate, created by accident. The film is set in Prague
of the twenties, and, at one point, the protagonists find
themselves in a theatre where Čapek's *R.U.R.* is being performed – a pleasant literary *hommage*.

Like *R.U.R.*, the play that gave first currency to the now
universal term 'robot', Nesvadba's story 'Dr Moreau's Other
Island' takes place on a remote island. A woman doctor follows
a research worker, Ivan, to this island, where she is stranded
after her helicopter crashes. She finds herself among amputees
who are presided over by a famous professor of surgery. She is
terrified. Ivan is also a victim of deep surgery.

The amputation is voluntary. The unnecessary has been cut
away. Art, music, sport, these mean nothing to the amputees, it
is science that attracts them. Pared down, they can economise
on weight in rocket ships and travel out into the cosmos.

The woman doctor tries to seduce Ivan in order to save him. 'I may have danced too, I don't remember, but suddenly I felt as though my own thoughts, my voice, my legs, thighs and breasts, the dark hair I was twisting with a silver ribbon, could all help somehow to save these men.'

It is not so. For the male, the attraction of science is too great. She believes herself to be confronted with a disease, one that may have been endemic since civilisation began.

The quality of fable in this story is strong, and reminiscent of another great European writer, the Pole, Slavomir Mrozek. 'Dr Moreau's Other Island' lacks the fascinatingly labyrinthine plot which is one of Nesvadba's specialities, but it bears other hallmarks of the writer, not least a sharp dash of the Absurd. People are set to follow and spy on each other, long reports must be made out, while many characters are involved with ludicrous and menacing institutions, of which my favourite is the Institute for Research into the Curvature of the Universe. Such ambitious projects are never resolved; for these stories were written in Kafka's capital.

The most effective weapon in an author's armoury is a proper deployment of plot – not as a mechanical device but as an integral expression of the author's attitude to life. I remember when I was in Prague that Nesvadba pointed out to me a certain balcony, linking it with the name of Eduard Benes, one of the founders of the Czech state (and, incidentally, a friend of Čapek's) and its last president before it became Communist; Benes had jumped from that balcony in 1948. 'Or maybe he was helped towards the ground.' There was a certain melancholy satisfaction to be derived from such a plot-twist.

Readers who believe that plot has no place in stories with intellectual pedigrees may like to consider that most of these stories were published originally in Prague in 1964. Since then, time had added a painful plot-twist of its own. With the Russian invasion of Czechoslovakia, these bureaucratic toils in which Nesvadba's characters labour have become tighter than ever before. A literary encyclopaedia, giving a brisk summary of Karel Čapek's life and work in a matter of six hundred words, concludes by saying 'His relativist humanism was characteristic of his age but did not fully come to grips with the problems posed by twentieth-century mass societies.' It is difficult to imagine any humanism succeeding in such a task; but Nesvadba's is another approach to the problem.

Although these stories are science fiction in a sense that Čapek or H.G.Wells would readily comprehend, their precognitive sense is nearer that of Kafka than Arthur Clarke. This emerges through Nesvadba's remarkable sense of humour, which deals strictly logically with the incredible.

Consider, for instance, some of the ingredients of the title story, 'In the Footsteps of the Abominable Snowman'. Because his wife is living happily with the yeti, Lord Esdale obeys a telephatic request and visits some caves in Spain. There, he almost gets killed by Franco's army, who happen to be taking over. He has already lost his fortune in the Great Slump. When he recovers, he goes to Moravia, to meet a man who forges prehistoric carvings; on the way, he passes through Vienna, where men are marching about in black boots and brown shorts.

Esdale disappears from the story with his faith in the power of reason quite undiminished, despite all he has seen and experienced. The narrator of his story is the man who forges the prehistoric carvings, who also has his own crazy preoccupations. He leaves his beautiful wife and goes potholing with his lordship, when he breaks his leg. Everything is in toto incredible, but entirely logical.

Nesvadba has a doctor's degree and is a psychiatrist by profession. He spares us the psychological depths of character to which much modern fiction has accustomed us. Instead, his characters are humours or traits, and the complexities of the human mind are expressed in multi-jointed plots. His immensely enjoyable stories belong to that rare order of science fiction which does not require us to take literally what it says. Lively surface detail and humour relieve the undercurrent of despair. In their tenacity, cynicism, mystification, and cheerful defeatism, they bring the Prague in which they were written vividly to mind. My one regret is that they could not have been presented in a paper bag.

Verne: The Extraordinary Voyage

In the lives of great science fiction writers there is always great fascination: they seem to act out some quality that is missing or, at best, latent, in their works. Whereas, in the lives of lesser writers, we meet merely a vacuum, the more noticeable for the magnitudes acted out in their writings.

The monstrous in the works of Jules Verne is kept reasonably under control, tethered to engineering possibilities or the limitations of the atlas. In his life, it leaps out at us. We are surprised when we read in a biography by his grandson* that Verne was 'fun', and bathed in the nude in Scotland; the image is always of a thoroughly dressed Frenchman who meant to run away to sea as a lad but was caught before he sailed, who thought in terms of iron and revolution, whose characters are caricatures and who was dominated by the work ethic.

Apart from the abortive attempt to run away to sea, incidents in Verne's life are few and far between, which is unhelpful to biographers. True, Verne was once shot in the foot by a nephew ('a family tragedy such as everyone encounters at one time or another,' says the grandson, airily), but that is not very important. He is a man with a carapace; he armoured himself against the world by taking to his desk the way some of his contemporaries took to their beds.

Chained to his desk, he was free. He could imagine. His publisher remarked that Verne had 'a sense of the perpendicular', meaning that he could extrapolate from known data. He certainly could grind out facts; had his immense edifice of work been English, we would have recognised its style by its lack of fantasy, its emphasis on horizontals and verticals, as Early Perpendicular.

His novels, solemn and slightly silly at the same time, occupy

* *Jules Verne: A Biography*, by Jean Jules-Verne, Macdonald & Jane's, 1976.

over one hundred volumes of the *Voyages Extraordinaires*. He remained labouring over them, even when he was dying, even when his eyesight had faded and he had to dictate to a secretary. He was blessed by the Pope for his good work and earned a million francs for himself during the course of his lifetime – plus ten million for his enlightened publisher, Hetzel (a fact that all authors would do well to remember).

Verne died in March 1905, at the age of seventy-eight, after an existence which was 'one hard single-minded grind' (the phrase is his grandson's). His life is almost exactly contemporaneous with that of two great English writers, Henrik Ibsen and Leo Tolstoy.

Since his death, Verne's reputation had never entirely died; nor has it been established. Verne still abides the question, although a French critical industry is at work among the cerements. The world has never learned to think of him as a novelist. Yet, if he has not graduated beyond the rank of story-teller, his books, even in bad translations, still give pleasure all round the world, that world he described so often, and most high-spiritedly in his most popular book, *Around the World in Eighty Days*.

Like many of his other stories, *Around the World in Eighty Days* digests facts. Verne's appetite for facts was formidable, in particular the facts revealed or generated by nineteenth-century technology. His training as a lawyer possibly assisted his fact-collecting technique. During the eighteen sixties, he compiled an illustrated geography of France and her colonies which was published in one hundred parts; this was followed by a six-volume work on voyages and discoveries, *Découverte de la Terre*. His life was a love affair with vicarious geography.

After that abortive attempt to run away to sea, Verne's fancy was never at home. He made an unexciting marriage and spent most of the rest of his life sitting at a desk, describing just about every revolution of note or country that counted throughout the nineteenth century. He writes a letter to a friend, describing a story in progress: 'I'm in New Zealand ... I'm down on the eightieth parallel and it's eighty below zero; I'm catching cold just writing about it ...' The desk was his quarter-deck. His works, particularly the more famous ones like *Twenty Thousand Leagues Under the Sea*, *Journey to the Centre of the Earth*, and

From the Earth to the Moon, are wholesome, serious, without female characters for the main part, and freighted with fact, pseudo-fact, and adventure – and something more, an unusual quality, intense romantic longing coupled with hard-headed political awareness.

Verne's novels illustrate as successfully as any writer's one aspect of the nineteenth century: its energy, and its abundant delight in the energy and enterprise of man and his machines. Verne's early heroes are the embodiments of Samuel Smiles's doctrine of self-help. The gospel of work, the little communities set up in the wolds, the rebellions and those personal eccentricities which denote individual rebellions, the machines and animals, and, especially, those oddly named English, French, German and American males, all rushing hither and thither by odd forms of transport – we regard the lot of them now with some indulgence. But our indulgence is properly tinged with envy.

Behind the rushing about lay a good deal of thought, the notes, as it were, which got no further than Verne's desk. M.Chesneaux has elucidated the thought in a gallant and unfashionable book*, liberally decorated by beautiful illustrations taken from the steel engravings which adorned the original French editions of Jules Verne's writings.

The best-known of the *Voyages Extraordinaires* are the early ones, with their trips to the centre of the Earth, the Moon, the bottom of the sea, or off on a comet. These are characterised by massive confidence in mankind's progress and a pride in his ingenuity in building large machines (machines not bound to large-scale capitalist production; nor does Verne enter the descriptions of how and where the machines were made, though the *Nautilus* is assembled from internationally fabricated parts). The machines, in other words, exist more or less independently of the social order, whilst the same is true of the flesh-and-blood heroes, who are usually rebels against society.

The novels span the last four decades of last century. They present a changing emphasis, which darkens towards the end of Verne's life. They start to clog with satanic cities rather than

* *The Political and Social Ideas of Jules Verne*, by Jean Chesneaux, translated by Thomas Wikeley, Thames and Hudson, 1972.

super-submarines, with Stahlstadt, Milliard City, Blackland. Things fall apart. The brave scientists show signs of deterioration, insanity, blindness. Benevolent Robur, hero of *Clipper of the Clouds*, returns in a sequel eighteen years later and attempts to conquer the world. As for Verne's great land of the future, the America which provides a setting in twenty-three out of his sixty-four novels, it develops alarmingly negative aspects; in comes dollar diplomacy, expansionism threatens the social framework, and the machine-mentality triumphs.

As M.Chesneaux points out, the three satanic cities are carefully planned. Stahlstadt, in *The Begum's Fortune*, is a steel city of the future, teutonic and totalitarian. It is militarised, and its separate sections are cut off from each other by water-tight bulkheads. Milliard City in *Propellor Island*, is the capital of Standard Island, and floats round the Pacific. It is rootless – a place of artificial luxury and artificial society, which eventually destroys itself. Blackland, in *The Barsac Mission*, is an artificial city in the desert, which relies on massive exploitation of black labour, and is broken up into strictly maintained zones, a proto-apartheid state.

These novels, published respectively in 1879, 1895 and 1920, are hardly prophetic, as some have claimed; rather, they coincide in their writing with a period when capitalism and imperialism in Western Europe were reaching their peak; Verne's satanic cities embody that phase not prophetically but symbolically.

From Verne's long panorama, one or two remarkable items are missing. His anglophobia is marked ('Sir Edward Turner, one of those men who think everything is permitted to them by the mere fact of being English ...' *Touché*!), but is directed mainly against British oppression. There is no word glorifying French conquests; Verne, to his credit, passes over the chance to make propaganda for his own nation. He's that rarity among science fiction writers, an internationally minded man. Even more remarkable is the way in which Verne, a Catholic and a pillar of his society, makes no references to priests, and builds no churches over all the great wilderness of his novels. His characters may call on God in their hour of need, but they swim ashore unaided, and work to save what's salvable from the shipwreck. Everywhere is the fight to be free; but neither the bondage nor the salvation comes from above.

Nowadays, Verne's gospel of work is out of fashion in the West, likework itself. Even antheism is drowning under wave after wave of nut-culture. Verne's vision of men and societies going down into eclipse is more acceptable to our sensibilities. Could Verne be reinstated with a new reputation as a serious writer?

Stranger things have happened. But reinstatement must wait until it is decided whether Verne is a novelist, however flawed, or a science fiction writer. That is a complex question.

I have always found difficulty in thinking of Verne as a science fiction writer, and remain open to persuasion either way. Peter Costello, in a recent book*, does not help me at all. He says, 'It is perhaps inexact to describe Verne as "the father of science fiction" ... I prefer to call him "the inventor of science fiction", as the mechanical analogy fits him better ... As I hope to show, Verne's particular contribution was a love of exact scientific detail, such as is often lacking in Poe or Mary Shelley.'

A love of exact scientific detail is the mark of a scientist, but not necessarily that of a science fiction writer. Verne clearly has some of the qualities of a sf writer; equally clearly, he lacks some. Two qualities in particular.

Verne has no use for strange entities – what the psychologist and philosopher Stan Gooch calls 'alternative persons' – and hence no use for paradox.

After defining 'person' as an ideal amalgam of Self and Ego, Gooch says,† '*Science fiction fails to write about the Person*. So, of course, does much other literature also. But this "fault" is characteristic of *all* SF – and only of *poor* literature outside SF. My statement is therefore something of a paradox. I am saying that *outstanding* SF shows qualities which are otherwise the trademark of *poor* literature.'

Gooch goes on to claim that sf has invented a new character, Man, and ranged against him androids, robots, aliens, machines,

<hr />

* *Jules Verne: Inventor of Science Fiction*, Peter Costello, Hodder & Stoughton, 1978.

† *Alternative Persons. The Entities of Science Fiction and Myth*, by Stan Gooch, *Labrys 1*, Bran's Head Press, 1978.

super-computers, etc. etc., which are creatures of the Ego.
Gooch defines the Ego as one of the two energy bases of
personality, the one centring round aggression, the other base
being the Self, centring round libido. In these terms, Verne's
writings are highly ego-oriented (and markedly lack Self), but
they contain none of those dramatic embodiments which,
according to Gooch's theories, characterise good sf.

The second quality which Verne lacks is another which
appears abundantly in most science fiction. He does not use time
as a dimension.

Not only do we find few stories taking place in the future (*The
Eternal Adam*, Verne's last book, is set far ahead in time), but
Verne structures his novels in a safely traditional way, setting
them a few years or perhaps a few months in the past, or using
the formula, 'In the year 186-', taking care to mention the date
of the occurrences, generally within a few paragraphs of the
opening of the tale. Thus he fails to make use of the medium
which, as I argue elsewhere, is the one most characteristic of
science fiction writers: plastic time. In this respect, we see that
he lacks qualities we associate with the fiction of Mary Shelley
(Frankenstein's monster, very much a creature of the Ego,
threatens the Self – 'I will be with you on your wedding night')
and of course with H.G.Wells's fiction (which is saturated with
a sense of the transience, yet voluminousness, of Time –
'Whatever memory I had of this life, this nineteenth-century life,
faded as I woke, vanished like a dream').

Verne possessed one paradoxical quality, however, which we
commonly find in sf writers: the past, and ruins which symbolise
the past, stirred him greatly.

The prevalence of ruination in science fiction even of the most
technological order might be taken as evidence for its modern
origins in the Gothic novel. No doubt that influence is there. But
mankind's interest in ruins goes far wider, far deeper, than that.
Rose Macaulay puts the matter squarely in the introduction to
her *Pleasure of Ruins* when she says, 'Since down the ages men
have meditated before ruins, rhapsodised before them, mourned
pleasurably over their ruination, it is interesting to speculate on
the various strands of this complex enjoyment, on how much of
it is admiration for the ruin as it was in its prime – *quanta Roma*

fuit, ipsa ruina docet – how much aesthetic pleasure in its present appearance – *plus belle que la beauté est la ruine de la beauté* – how much is association, historical or literary, what part is played by morbid pleasure in decay, by righteous pleasure in retribution (for so often it is the proud and bad who have fallen),* by mystical pleasure in the destruction of all things mortal and the eternity of God (a common reaction in the Middle Ages), by egotistical satisfaction in surviving – (where now art thou? here still am I) – by masochistic joy in a common destruction – *L'homme va méditer sur les ruines des empires, il oublie qu'il est lui-même une ruine encore plus chancelante, et qu'il sera tombé avant ces débris* – and by a dozen other entwined threads of pleasurable and melancholy emotion, of which the main strand is, one imagines, the romantic and conscious swimming down the hurrying river of time, whose mysterious reaches, stretching limitlessly behind, glimmer suddenly into view with these wracks washed on to the silted shores.'

My own preoccupation with ruins rises before my mental view as I copy out Rose Macaulay's words. In *The Shape of Further Things*, I spoke of a dream recurring throughout my life, a dream of a new and humbler building built in the shade of and from the substance of a grander ruinous structure, that image embodied in a Piranesi engraving showing the mausoleum of Helen, mother of Constantine, in decay, with an eighteenth-century villa nestling in the middle of its ruination. Echoes of that archetype sound in *Frankenstein Unbound* (written after *Shape of Further Things*) but I realise only now, typing this Verne essay, that both my early novels, *Non-Stop* and *Hothouse*, can also be read as embodying that same archetype.

Returning to Verne, we find that he too responds to themes of ruination and regeneration, and with what is cryptic in ruins. Alantis is a theme that haunts him – not only the ruinous Atlantis of *Twenty Thousand Leagues Under the Sea*, but in several novels from *Captain Hatteras* to *The Eternal Adam*.

Theories of evolution have probably increased the power of ruins over our imaginations by fortifying our empathy

---

* Thus conforming to my pocket definition of sf as hubris clobbered by nemesis.

with decay and past epochs. Mary Shelley, pondering over the pronunciations of Erasmus Darwin, provides us with the key-figure, a man, Frankenstein's creation, built from the ruins of earlier men. Verne also goes beyond ruins to vanished days in an evolutionary reverie which recalls remarkable passages in Gerard de Nerval's *Aurélia* (1855), which appears in chapter 32 of *Journey to the Centre of the Earth*. It has been remarked on by Kenneth Allott in his book on Verne, but it bears quotation here, as a reminder that not all Verne is homogeneous.

Young Axel is lying on his raft, drifting on the central sea.

'Now, however, my imagination carried me away among the wonderful hypotheses of palaeontology, and I had a pre-historic daydream. I fancied I could see floating on the water some huge *chersites*, antediluvian tortoises like floating islands. Along the dark shore there passed the great mammals of early times, the *leptotherium*, found in the caves of Brazil, and the *merycotherium*, found in the icy regions of Siberia. Farther on, the *pachydermatous lophiodon*, a gigantic tapir, was hiding behind the rocks, ready to dispute its prey with the *anoplotherium*, a strange animal which looked like an amalgam of rhinoceros, horse, hippopotamus, and camel, as if the Creator, in too much of a hurry during the first hours of the world, had combined several animals in one. The giant mastodon waved its trunk and pounded the rocks on the shore with its tusks, while the megatherium, buttressed on its enormous legs, burrowed in the earth, rousing the echoes of the granite rocks with its roars. Higher up, the *protopitheca*, the first monkey to appear on earth, was climbing on the steep peaks. Higher still, the pterodactyl, with its winged claws, glided like a huge bat through the dense air. And finally, in the upper strata of the atmosphere, some enormous birds, more powerful than the cassowary and bigger than the ostrich, spread their vast wings and soared upwards to touch with their heads the ceiling of the granite vault.

The whole of this fossil world came to life again in my imagination. I went back to the scriptural periods of creation, long before the birth of man, when the unfinished world was not yet ready for him. Then my dream took me even farther back into the ages before the appearance of living creatures. The mammals disappeared, then the birds, then the reptiles of the Secondary Period, and finally the fishes, crustaceans, molluscs, and articulated creatures. The zoophytes of the transitional period returned to nothingness in their turn. The whole of life was concentrated in me, and my heart was the only one beating in that depopulated world. There were no more seasons or climates; the heat of the globe steadily increased and neutralised that of the sun. The vegetation grew to gigantic proportions, and I passed like a ghost among arborescent ferns, treading uncertainly on iridescent marl and mottled stone; I leaned against the trunks of huge conifers; I lay down in the shade of *sphenophyllas*, *asterophyllas*, and *lycopods* a hundred feet high.

Centuries passed by like days. I went back through the long series of terrestrial changes. The plants disappeared; the granite rocks softened; solid matter turned to liquid under the action of intense heat; water covered the surface of the globe, boiling and volatilising; steam enveloped the earth, which gradually turned into a gaseous mass, white-hot, as big and bright as the sun.

In the centre of this nebula, which was fourteen hundred thousand times as large as the globe it would one day form, I was carried through interplanetary space. My body was volatilised in its turn and mingled like an imponderable atom with these vast vapours tracing their flaming orbits through infinity.'*

In this passage, Verne seems almost to be having his cake and eating it, to be able to believe in both Darwin's findings and the Bible; it is probably nearer the truth to say that in 1864 he merely reflected a popular confusion. What is certain is that he here attempts to cope with one of those 'grand gloomy ideas' referred to in the first essay in this book. Moreover, he rejoices – even though his body becomes volatilised – in the enormous new freedoms of speculative time.

So we can see that, despite his difference with sf writers who followed him, Verne had much in common with them. Equally,

* Robert Baldrick's translation (Penguin).

in his concern with historical processes and social issues, he has something in common with such contemporaries of his time as Tolstoy and Ibsen. People with a mania for categorisation will find Verne difficult to categorise; nor, having categorised him, should they think that they understand him thereby. He remains a bit of a mystery, like one of his cryptograms; in his life we find a poignance often missing from even the most extraordinary of his *Voyages Extraordinaires*.

Vonnegut: Guru Number Four

With what mixed emotions, as leader-writers used to say, did some of us read in the columns of *Harper's Bazaar*, that arbiter of literary fashion, an edict to the effect that Kurt Vonnegut Jnr was one of the top four or five gurus on the American scene! Unlike poets, gurus are neither born nor made, but fabricated rather. All the same, one can see that Vonnegut, who has always had a talent for gnomic utterance and lucid obscurity, is a likelier candidate for the cosmetic process than most.

'By Jingo,' a hypothetical reader of *Harper's Bazaar* might be supposed to cry, 'if this is what we get from Kurt Vonnegut Jnr, what must the writings of Kurt Vonnegut Snr contain?' And well they might cry it; but here – particularly since *Harper's Bazaar* had now amalgamated with *Queen* – I would prefer to look at what some might regard as the more junior aspects of Junior, his earlier works.

Vonnegut appeared on the literary scene in the early fifties with stories that were perhaps as tricksy as they were captivating. One might take as an example 'Report on the Barnhouse Effect', the first story in the 1961 Gold Medal collection, *Canary in a Cat House*. 'The Barnhouse Effect' is a short story first published in 1950 about a Professor Barnhouse who develops an unusual power of mind by re-aligning his brain cells. He calls this power 'dynamopsychism'. The time is World War II. At first the power is weak, and the professor can do no more than roll dice the way he wants them. Later, he cultivates the power, he comes under government protection and can destroy warships or bombers or nuclear weapons at long range. He is his country's perfect defence.

'Charges that Professor Barnhouse could have won the last war in a minute, but did not care to do so, are perfectly

senseless. When the war ended, he had the range and power of a
37-millimetre cannon, perhaps – certainly no more.'

The story is told by a pupil of Barnhouse's. The pupil also
picks up the power, which depends on straightening out the
brain with a certain sentence, and – like Barnhouse – he
disappears into hiding rather than work for the government;
instead, he will devote himself to bringing peace on earth in his
own way, wrecking military equipment all over the world.

It can be seen how remarkably like late Vonnegut is this early
Vonnegut. Early Vonnegut is also remarkably like much early-
fifties science fiction, which was similarly preoccupied with
power politics and paranormal mental powers.

Deep in the mind, it is said, there is no distinction between
Wish and Deed – a frightening thought which makes all enjoy-
ments equal. There is a certain childishness in wishing; wishing,
that is, without following the wish by action and initiative.
However, it is towards childishness that powerful states push
their citizens, by denying them action and initiative. And hence,
I suppose, the popularity of science fiction stories dealing with
unlimited mental powers, telepathy, psychokinesis, and dynamopsychism, or whatever fancy name we call it. Hence the continued interest in the researches of Dr Rhine, long after his
results have proved how dead is the trail he follows.

But to turn from similarities between Vonnegut and sf to
similarities between early and late Vonnegut. 'The Report on the
Barnhouse Effect' is written as a report; in the second
paragraph, there is a reference to 'readers of this *article*'. Vonnegut's method is generally to dress fantasy as fact, or to mix
hard fact with fantasy as much as possible. In *Slaughterhouse
Five*, it is difficult to decide whether the actuality of Dresden is
mixed with the fantasy of time-travel or vice versa; in *Mother
Night*, Vonnegut's most successful novel, elaborate care –
editorial notes and so on are appended – is taken to add to the
general verisimilitude. In *The Sirens of Titan*, chapter heads are
often provided by quotes from the books supposedly written by
the characters therein, while the technicalities of chrono-synclastic infundibula are defined – a skilfully comic touch – by
reference to an entry in the fourteenth edition of a fictitious
reference book.

Humour is certainly present in the early tale, though by no means as richly, as integrally present, as in the later writing. Vonnegut's humour is difficult to define; it is too dark to be called mirth, too broad to be called irony, too benevolent to be called satire – though it has been called all those things. It is perhaps the most vonnegutian thing about Vonnegut. It is a very surrealist sense of humour. Quirky is another word that springs to mind in this connection.

Then again, Vonnegut's message hasn't altered much over the years. He's still for peace and the collapse of governments and the preservation of the American small town. I put it like this deliberately because the message, however palatable, however worthy, is banal; and especially banal when Vonnegut does a late-Ray-Bradbury act and serves up stories about rather nice helpless people who kinda love each other in little insignificant towns called North Crawford or Barnstable Village. *Welcome to the Monkey House* contains several examples of Vonnegut's Bradburian folksy side.

Of course, Bradbury is a guru, too. He may have made the Top Twenty, for all I know. It suggests that the recipe for guru-ism is fairly simple. One must be the voice of the times, which means thinking what a powerful youthful minority is going to think, a year ahead of them. The Vonnegut message is essentially the Bradbury message: distrust rulers, make – if not love – affection rather than war, opt – if not out entirely – out of the American technological dream. Read this way, the message, with its qualifications, can appeal to bourgeois and hippie alike – and nothing less than both barrels can blast you to the position of Guru 4.

What could push Vonnegut even further up the guru charts is his fashionable derision of organised religion, coupled with a constant preoccupation with way-out creeds – The Church of God the Utterly Indifferent in *Sirens of Titan*; Bokononism in *Cat's Cradle*. While Rosewaterism is itself almost a religion in *God Bless You, Mr Rosewater*, there are other creeds, like the New Ambrosian cult, which has degenerated into a picture on a beer label; The Iron Guardsmen of the White Sons of the American Constitution in *Mother Night*; and the 'So it goes' philosophy of Tralfamadore in *Slaughterhouse Five*.

Whatever the fake religion, in its beginning, for Vonnegut, is the word. He can build whole structures of belief on a grammatical *jeu d'esprit*. 'God smiles on the Meadows,' says Dr Gelhorne in *Player Piano*. ('Doctor Gelhorne said so many memorable things, it was hard for a person to stow them all away in his treasure house of souvenirs.')

Vonnegut is rather more palliative than challenge, for all his appearance of rebellion. If there were no more to his writing than the qualities I have outlined, he would be no more worth reading than (to be invidious) late Bradbury. But there is more. Even within the limitations of his message, for instance, he does not just deliver the cliché of distrusting governments: he produces good reason why they should be distrusted. And his good reason is the best reason: because governments are allowed into power by, and composed of, people like us; and the individual cannot be trusted. There was nothing abnormal about Eichmann; he just was instrumental in destroying six million humans through official channels.

Eichmann makes a personal appearance in the revised version of *Mother Night* (the one Cape published in hardcover in 1968, not the US paperback version of 1961). The central character, Howard W.Campbell Jnr, meets Eichmann in Tel-Aviv before they both go on trial. Eichmann delivers one of those cryptic messages so beloved by Vonnegut: 'Relax. Just relax.' This novel, incomparably Vonnegut's sharpest and most ingenious, takes as its central preoccupation the relationship between the individual and power – power in large manifestations like Nazi Germany, and small, like the Rev. Dr Jones, publisher of *The White Christian Minuteman*. Rather curiously, Vonnegut's introduction to this Cape edition mentions his wartime experience in Dresden, even mentions *the* slaughterhouse; perhaps it was the writing of this introduction that launched him on *Slaughterhouse Five*.

As to what else Vonnegut has to offer, defence need present only one item: his divine ingenuity. Ingenuity is the key to most of his novels. The ingenuity in *Mother Night* is so vast, so all-encompassing, so integral, that this writer tiptoes away from any attempt at analysis, hoping that readers who do not know the novel will hasten to do the right thing by themselves. Even in

Vonnegut's first novel, *Player Piano*, ingenuity is solidly there, but kept cautiously under control. In *Cat's Cradle*, it rules the roost, not entirely to the novel's advantage. In *Sirens of Titan*, it is in perfect equilibrium with the other elements.

To instance a little of *Sirens'* plot. Winston Niles Rumfoord and his dog Kazak are little more than wave phenomena since they were caught in a chrono-synclastic infundibulum; they stretch from the sun to Betelgeuse; but they have synchronised with the orbit of Titan, one of Saturn's satellites, and are permanently materialised there. They share the world with Salo.

Salo is a machine who had been stuck on Titan for two thousand years – a mere drop in the ocean to Salo, who is eleven million years old (Earth years, that is). Salo was travelling from one end of the universe to the other when his spaceship broke down. The name of his home planet was Tralfamadore which, one might as well add, since Tralfamadore also appears in *Slaughterhouse Five*, means both 'all of us' and 'the number 541'.

With him, Salo is carrying a message sealed in a thin lead wafer, which he considers it important to deliver. He signals back to Tralfamadore for a replacement for his spaceship and awaits developments, passing the time by watching events on Earth through his viewer.

'It was through his viewer that he got his first reply from Tralfamadore. The reply was written on Earth in huge stones on a plain in what is now England. The ruins of the reply still stand, and are known as Stonehenge. The meaning of Stonehenge in Tralfamadorian, when viewed from above, is: "Replacement part being rushed with all possible speed."

Stonehenge wasn't the only message old Salo had received. There had been four others, all of them written on Earth.

The Great Wall of China means in Tralfamadorian, when viewed from above: "Be patient. We haven't forgotten about you."

The Golden House of the Roman Emperor Nero meant: "We are doing the best we can."

The meaning of the Moscow Kremlin when it was first walled was: "You will be on your way before you know it."

The meaning of the Palace of the League of Nations in

Geneva, Switzerland, is: "Pack up your things and be ready
to leave on short notice." '

This local accident of having Salo grounded on Titan has
warped the whole of Earth's history. Eventually, the spare part
turns up on Titan, brought by young Chrono, who arrived with
his mother, Rumfoord's ex-wife, and his father, Malachai Constant; Chrono believes the replacement is just a good-luck charm.

Eventually, Salo opens the message he is carrying, the
message responsible for the major disruption of life in the solar
system. The message says: 'Greetings.'

It is absurd. It is pointless, nihilist, dadaist. And it has the
profundity of anti-meaning. What, after all, could more
profitably be carried round the universe than greetings? *The
Sirens of Titan* is good surrealism. Appollinaire took as his
motto: 'I astonish!'; André Breton said: 'The marvellous is
always beautiful, anything marvellous is beautiful'. *The Sirens
of Titan* is astonishing and beautiful. Like other surrealists, Vonnegut is trying to unite thought and feeling by the shock of the
inconsequential, to mend that classical Western division between
head and heart, thought and feeling.

Perhaps a postscript on Guru 4 needs to be added for those who
have come to him recently – for instance, tempted by that
staggering recommendation from Mr Graham Greene, tacked
on the cover of *God Bless You, Mr Rosewater*, like a Queen's
Award for Industry seal: ONE OF THE BEST LIVING AMERICAN
WRITERS.

It seems almost too obvious to require mention that Vonnegut
is a science fiction writer. He has denied this charge himself, thus
causing much anguish to lesser writers back in the sf ghetto, far
from guru-dom, who believe that he should remain in the leaking
house with them, sharing their sense of martyrdom and neglect.
His reasons for denying the charge are surely both obvious and
good; he wishes to be judged on his own merits, rather than
damned for their shortcomings; he needs independence. The cli-
quishness of sf writers is something every right-thinking author
zooms away from just as soon as he earns an advance large
enough to buy gasoline.

For all that, Vonnegut owes a tremendous debt to the sf field
– and admits it, in some of the more amusing passages of his
least inventive novel, *Mr Rosewater*, where he good-naturedly
joshes the sf writers at a Milford convention for their fraternal
spirit ('We few, we happy few, we band of brothers'), and for
their worrying over the way the world is going ('You're the only
ones zany enough to agonise over time and distances without
limit, over mysteries that will never die, over the fact that we are
right now determining whether the space voyage for the next
million years or so is going to be Heaven or Hell'); he also
invents – and quotes from – an old science fiction writer,
Kilgore Trout, who appears again in *Slaughterhouse* and
Breakfast of Champions.

The sf field is a field of gurus manqué. The messianic
complex, of which Vonnegut has more than his share, is evident
in writers who either save or destroy the world. L.Ron Hubbard
wrote *Fear*, *The Typewriter in the Sky*, and novellas under the
name of René Lafayette before arising and founding Dianetics,
later Scientology. Arthur C.Clarke almost got a patent on
communication satellites. Robert Heinlein wrote *Stranger in a
Strange Land*, a compulsory campus novel some years back;
while the cult now is for Frank Herbert's *Dune* – both books
were mentioned in the recent Charles Manson trial. Scratch an
sf writer and you tickle a prophet. The disease is known as
H.G.Wellsitis.

Sirens of Titan resembles in its bounce and invention Alfred
Bester's *Tiger Tiger* (something of a cult book among later sf
writers); the verbal felicity may owe something to Theodore
Sturgeon, while the general theme of an oblique battle between
good and evil is most reminiscent of the novels of the prolific
Philip K.Dick.

I'm taking bets that Dick will rise to be one of the next gurus.
Meanwhile, it's good to see that Vonnegut has made it out of the
ghetto. Greetings! Relax. Just relax.

Barefoot: Its First Decade

Strange things happened in the nineteen-sixties. More children than ever before came crowding through flimsy gates of flesh into our world, more would-be-babies than ever before were quenched before they had knowledge of life. Maybe it was because of all the overcrowding, but the sixties was also the decade when more and more people decided to throw away an old life style and wear a new one.

New concepts of the city — themselves products of over-population — encouraged new ways of life. While think-tanks like the Hudson Institute were smuggling in enormous Magritte-shaped chunks of the future under our noses, and man was firing his hardware into the near reaches of space, Dr Doxiadis, Greek architect and guru, was proposing an open-ended world-city, Ecumenopolis ('The Inevitable City of the Future'), to creep over the globe in a continually lengthening echelon.

Whether in space or in Ecumenopolis, the postulated Anthropos was going to be a different kind of creature. In the sixties, we felt Anthropos breathing down our necks.

Old ways of life appeared unsatisfactory. All kinds of new ways were invented. Their very newness made them exciting and dangerous. The danger was often increased by use of drugs. Drugs help you throw your old mind away; many people never found need of another one. The decade ended with the Sharon Tate murders and the trial of Charles Manson, hippie Christ, rapist, murderer, life-style man. It certainly was bloody sunset.

When I wrote the first fragment of *Barefoot in the Head*, towards the end of 1965, the decade looked different. Not sunset; high and early in a golden afternoon. In England, we had had the flower-power thing; succulent post-pubertal voices were still singing about Coming to San Francisco, while the Beatles tried to persuade us that all we needed was love. It was a lie, but the high count of discarded foetuses and mutilated daughters in the garbage-cans of Haight-Ashbury was not then public knowledge. The good trips Aldous Huxley had enjoyed on acid still lent their blessing to a whole lot of squalor.

The drop-out acid movement, in other words, sounded pretty good. Especially when you compared it with that big machine of the going political world, where it was observable that many nasty things were going on in a generous selection of countries, under the holy name of Law and Order.

I'm just a timid middle-class man, with the in-built predilection of my class for Law and Order. What I don't want is too much Law and Order. Also, I have a sneaking respect for the squalor, from the literary squalor of what used to be called *la vie bohème* onwards. I need to enlarge on that point, because it is an important part of *Barefoot*.

'Civilisation is the distance man has placed between himself and his excreta.' That was the epigraph I used in my 1964 novel, *The Dark Light Years*. Every now and again, civilisation to a younger generation suddenly looks more like a psychosis than an achievement. That's when I think of my epigraph, because there is something sick in the way mankind tries to forget or ignore its animal nature. The most expensive invention in history is not the internal combustion engine, getting such a bad press these days, but the flush toilet, which has propelled us further from Mother Nature than rocket ever took us from Mother Earth. It is the most basic discontinuity in all ecological cycles. That which was of the soil is returned not to the soil but to a sewage plant and thus to the sea – while nine-tenths of our domestic water is expended launching it on its voyage. (I'm aware that Sweden now has a vacuum-extraction process; but bucket and shovel are better for crops and humility.) *Dark Light Years* thought along these lines, comparing the hygiene-phobias of mankind with the mysticism of a perfect gentle race of creatures the utods, who accepted their own excrement without revulsion.

Law and Order – or anarchy and excrement? I was not sure which was better. I wrote *Barefoot* to find out which I preferred. Not to keep you in suspense, I came out on the side of . . . well, against anarchy, let's say. Part of the excitement many people have found in *Barefoot* is because the debate was live to me as I wrote it.

Which brings us to the parallel theme. The trouble with anarchy is that it takes you back in time. The world is now too thickly populated for anarchy. You have to accept Organisation, if you accept reality, and urbanism rather than some bum rurality.

The hero of this novel is Charteris. Charteris goes on a trip and comes to see himself as a sort of Messiah. Others con him into accepting the role. Charteris and his followers drive off through Europe, ironically tracing the fantasy map of Doxiadis's megalopolitan system for Europe 2000 AD. They imagine that their anarchy is taking them in a new direction. Instead, they go speeding straight down the old roads to the Stone Age.

They are retravelling history. That must be a mistake. That's why I could not accept the idea of a 'hippie culture' intellectually, however sympathetic I was emotionally: you wind up with a Crucifixion. As so often happens, Nature followed Art, and Charles Manson emphasised my point for me.

There's also a strain in the novel and the poems which asks whether we are yet able to embark on any further evolutionary progress. We belt across the M-roads of our Western culture — the automobile may be new but we are equipped still with the brains, eyes, reflexes of the Stone Age.

I speak diagnostically, trying to conceal the warmth I still feel for my canvas, and for the figures moving in its tragic landscape. If I make it sound past-derived, that's not so. It's a future-derived book. Let's use that word *humility* again; if the West shows continued arrogance, fails to acquire humility, then one day, some way, the Third World will reach for a larger share of Earth's riches. They may strike as they strike in *Barefoot*. Psychotomimetic chemicals are so cheap to make and deliver; a blanketing of LSD-derivative is as effective as a nuclear strike. And takes you back to the Stone Age just as fast.

Barefoot is a poetical novel of ideas. Its language will have to speak for itself. I dwelt inside the idiom, with the results you encounter in the book.

There's philosophy in it, too; mainly the rather suspect

philosophy of Ouspenski and Gurdjieff, because that fitted my theme exactly. Those two buffoon-thinkers camping out in towns, half-eating, mashing science to fit their maze of ideas, are the very mirror of hippie philosophers. In such cases, philosophy, which should be a coherent system of ideas, is worn like a patched coat over anarchy of thought. So with Charteris. And Charteris is not his real name.

But we all travel through life under our aliases . . .

Barefoot is a European novel, notes for which were often written in the actual situation, from Jugoslavia and Strasbourg to Italian autostrada and Belgium, where I saw the broken STELLA ART sign glowing in the dark ('Stella Artois' is a drinkable Belgian beer) and began to get the message. There's a passage in 'Drake-Man Route' which was written in a SAS plane just after we had taken off from Arlanda Airport, heading south for Copenhagen. Other bits were written on the beautiful stretch of the A6 south of Loughborough. I slept in the Metz hotel and on Ostend beach.

It took me over three years to put all the pieces together. I used up all I knew about fiction or science fiction, about scientific processes, historical cycles, philosophical reasoning, and men and women. I shot my bolt, and for a while believed I would never be able to write sf again.

Since then, I must have learned some new things. Or forgotten caution.

The Gulf and the Forest: Contemporary SF in Britain

British sf has come a long way since *Beowulf*. Perhaps the first thing to be said about the British scene is that we have more science fiction writers than ever before. Many of them are independent-minded men who have taken the plunge and become full-time writers. Only when you write full time can you sample to the dregs authorship's despairs, its isolation, its occasional keen joys. Only then are you dedicated. It is what is known in the vernacular as putting your balls on the chopping-block.

Let's name some of the independent writers. Recent declarations of independence have come from Ian Watson, Andrew Stephenson, Rob Holdstock, Chris Morgan, Mark Adlard, Bob Shaw, and Philip Dunn (who also runs a one-man publishing business). Of these writers, only Bob Shaw can be said to be established. All willingly embark on hazardous waters, as I remember doing twenty years ago.

Also independent are Richard Cowper, Edmund Cooper, Christopher Priest, Duncan Lunan, Lawrence James, Tanith Lee, Barrington Bayley, Michael Coney, D.J.Compton, Angus Wells, and M.John Harrison. Some of them are content to live on potatoes as long as they can write. Others are among the highest-paid writers in the world, earning say £50,000 a year.

Then there's an older age group which includes such stalwarts as Kenneth Bulmer, John Brunner, E.C.Tubb, John Christopher, Michael Moorcock, J.G.Ballard, and me. I'd better exclude Fred Hoyle, a frier of other fish. I also exclude expatriates like Charles Platt, Bertram Chandler, and Arthur C.Clarke; and there are people whose reputation lies mainly in other fields of writing, like Angela Carter, Nigel Kneale, Peter Dickinson, Roald Dahl, and Terry Nation, creator of The Daleks. Excluding them, I've listed twenty-five people who live the lion's life of an author. That says a lot for the state of the art, and for our healthy independence of mind. No other country can claim as much.

We rely on our living on selling outside the British Isles. We rely on Australia, of course, where authors are now learning the hard way to become independent themselves, and where much excellent sf criticism is born. We rely on Scandinavia, on the continent of Europe, and particularly on France, where sf thrives as never before. On Japan. And on the United States of America.

You'll have to forgive me when I remind you that sf originated in Britain. (French, German, Hungarians and Russians mistakenly believe the same about their countries.) But, no matter what country gave birth to the poor bastard child, the US certainly became its orphanage.

The States has been so generous to sf that it thinks of it as its own child. Well, damn it, for a long while nobody else applied for adoption. The States provides the world's largest and most lucrative market for sf, a magnet for writers everywhere. So big a magnet that it has tempted many British writers to adopt a Yankee idiom and compete with the natives. Often with some success.

Until World War II, there was very little British sf, despite the fact that Wells and Stapledon and others were still alive. One reason for this, I believe, was that less gifted writers than Wells were tempted to try for publication in American magazines, where they were hospitably received.

After the war, things changed. Arthur Clarke wrote English stories. And so did John Wyndham. The vogue for Wyndham is past, I suppose, but his career remains significant. In the early thirties, he won a small prize in Gernsback's *Air Wonder Stories*, and after that appeared quite regularly in magazines like *Wonder* and *Amazing* under the name of John Beynon Harris. Following the war and a spell in the army, he had to start his career again. He adopted a markedly English style and English subjects. At once, his first novel, *The Day of the Triffids*, was serialised in *Collier's* and published in Britain in hardcover, where it became an enduring best-seller. *The Kraken Wakes*, known in the States as *Out of the Deeps*, was almost as successful. For over a decade, Wyndham produced a novel every other year; some, like *The Chrysalids* (or *Rebirth*) were real beauties.

Wyndham's novels appeared in Penguin Books, then a British institution like the BBC. As a result, Penguin Books turned to science fiction. I'm by no means a mercenary man, but I must point out that Penguins immediately began to pay twice as much as any previous British paperback publisher. I know because I was the first editor of their sf series. I also edited three Penguin sf anthologies published in 1961, 1963 and 1964, which introduced many of my favourite American writers to an English public, where they have thrived since. (Those three volumes, now issued as an omnibus, have sold almost a quarter million copies and must represent the longest-lived of all anthologies.)

Wyndham, that conservative man, was the true begetter of the New Wave. It was he even more than Clarke with interstellar subjects or Tolkien with his brand of ur-history, who proved to those who had forgotten their H.G. Wells that you could write ordinary local stories about time paradoxes or perambulating vegetables and hold an audience, without necessarily imitating Heinlein or Van Vogt.

It must be hard for American connoisseurs of sf to comprehend the origins of the British New Wave. From where I stood at the time, I saw its first achievement was to chuck out from the two British magazines, *New Worlds* and *Science Fantasy*, the chaps who were filling them with American forgeries. That is to say, the British writers who tried for American markets and failed, selling instead to the cheaper British magazines. I was for chucking them out. Imitations are no good.

Since that palace revolution in the mid-sixties, British writers have contributed as never before to world sf. For us, that cleansing was an absolute necessity, just as it was necessary for John W. Campbell to chuck out the old guard when he assumed control of *Astounding*. Michael Moorcock was doing Campbell's work in a different context. Maybe we didn't like – or understand – all we read in the new *New Worlds*, but by God we knew it had a creative impulse behind it. Those were fighting days.

The new fiction brought a more lively audience to sf which it has never lost. In place of the old suffocating atmosphere, breezes blew from outside. One practical result of this has been the re-introduction of science fiction as an ordinary part of the average reader's diet – part of the roughage along with Richard Adams or Margaret Drabble or Edna O'Brien. It has also meant that there are critics and editors and publishers with a sympathetic insight into science fiction. And they see it as a creative force, not just a marketable commodity.

A fanzine called *Cidereal Times* landed on my desk this morning. (Cider is a Somerset drink and this is a Somerset SF Society publication.) Michael Elvis writes in an editorial, 'What I think is needed is a return to the New Wave of ten or so years ago, not necessarily in content or even in style, but in vitality, which is what SF seems to lack, today.' It may sound like Chairman Mao's prescription for perpetual revolution, but discomfort is better than stagnation.

Perhaps I'm wrong in thinking that our revolution was widely misunderstood in the States just because a few established American writers spoke against it. It was anti-bunk, not anti-American. But a gulf opened then which is only just being bridged.

That gulf has helped us become independent, made us seek our own role. The same process takes place in every country; because it is always directed towards originality, against imitation, it deserves understanding rather than a load of bullshit about stamping it out. Just last year, I witnessed the attempt not to remain subservient to Anglo-American sf taking place in Italy and Denmark and Sweden. The hostility that was expressed towards our revolution has led some English writers to welcome the gulf, take less jam on their bread, and ignore the American market.

I prefer bridges to gulfs. Even if you have sentries at both ends of the bridge. My first novel, *Non-Stop* (*Starship* in the States, alas) was dialogue with American premises; I still see the democratic ideal as enshrined in your country as of utmost value in our embattled world. My discourse is intended as much for the States as for the Europe to which I belong.

The gulf is also bridged by American writers who have derived encouragement from this side of the Atlantic. Early birds like Norman Spinrad (Hero of the Resistance, damned in the House of Parliament!), Thomas Disch, John Sladek, Stout Trooper Harry Harrison, and others arrived a while ago. Without leaving home, such writers as Philip K.Dick, Frederik Pohl, Robert Sheckley, and Ursula Le Guin have found, I believe, some temperamental affinity with England, as did the late James Blish. They have won large supportive audiences here.

So far, I have written of safe, non-controversial matters. Now I need to launch out more widely. Even in an age sprouting new media, literacy remains of paramount importance. No invention supersedes literacy – even totalitarianism. Perfection is achieved only on paper, and the written word is the means by which we perpetuate, not our species, but our civilisation – without which our species is worth a questionable amount. Voyager spacecraft are a test of the reality of the alphabet.

Literature is always under threat, writers always under pressure, and so it should be. One element that menaces literature is Formula. Formula is the enemy within, the hardening of the arteries. In the present day, commercial fiction of most kinds relies on formula at all stages of production, whether it is Gothic, supernatural, tough tec, western, hospital romance, or whatever.

There is much to be said for formula. It makes the whole performance easier for writer, reader and publisher. Formula fulfils expectations; if life proves disappointing, then we want to read that love and constancy win in the end, that the international communist dope-smuggler gets his come-uppance, that the corrupt city can be cleansed by one disillusioned hero. A world in which Superman breaks a leg falling downstairs or Maigret fails to solve his case is worse than silly, it's pointless. The whole point of formula is that it first teases and then satisfies expectations, one hundred percent of the time. Anything else is bad business.

My faith in sf as a medium lies in the belief that it can never become entirely formularised; that by its nature it keeps breaking out of its shell, that it challenges us, enlarges us.

Yet now as never before sf is threatened by formula, simply because it is so commercially successful. Hence it is packaged on both sides of the Atlantic as formula writing, with formula covers and formula blurbs. It is easier to sell a novel if it runs to formula, easier still if it forms part of a formula series.

An example of sf formula: the galactic empire. Imperialism is a dead duck in the real world, an exhausted topic, a nineteenth-century hangover, yet it still passes for live in many a ritualistic fantasy.

Edgar Rice Burroughs and E.E.Smith have much to answer for. Though you can't blame them for their imitators. They discovered and capitalised on certain formulas now widely used without thought. Formula, as I say, is not to be despised, in that it meets certain deeply felt requirements and allays anxiety by showing us that the world is what we expect. This is precisely the message sf should not deliver. Astonishment is everything. Literature is in any case not designed as a soporific; it should awaken us.

More to be blamed than Smith and Burroughs are the supercilious critics of literature. They have in the main resolutely turned their backs on sf, refusing to seek its virtues, thus discouraging those writers who strive to forge individual work; for those same writers less readily find the security offered by a mass audience, although they are the ones who in fact maintain forward momentum.

Sometimes, new prescriptions emerge. We leap to our feet cheering. It happened with Gernsback at first, with John Campbell at first, with the advent of *Galaxy*, with the advent of *F&SF*, and with Moorcock's *New Worlds*. Everything demands form if not formula. But vain repetition is the death of any literature. How many institutions of Doc Smith or Tolkien or *Dune* or Perry Rhodan have you seen and (I hope) passed by this year?

And this is where British writers are valuable to the American audience. I won't claim that we disdain formula – that would be daft. But we are conscious of being part of a literary tradition which is not outcast, and so we sometimes manage to write freshly; living outside your pressures, your society, but sharing your language, we can be relied upon for a different approach.

To this should be added a marginal thought. British sf writers are not segregated from other writers. We just form a healthy part of the cultural scene. Conversely, there are British writers like Anthony Burgess, Doris Lessing, Emma Tennant, Kingsley Amis, Martin Amis, Martin Bax, Adrian Mitchell, and others who sometimes write novels you might easily mistake for science fiction. Our publishers are not so obsessed with categories – and that goes for the writers too. I prefer writing something out on a limb; the old sense of adventure retains muscle-tone that way.

So far, this article has dealt with differences between American and British sf. Those differences fade when we begin looking at what we have in common. I refer to the language itself – and here I draw on something I wrote for a British fanzine, *Maya*. We will talk not of gulfs but of forests.

We are accustomed to looking towards the future, but to assess the contribution Britain makes to science fiction, we must glance backwards to periods long before sf existed.

The English language has been growing like a great forest for over a thousand years. The first leaves of that forest survive from the sixth century. Among those leaves are such poems as *Widsith*, *Beowulf*, and *The Wanderer*, which convey a kind of awe for the world and its strangeness which we can recognise as the spirit which, at least in part, informs contemporary science fiction.

As the forest has developed in response to changing conditions, so has the response to the wonderful, but that response is present in some of our greatest writers. The Langland of *Piers Plowman*, Chaucer, Marlowe, Shakespeare, Bunyan, Milton, Thomas Browne, Johnson, Pope, the Romantics such as Shelley and Byron, and the novelists and poets of last century – all in this long and illustrious line preserve a vision that escapes from the dull appearance of everyday. I do not know enough about other literatures to make useful comparisons; but a glance at Racine and Molière as compared with, say, Shakespeare and Congreve is revealing. The unities of drama were certainly not invented in this country; here, joy is never at home.

This tremendous green bank balance of the imagination is something on which British science fiction writers draw. Our language is so much one of metaphor and metonym, of shifting light and shade, that we have only to say 'the dew is on the rose' to flood our minds with a host of associations about early mornings and English summers and so on – associations both vague and powerful.

The opening sentence of John Wyndham's *The Chrysalids* is this: 'When I was quite small I would sometimes dream of a city.' So powerful are the associations here that we are immediately prepared for a novel of visionary intensity. Yet, simplicity apart, there is nothing in the sentence which can be labelled as particularly Wyndham's – apart from the way in which the grand, fruitful traditions of the language are at Wyndham's and his reader's disposal.

Turn to the first novel in our language which is unmistakably science fiction, Mary Shelley's *Frankenstein* (1818). We can see an imaginative tradition behind it, in particular the translation of the Bible, Milton's *Paradise Lost*, and Mary's father's novel, *Caleb Williams*. The text makes specific reference to *Paradise Lost*, just as Kingsley Amis's *The Alteration* scrupulously makes reference to Philip Dick's *The Man in the High Castle*.

After *Frankenstein*, it is easy to trace that imaginative tradition forward. H.G.Wells, an innovator of thematic material, belongs to the tradition which includes Defoe, Swift, and Mary Shelley. Olaf Stapledon apart, all British sf writers write within this tradition, however debased it may become in their particular case. Writers who show loving care for the language, like Ballard, Cowper, Masson and Moorcock, revivify the tradition without rebelling against it. In some of his most recent and best books, Moorcock exhibits remarkable synoptic grasp of the English past, its language, its tropes; I'm thinking in particular of *The Dancers at the End of Time* series, and *Gloriana*.

Moorcock is the Old Inextinguishable, and makes most other British writers seem pale and constipated by comparison.

In Shelley's time, technology had begun to advance with steadier tread. As C.S.Lewis put it, 'The sciences long remained like a lion cub whose gambols delighted its master in private; it had not yet tasted man's blood.' The Frankenstein theme of man's creation out of control is probably sf's major theme; it is a British coinage.

If one characteristic of our science fiction is to be singled out, it

must be continuing scepticism; above all, scepticism about
man's supremacy over nature and the benefits of unremitting
technology. We have no writer of the standard of even, say,
Larry Niven, who celebrates the extension of white
technological power into the far future in a series of action-
fantasies; true, there is always Arthur C.Clarke, but in Clarke's
technological futures the human beings are generally rather
passive or else are observers (as in *Rendezvous With Rama*), not
supermen of the Van Vogtian mould.

We have bred no thorough-going technocrats such as Gernsback, E.E.Smith, Campbell, Asimov, or Heinlein. Ours is, on
the whole, a technological culture. Technology means power,
and the great bulk of magazine and paperback sf is power-
fantasy, escapism with strong action heroes. Most fantasy can
be written very fast − hence the productivity of sf's most
characteristic exponents. It's the plot that matters, not refine-
ments of character or reflections on life, which are a mainstay of
real novels.

Here I find myself wondering about my old friend Harry
Harrison. Consider the way in which he does not fit into
categories, or into any of the sweeping generalisations I have
made here, and then ask whether this is not the cause for a
general underestimation of his work − for readers prefer a writer
they can categorise easily.

To all intents and purposes, Harrison is a technocrat in the
lineage of Smith, Campbell, and Heinlein. Most of his books
centrally concern the use of power, whether power as a gigantic
machine or as a pill (the inimitable Stainless Steel Rat is a pill-
taker of the first order). But Harrison possesses a powerful
mickey-taking sense; the boot is forever going in. Hard.
American writers who are sceptical about the benefits of
technology are often forced to adapt a jokey tone; we see this in
Vonnegut, Sheckley, John Sladek, and Ron Goulart − and in
Harrison, but Harrison has a ferocity that the others lack.
Harrison is a rebel.

There is a reason why Harrison, an American, has settled
over this side of the Atlantic, as there was a reason why Blish
did so; and that reason is not simply because Harrison finds the
British endlessly funny. It is because he experienced, early in his

career, a sense of disaster, and a sympathy with the underdog (or rather a hatred of the overdog) which estranged him from the mainstream of Campbellian sf. I suppose that novels such as *A Transatlantic Tunnel, Hurrah!* can be read, not just for their own sweet sake, but as tokens of his alienation from American dominance and his affection for the land of British Rail and English beer. Transcending his origins, travelling compulsively, Harrison can hardly be claimed for British sf; since he established World sf, we must leave him as an international figure – one of the first.

Preoccupations with power in science fiction stories tend to exclude tender relationships between the sexes; so that such relationships in power-fantasy tend to the formulatic (boy gets girl in final paragraph) or are censored out entirely. Away on alien planets or zooming in their space-ships, the tough guys are safe from female complications.

British sf, not having this preoccupation with power, is generally more liberal with sexual encounters. Incidentally, the New Wave was anti-technological and anti-power orientated, with a resulting powerful release of libido. Significantly, while the New Wavers paid due tribute to their more illustrious hard sf predecessors, the technocrats could find no good in what was new: it had dirty words, guys did dirty things to girls, people went to bed instead of to Mars. The technocrats felt themselves threatened.

With scepticism goes another frequent English usage, irony. This quality one finds also in those American writers I mentioned earlier as bridging the gulf, Philip Dick, Ursula Le Guin, and Fred Pohl. Irony is rarely found in formula writing, for obvious reasons. Formula writing's basic function is reassurance, whereas irony works by questioning the reader's values.

Our best writers use sf to explore that irony formulated by Shelley long ago when he claimed that man, having enslaved the elements, remains himself a slave. This disturbing premise is also used by Wells, Aldous Huxley, George Orwell, C.S.Lewis, and J.R.R Tolkien. Those names rank among the most honoured of science fiction writers anywhere in the world.

All of which suggests that British sf is simply, or not so

simply, a branch of literature, and concerns itself with the peren-
nial questions of good and evil within us, adapting this concern
to the surrealist environments of change. Characteristically,
landscape plays a large role in the genre. Disaster novels – an
English speciality since Wyndham's day – are often exercises in
landscapes. Characteristically, the alien is absent from British sf.

It is American sf which confronts us with the alien
personalised. There are probably historical reasons for this –
white and black Americans being themselves aliens in a red land
– but, whatever the reasons, the effect is generally to make us
(the Earthmen) goodies and the intruders baddies. Much drama
is to be had from such confrontations, but it is surely more
sophisticated as well as better theology to recognise evil within
ourselves rather than as an external phenomenon. Pretending
otherwise leads to the pastoral of *Star Trek*, where half a dozen
sexless saints go forth and impose American diplomacy on a
naughty galaxy.

A matter-of-fact acknowledgement of evil and corruption,
implicit alike from Wells's Dr Moreau to Ballard's Dr Nathan,
leads to the often-heard charge that British sf is 'too pessimistic'.
If one wants optimism, one must turn, not to the States, but to
the Soviet Union, where optimism is official. There you are
required to be 'positive' about the Soviet future or they take
away your typewriter and give you a shovel instead.

Perhaps British science fiction is not ambitious enough. Yet I
have just read five recent novels which are enjoyable, well-
written, and generally enhance life. They are Christopher
Priest's *The Space Machine*, Bob Shaw's *A Wreath of Stars*,
Michael Moorcock's *The Hollow Lands*, Michael Coney's
Brontomek!, and Kingsley Amis's alternative world, *The
Alteration*. All have that modest British virtue of modesty,
together with an enormous competence which, like a Harris
Tweed coat, stems in part from the traditions behind them. I
cannot imagine that any other country will produce five such
pleasing novels this year – though they may make more noise
over fifty inferior ones.

Science fiction, however, is not simply a few authors and the
texts they produce. These days, it is very much more. It is an
industry with various departments. All these departments are

almost totally lacking in Britain. This applies particularly to the critical department.

Foundation under Malcolm Edwards and *Vector* under David Wingrove are two journals which publish interesting criticism of an informed order, but they are exceptions in this country rather than the rule. In the States, matters are different. Science fiction appears increasingly as a subject on university curricula and the result has been that admirable American phenomenon, an immediate response. The immediate response has come in the form of a whole new school of critics, many of them members of the SFRA (The Science Fiction Research Association, a branch of the MLA). They publish a great many papers, and organise their own conventions.

Their papers may be published in the doyen of critical magazines, Dr Darko Suvin's *Science Fiction Studies*, published from McGill University in Canada, or by new publishers like Taplinger which specialise in science fiction criticism (for instance the Writers of the 21st Century Series, edited by Joseph Olander and Martin H.Greenberg) or the excellent Borgo Press in California. This activity would have been unthinkable ten years ago.

Certainly some of the criticism is clumsy, and some of it comes garbed in ugly Marxist phraseology, but its direction on the whole is admirable, and useful for the field, a counterbalance to the increasing popularity and trivialisation of sf. The new critics are often more concerned with establishing a methodology and their own pecking order than in elucidation and in communication with the ordinary reader; we have to see that as inevitable, an opening phase in an innovative game. Good things can derive from it. If sf is a new literature, it must have a new criticism.

Only in America is there the dynamism to produce it.

Hoping

Looking Forward to 2001

The Oxford Union is one of Britain's leading places of debate, the traditional training ground for Oxford University students who have, or hope to have, a political career ahead of them.

What follows is my one and only speech in the Union, in support of the motion that 'This House is Looking Forward to the Year 2001'. Other speakers included James Cameron and Lord Kennet.

Mr Chairman, Fellow Mortals,

I suppose you all know what death is. It's that last great MOT Test in the skies, that undiscovered bun-fight from whose custard-pies no traveller revives. Undertakers used to charge £95 per head for it; this week, it's gone up to £120 per head, and I daren't tell you how much for the body.

Even those of you who are not actually dead yourselves will have had a loved one die: a cherished brother, a little old Irish grandmother, a favourite fishmonger, a pet tortoise adored for its associations with your first sweetheart, from whom you rescued it, or vice versa. You will know of its sting, its bite, its – if I may phrase it this way, Mr Chairman – its appalling waste of human life.

Some of my best friends are in the EEC, the East Ealing Cemetery. Others are in publishing. The remainder are being remaindered.

You know what mortality is? It's when dental decay spreads to the rest of the body, converting it into a body at rest. If you find the subject distasteful, remember that death is just nature's way of telling us to slow down, to cool it.

Recall the words of William Shakespeare, great poet, great dramatist, quite funny in his own way too: 'We are such stuff as dreams are made on, and our little life is rounded out by a good old plateful of pig's trotters and mash – with croutons if you're lucky.' But there, that's poetry. Immortal Bard they call him. Immortal? Nonsense. Shakespeare's dead – I read it in the papers. Defunct, deceased, his skull selling in antique shops all over the world. He's not looking forward to 2001.

When our distinguished chairman asked me if I was looking forward to 2001, I said I had already seen it four times. A natural confusion. I dropped a Kubrick. Now I understand very well what the motion before us means. It means that we approach the future with excitement, empathy, and tolerant amusement. Of course we do. When we cease to experience excitement, empathy, and tolerant amusement, we are dead.

The gentlemen speaking against the motion will probably seek to confuse us with talk about the present world crisis and the disastrous state of the British economy. They will strike out at us, like Moses with a fist full of bulrushes, warning us of bankruptcy, anarchy, spiritual deserts, dearer coffee, and the agony of British Leyland. They will conjure up the spirits of the illustrious dead – Keynes, Karl Marx, Bertrand Russell, Mary Whitehouse – with which to terrify us. They may even go on about Spengler's *Decline of the West*. There's a vague possibility that they will try to kid us that things are going from bad to worse, and that 2001 will be practically uninhabitable.

Don't listen. Plug your ears with old copies of that fun book, *A Handbook to the University of Oxford*. The earliest scrap of papyrus exhumed in a prehistoric Babylonian latrine, states, when interpreted, that things ain't what they used to be. When the Lord Almighty (as He was then) created the World, He walked around it on the Seventh Day and His first words to Adam – His very first words to Adam – were, 'I liked this place better the way it was on the First Day.'

Let me assure you all that the miseries of public life and public events have precious little to do with our private and personal experiences. Every century had brought with it one crowning horror or another, yet human life has gone on, from Chaucer and the Black Death to Alistair Maclean and myxamatosis. That's what Henry Ford meant when, summing

up a weight of academic learning of which even this great
university might be proud, he said, 'History is bunk.' Despite
history, private life goes on. The Hundred Years' War is nothing
beside the girl next door.

No deterioration, you see, just evolutionary change. Institutions decline and fall — and this Union could do with a coat of
paint — other institutions rise. Down goes Greece, up comes
Rome; Spain goes down, Britain comes up; literature goes
down, science fiction — but that's another story ...

If you have any appetite for life at all, the only catastrophe
that matters is the brevity of life itself. You have just learnt to
read the thrilling serial story of our civilisation when you are
snatched away in mid-instalment — and will never know how it
all ends.

What appears to be happening, as far as one can interpret
global trends, is that the momentum of the Renaissance, which
was born in Europe, is dying in Europe. After centuries of good,
even riotous, living, spending beyond our means in the form of
war, we find the bills coming in. The norms of that Renaissance
have been fulfilled, often in unexpected ways, often to super-
abundance. But we have hit the law of diminishing returns; it is
no longer possible to paint like Tiepolo, invent like Farraday, or
anticipate a good ten cent cigar.

Not that Europe has run out of dynamism. Not that it shrivels
under the cold winds from the East. Not that it has become
merely a developing country compared with the over-developed
country, the USA, which has most successfully adapted Europe's
methods to a New World. Not exactly any of these things,
perhaps; rather that Europe has run out of a guiding philosophy.
The people cannot live without a religion, a myth, as someone
must have said.

But perhaps this theory is not correct. Perhaps we may yet
see the old master, Europe, leap up refreshed in the eighties or
nineties — the revival of the fittest, as it were. Who knows? I
want to be around in 2001 to find out.

And the rest of the world. All of it ticking at different times
like the circadian clocks of an enormous anatomy. Is it true that
it has by and large opted for the European way of life, or imitations thereof — for Western medicine and high productivity and

parliament and grouse shooting and the pursuit of foreign markets – without being able to grasp entirely the spirit of humanism and enquiry which informed the Renaissance ideal? I want to be around in 2001 to find out.

And the Soviet Union. There are no real signs that any amelioration is taking place in that oppressive régime. Yet nothing remains unchanged for long; how will that change manifest itself in Russia? In a genuine change of heart and personnel at the top? In a grass roots revolution or reformation? In a war with the West or China? I want to be around in 2001 to find out.

And the United States. Now that the Vietnam war is removed from their shoulders, will they find the will to tackle all those challenging problems which always remain just beyond solution? Will they find presidents of the stature of Roosevelt and Truman? Will they be able to turn their exuberance to truly creative ends? As a firm admirer of America, I want to be around in 2001 to find out.

And South America. Argentina seems to be vanishing down a well of inflation. Will she emerge? Will Brazil eventually dominate the hemisphere? Will the great contemporary problem of individual versus state – as acute in South America as anywhere – be worked out there? I want to be around in 2001 to find out.

And China, ever the mystery. With its long history of stasis in territory, government, and philosophy, will China throw off its present disorders and rise to become the major world power which finally imposes peace and even unity on the world? I want to be around in 2001 to find out.

And here at home. Are we going to live in a corporate state, with trades unions wielding all the power, or will a strong man of the Right with an Esher accent emerge? Will Scotland, Wales, Northern Ireland, Cornwall, the Isle of Wight, gain independence and cease sponging off England? Will we have sold off Centre Point and Sandringham to Brussels by 2001? I want to be around to find out.

And of course it's far from being merely a matter of nations. Ecological problems also require resolution. Will our industries fill the air with carbon dioxide until a hothouse effect builds up and we cook ourselves? Or is another Ice Age on its way to freeze us – and can we prevent it? Will science ever achieve a straight banana? I'd like to be around in 2001 to find out.

What turn will morality take next (this is one for you, Mr Chairman)? Is the permissive society going to materialise at last, just when I'm too old for it? When are film-makers going to give us dirty Westerns? Or will the next Archbishop of Canterbury bring back the Ten Commandments and enforce them by law? I want to find out. (Not much, but a bit).

Besides, there's absolutely no guarantee that 2001 is going to be all that atrocious. Pessimism is just a fashion, like jeans, Scott Joplin, modes of coitus, and Robert Redford. 2001 will be different, but to the 2001 generation it will not be dreadful. Let me sketch for you a day in the life of an ordinary Englishman, 15 May 2001.

'His name is Mike Singh. He's half-Irish, half-Pakistani. His son rouses him at five-thirty in the morning, with a cup of real hot water. None of your dehydrated stuff. Mike drinks one half and washes in the other half. He breakfasts on a handful of rice-and-chips, garnished with a radish grown in his window-box.

Fossil fuels have become too expensive for Britons like Mike to afford, owing to an astronomical trade deficit with the Pan-Arab Empire. As a result, artificial fertiliser is scarce and prohibitive in price. So all human dung is now conserved and used on the land and in window-boxes like Mike's. This has the beneficial result of making coastal waters fit to bathe in by tourists.

The British have indeed become a healthy nation, whereas the rest of Europe is suffering from the diseases of prosperity such as cardiac arrest, cancer, obesity, satyriasis and piles.

Mike Singh goes to work in Dover, where he has been directed by the Ministry of Labour and Moral Uplift. In fact, he drives an uplift truck, moving goods at the entrance to the Channel Tunnel. Yes, the Chunnel's built at last, because most of the British can afford only to walk to the Continent. From the French side, scores of vehicles are emerging, mainly dashing towards London to sample Marks and Spencer and *le vice anglais* and Double Gloucester. As the travel posters enticingly say, COME TO BRITAIN – GROTTY BUT CHEAP. To pander to the ever-increasing tourist trade, Britain is gradually abandoning driving on the left of the highway; at present, everyone drives in the middle.

In his lunch-break, Mike Singh drifts down to the flea market by the harbour, picks a few pockets, and sells some woven-grass teacloths his two wives have made. He is holographed by tourists from Tokyo, Kuwait, Seoul and Strimini, in search of local colour. Oh, you may not have heard of Strimini, which hasn't been built yet owing to the present deplorably slow rate of the population explosion, but by 2001 you will have done right enough. It's where all the world's traggeters are manufactured.

Content to be photographed, Mike sits on the harbour wall watching the boats – those beautiful crewless fully-automated nylon-sailed computer-controlled windjammers – sailing along in the Common Channel. Spiralling gasoline costs mean that clippers are back on the high seas, replacing air freight. British Rail also operate Rafts to Rotterdam.

Back at work, Mike finds that a game of cards helps the afternoon pass. Packs now consist of forty-two cards, owing to the paper shortage. Mike also chats with other supervisors (the word "worker" is out of fashion); some of them are incensed because the Prime Minister has admitted to privately owning his house – and him callin' hisself a communist an' all.

On his way home that evening, Mike stops to take a look at the big television screen over the post office. The Moon War is still going strong, with the US holding her own against Brazil and China. That's good news for the British economy. British factories turn out two million zips for the flies of US combat trousers every week the war lasts. Heavy industry is on its way back.

Still more cheering news. Birds are not extinct as feared. A pair of breeding sparrows has been observed in Newcastle-under-Lyme. The government is sending in a detachment of troops to protect the birds, in view of the proximity of the local political prisoners' camp.

Mike's wives give him a good tea of curried Scotch reindeer, after which he goes out for the evening with his mates. His favourite hobby is coxing an eight-man team which crews a muscle-powered sailplane.

Since he still has some of the week's drink coupons left, he rounds off the evening with a visit to his local for a litre of fuzzy pink National Beer ("Forget the Rational with National").

He returns to home and bed, sleeping securely between his two chubby wives, Fatima and Fatimama. Since he was sterilised at the age of twenty-one, at the same time he had his rabies injection, he can have fun without fear. And a drag of Benson & Hedges Lornox Grass sends him off to a peaceful night's sleep.'

I can't guarantee it will be exactly like that – but we can hope. I'm more than curious, I'm positively impatient, to see what will be happening in 2001. It is true, of course, that they may have to wheel me out in a wheelchair to see in the twenty-first century, but I'll be there at the celebrations if I can make it.

So what I am saying is simple and inarguable: (though the ineffable gentlemen of the Opposition will argue it) even the most awful event is more fascinating than it's awful. It's a privilege, the luck of the draw, to be alive. 'A million million spermatozoa, and out of them but one poor Noah . . .' We're allowed just one glimpse of this thrilling serial story of our civilisation, which is built on the daily life of our ancestors and is to be continued yet for countless generations to come. Just the one precious glimpse! You mustn't miss it.

> Breathes there a man with soul so dead
> Who never to himself hath said
> 'Though every damned thing has me vexed —
> I long to see what happens next!'

If only by dint of intellectual curiosity alone, yes, yes, of course we are looking forward to 2001. Otherwise we're dead – and not only from the neck up!

The motion was carried, surprisingly.

Living

The Hiroshima Man

Just after the midnight of 5 August 1945, on a small atoll in the Pacific called Tinian, a chaplain offered up a brief prayer for airmen about to fly on a dangerous mission. 'May the men who fly this night be kept safe in Thy care and may they be returned safely to us . . .'

The men concerned went off to a midnight breakfast consisting of eggs, sausage, and good American coffee. An hour later, a B-29, 'Straight Flush', a weather plane piloted by Captain Claude Eatherly, took off. Within an hour and a half, it was followed by 'Enola Gay'. Both planes headed towards the Japanese city of Hiroshima. In the belly of the 'Enola Gay' lay the atomic bomb affectionately christened 'Little Boy'.

It is, of course, a cliché – and none the less true for that – to say that the atomic age was born with the dropping of that bomb. It was a very difficult birth, just as its last years have been difficult and complex enough, full of enough ambiguities, to satisfy even a science fiction writer. The story of the birth of our age is related, concisely and impartially, in an American book* just published in this country.

This is a popular book, not littered with footnotes. It earns its place on a crowded shelf by being a model of clear reporting on the steps, mainly political, which led to the dropping of the bomb.

The ill winds of the century, scientific, economic, psychological, national and political, whirl over Hiroshima, making it the eye of the storm for a moment, before blowing outwards again in new and more ominous patterns. The dropping of the bomb, the last military act of World War II, was the first political act of the Cold War, aimed as much against the Soviets as against Japan. Since then, we have had to accommodate

* *The Decision to Drop the Bomb*, by Len Giovannitti and Fred Freed, Methuen, 1967.

ourselves to a world of political acts; the more thoroughly science interpenetrates our world, the more our lives enter the political arena. In cases of drought we now phone the Water Board, where our grandfathers bowed their heads to the Almighty.

Juxtaposed in the book with a picture of the 'Enola Gay' returning from its mission is a key photograph: the Big Three at the 1945 Potsdam Conference. There is Generalissimo Stalin, then known to and loved by the British public as 'Uncle Joe', with President Harry Truman, who had so recently taken over from Roosevelt, and Prime Minister Churchill, clutching his customary cigar. These leaders, whatever else they had done, had concluded the war against Hitler; the terrible facts about Hitler's extermination of the European Jews had recently come to light and were being digested, as far as that was possible. In two bombing raids on Dresden, 25,000 people had been killed and more injured; 83,000 people had been killed in Tokyo during one fire raid; over 1,000 V-rockets had fallen on Britain; the Russians had lost an estimated twenty million military and civilian dead.

Against such megalomaniac facts the decision was taken to drop the bomb. It was a way of ending the war quickly, the easy way; the alternative was to inflict more fire raids on Tokyo and to launch a full-scale invasion on the Japanese islands, when the death toll on both sides would have mounted enormously. And there was another consideration; at any moment, Russia would enter the war against Japan, and grab more territory to the East, as it had to the West.

In May 1945, Churchill had first used that drab phrase 'the Iron Curtain', which we were to grow to love so well. The multitudes who had survived the war had reluctantly to turn and face the spectre Churchill had identified long ago − perhaps when he delayed the Second Front − and realise that good old Uncle Joe was a figure more terrifying and more secure in evil than Hitler. Stalin was the world's richest poor man, the apotheosis of Communism; he had no income because he commanded all Russia. He was one of the new improved-model bogeymen who have made this century what it is.

In Washington, a belated realisation that Russian Communism was more to be feared than British imperialism produced nifty footwork. The testing of the atomic device was hurried forward. Pressure had been brought to bear on Stalin to enter the war in the Far East; that pressure was speedily relaxed. The idea of the Russian armies poised on the Manchurian border became hideous, the thought of Russian and American zones of occupation in Tokyo unbearable. Besides, the Russians wished to do away with the Emperor; the Americans saw that he represented stability in Japan. Without the Emperor, Japan might relapse into chaos — which of course would encourage Soviet adventuring in the Pacific zone. The war had to be finished, but fast. What made it a little bit awkward was that, by June, the Japanese were putting out peace feelers through the Russians.

So, who did decide to drop the bomb? The traditional and correct answer is, of course, Harry Truman. But, as the authors of this book observe, a positive decision was scarcely needed.

A doubt remains as to whether a clear-cut formal decision was ever taken. The decision to use the bomb was implicit in the initial undertaking to make the bomb; the bomb had to be made, the argument went, in case Hitler was manufacturing one. The Manhattan Project and its allied projects got under way, following Einstein's suggestion to President Roosevelt that a thermonuclear bomb would work. Later, many of the physicists and chemists involved had qualms of conscience and protested; but the impetus of events proved too strong for them; there was two billion dollars of tax-payers' money on the ball and it was rolling too fast. And so it was that the bomb designed to be used against Nazi Germany was dropped on Imperialist Japan as a warning to Soviet Russia.

For all that, there was conscientious debate on the question of using the new weapon; one cannot exactly charge such men as Secretary of War Stimpson or the cautious Secretary of State Byrnes with indifference; but it seems that they were no longer as much in command of events as we might have supposed, because the world and its events had become too complex.

Japan could have been warned that the new weapon would be used if she did not immediately surrender. But that surrender might not have been forthcoming, following a mere warning;

even after the two bombs had fallen on Hiroshima and Nagasaki, there remained a division of opinion within the Japanese government as to whether they should fight on to the death.

And, in sober fact, perhaps it is only because we have been confronted with those two acts of destruction that no more have been dropped in anger in all the succeeding rancorous years. The effect of that filthy hot cloud boiling up over Hiroshima with whole buildings sailing in it has been lasting. We have experienced peace – even Poland has experienced peace. Perhaps future historians will see that Europe lost its nerve after Hiroshima: the bomb that deterred Stalin did ultimately serve Marxism.

One of the Americans who was uncomfortably close to the scene of the crime was Captain, later Major, Claude Eatherly who piloted the weather plane 'Straight Flush'. It was he who reported that cloud conditions over Hiroshima were satisfactory, thus sealing the fate of the city.

Eatherly has since become something of a legend, which is re-examined in another book.* Nobody could pretend that this volume offers anything like the lucid reasoning which is a feature of *The Decision to Drop the Bomb* (which mentions Eatherly only once in passing), but it is equally expert in showing another face of twentieth-century sickness.

When the 'Straight Flush' had made its weather report, it turned around for home. The highly trained crew debated whether they would stay to see the special new bomb dropped but decided not to wait, as otherwise they would miss the after-noon poker game back on Tinian. Eatherly was a tough young Texan of twenty-seven, devoted to gambling and drink and women, with perhaps the occasional quieter moment when he would look through a comic book.

His buddies called him Buck. His patriotism was beyond question. None of his friends or crew members recalls his saying anything 'in the slightest degree philosophical, profound, or even serious'. He was full of horseplay, a swashbuckler, and was disappointed that his boys never got to drop a bomb on Japan themselves. Japan caved in before that could happen.

* *Dark Star: Hiroshima Reconsidered in the Life of Claude Eatherly*, by Ronnie Dugger, Victor Gollancz, 1967.

After the war, swashbuckling went out of fashion. Buck's mother died, he got into trouble with the Air Force and had to leave. Like a Battle of Britain hero, he found it hard to settle in Civvy Street, and was soon engaged in some shady business involving arms-running to Cuba. He was lucky not to be arrested.

He drifted into minor jobs, working in a Texaco service station. There was a scare because his wife had a miscarriage; when doctors examined him, they found he had a defective sperm count. It might have been caused by his flight through an atomic cloud, when he acted as an observer at Bikini. But nothing definite emerged.

So what factors caused what Dugger quaintly calls 'the first hard tug on Eatherly's soul from the demiurge of atomic warfare'? It seems – again, things are none too definite – that he began to have nightmares in 1947 or 1948. He was drinking and gambling a lot. He started passing dud cheques. In February 1950, he tried to commit suicide, and returned to consciousness to find himself in a veteran's mental hospital.

Discharged from there, his character, on Dugger's evidence, deteriorated. He drank more, passed more dud cheques, tried to commit suicide again. Hiroshima was scarcely mentioned; the legend was merely gestating amid the litter of the Cold War.

When Eatherly was in jail in 1954, charged with forgery and theft, he wrote to an attorney called Joseph Gowan, who, says Dugger, 'believes in the power of prayer, in Unity, a religion he says is similar to Christian Science, and in Scientology'.

Gowan went to see Eatherly and, in Gowan's reported words, 'I brought out the psychiatric gimmick, which is true, that he felt like he ought to be punished . . . I occasionally suggested to him, as a sort of word to the wise, that it would be foolish to go on hurting himself out of a subconscious idea that he was responsible for Hiroshima . . .'

The tumblers of the lock were turning. Guilt, disappointment, hope, frustration all took their turn; scientology and the menacing backwash of the thoughts of Hitler, Hirohito, Churchill, Stalin, and Truman all swilled together above Eatherly's head. From now on, Eatherley's story was to be increasingly in the public domain, and he less an actual person than a case, a

problem, a myth, as the four magi figures of our culture –
publicists, politicians, psychiatrists and preachers – took over.

While the legend of the guilt-laden Hiroshima pilot grew,
Eatherly himself, after another spell of tranquillisers and shock
treatment, became a small-time hold-up man, stealing petty cash
from the tills of the little dried-up towns of the southern states.
At one grocery store, he did the hold-up with a gun that was
broken and unloaded; Dugger emphasises the point as if it were
important. 'He was nice,' said the store-owner later. Early in
1957, the Veterans' Association rating board, in Dugger's
picturesque phrase, 'escalated his mental disability rating to one
hundred per cent', and boosted his pension. A couple of weeks
after that, Eatherly was clapped into jail in Fort Worth.

Meanwhile, the Eatherly story was growing larger and even
more inaccurate than life, as newshounds all round the world
took it up. There is reason to believe that Eatherly himself was
as impressed as anyone by the stories. Maybe *Newsweek* was
right; maybe he did have the DFC, maybe had flown over
Nagasaki. We believe what we want to believe, and what we
want to believe is generally the best story. Even the logician,
Bertrand Russell, wrote that Eatherly *dropped the bomb* on
Hiroshima.

The Christians, as represented by the Fellowship of
Reconciliation, got to Eatherly. The Catholic *Commonweal* said,
'Mr Eatherly, it seems clear, has taken on his shoulders guilt a
whole nation would find hard to bear,' while *Christian Century*
asked, 'How will the psychiatrists deal with a man whose
tragedy is the tragedy of a whole generation of Americans?'
John Wain wrote an Eatherly poem which was published in the
Listener; George Barker also wrote one – his was published in
the *New Statesman*. (Dugger is sound on such details).

Inevitably, perhaps, Eatherly began to scribble letters to all
and sundry from his cell. He wrote to a Japanese newspaper
saying, among other things, that he also was a victim of
Hiroshima. If this is true, and if it is also true that he bears his
nation's guilt, this leads to an uncomfortable train of thought.
Eatherly lives today the same sort of life he always did, in the
sweaty Gulf port of Galveston; his country and its chief
adversary, the USSR, perform huge old-fashioned activities like

power politics and shooting astronauts and cosmonauts beyond the atmosphere in glamourised versions of Hitler' V-weapons, while the truly modern nation is the one that received the baptism of atomic fire: Japan, which showers the world with a glittering fallout of toys – video machines, calculators, printed-circuit television sets and programmed watches to computerised cameras, racing cars, oil-tankers, and hard-core sf films.

The Germans also became involved in the Eatherly business. Günther Anders, who knew the States well and was living in Vienna, began to write to Eatherly. Their exchange of letters was published as a book entitled *Burning Conscience*, with a preface by Bertrand Russell. Eatherly was taken up by the unilateral disarmers, while the American authorities seem to have been notably unauthoritarian. In this country, he would at least have been chaired by the CND freaks all the way to Aldermaston. The Editor of the *New York Post* said, 'one almost gets the impression that somewhere in Washington there has been a decision to treat him as a "non-person" . . .'

We all have myths about ourselves; eventually, it may only be that which distinguishes us from androids. Eichmann, whose spirit is invoked in Dugger's book, believed himself to be 'a man of average character'; that was his myth. Eatherly's navigator, Grannan, said of Eatherly, 'He was the Hollywood conception of a pilot . . . He unconsciously tried to live up to that image.' That was Eatherly's myth. Back in 1945, he was already striving towards non-personality.

And today? Dugger obviously liked the subject of his book. One feels perhaps that he would have preferred the role of debunker, but the bunking forces of the present prove too strong for him, and in the end he give us a romantic portrait of Eatherly today, as almost another Hollywood figure:

> 'He whiled away hours in the clubs of the dark pastels, talking, dancing to the melancholy songs, drinking, thinking. He likes cities because he gets lost in their corners like these. This is where he is, among drifters . . . wedding-goers, stopping for a drink . . . tourists in beach clothes . . . a lonely fellow at the bar, staring at the front door, his jaw lax.'

This is where he is . . . surrounded by dislocated grammar and bits of the legend of our age, overtaken by Vietnam veterans and rock rowdies. Whether he ever felt truly guilty is not a question to ask; he was a focus for the guilts of others. And whether their guilts were strictly what they believed them to be is another unaskable question. Guilt is one great romance of the twentieth century; it should not be long before some archaeologically minded operator gives us a musical based on Eatherly's life: *The Hiroshima Man*.

Meanwhile, perhaps it is enough, and sad enough, to say that Eatherly remains eternally the most spectacular victim of the atomic bomb.

From History to Timelessness

He was a pleasant-looking man in his fifties, with a good career behind him. His wife sat beside him, smiling a little tensely, trying not to watch him too closely.

On the table before him, the specialist had formed a four-pointed star with eight matches. It was a simple figure. The man sat there with another eight matches, trying to build his own star beside the first, using his right hand. He could form only the point on the left. The other points proved beyond him.

'No, I can't manage it,' he said at last. 'I can't seem to make a gap to cover the gap where the gap seems to be. If that makes sense to you.'

Two of his matches made a V. The others lay nearby, disorderly, on the highly polished table top. He looked down at them, sorrowfully, then gave his wife a quick reassuring smile. He had suffered a cerebral thrombosis in the right hemisphere of his brain. Something had been lost.

The right hemisphere is primarily responsible for spatial orientation, artistic endeavour, body image, recognition of faces, and, in general, rather diffuse things; whereas the left hemisphere of the brain is much more 'scientific'; it works on linear time, and specialises in such matters as language and mathematics. It can add any number of matches, but cannot make a star pattern out of eight of them.

The powers of the two complementary hemispheres are not balanced. We all specialise, and belong to a culture which specialises. One side or other of our heads may tend towards atrophy, like the poor Selenite in Wells's novel, who came to exist solely as a functional digit. Scientists and writers are left-hemisphere oriented, whereas musicians and painters are right-hemisphere oriented. The difference is between intellectual and intuitive. Obviously the two functions work in concert as they were designed to do; thus human is separated from beast.

One may speculate how this news about the physical nature of the brain fits with older theories about the conscious and the unconscious, or the Self and the Ego. My guess is that the relationship could be a fairly direct one, with the Self seated in the right hemisphere and the Ego in the left. Our highest achievements, as we should expect, unite and integrate the duality.

Most of our waking day is spent in linear pursuits, bound to a timetable of moving from house to office or factory to canteen or restaurant back to home and eventually to bed. But in bed we experience the non-linear world of dreams, when the right hemisphere is given, so to speak, its head.

In my introduction, I spoke, somewhat playfully, about the contrast between the sf novel and the ordinary novel. (Not that I wish to imply thereby that that makes it *better* than the ordinary novel.)

There are pointers to this possibility. On the understanding that this whole argument can only be tentative, since it is based on wild generalisations about what constitutes an 'ordinary' and what an 'sf' novel, perhaps I may be allowed to offer a table of the two modes of consciousness, which I have adapted from a table in Dr Robert Ornstein's book *The Psychology of Consciousness*.

LEFT HEMISPHERE	RIGHT HEMISPHERE
Day	Night
Time, history	Eternity, Timelessness
Analytic	Gestalt
Time	Space
Verbal	Spatial
Science	Magic/mysticism
Proof	Belief
Objective	Subjective
Day light	Subterranean
Human	Animal/alien

Towards the end, I moved in a few terms of my own. The

paired terms are not antonyms necessarily, though some are
('objective' and 'subjective', for instance). Still less do they
represent qualities we associate with the left hemisphere of the
brain which, according to the findings, controls the right side of
the body; the terms on the right are associated with the left side
of the body, the sinister side (Latin, *sinistra*, left). And we can
see that they are, on the whole, more mysterious than their
counterparts in the left-hand column.

It is clear that the qualities in the left-hand column are those
which make up the ordinary realistic novel, by and large. Henry
Fielding, Anthony Trollope, George Gissing, C.P.Snow, Arthur
Hailey, are residents of the left-hand column. It is equally clear
that the qualities in the other column are those we associate with
a wide range of fiction like fairy stories, allegory, fables, the
Gothic novel, and science fiction. Here live the Brothers Grimm,
the author of *The Tempest*, Mrs Radcliffe, the Brontë sisters,
L.P.Lovecraft, and Fritz Leiber.

The most marked exception to this observation, when we talk
about sf, would seem to be 'Science'. But the science in science
fiction has always worked like magic, with grand transformations like the pumpkin scene in *Cinderella*; we recollect Arthur
Clarke's remark that tomorrow's science is the magic of today
(or did he say that tomorow's magic is today's science?); and
the 'hard science' editor of the field, John W.Campbell, cheerfully ran a magic magazine, *Unknown*, besides *Astounding*,
to which all his hardline authors like Heinlein were happy to
contribute.

I do not wish to press this distinction too far, but a word about
the Proof/Belief dichotomy is necessary. There is a famous
story, 'Noise Level', by Raymond Jones, still popular after many
years, which is about the invention of an anti-gravity device. The
inventors are shown (faked) proof of the existence of such a
device; so they then go ahead and invent it. The continuing
attraction of this story is that it appears to be about left-
hemisphere oriented thinking (proof), whilst in fact being about
right-hemisphere oriented thinking (belief).

Many of sf's most popular stories exploit this left-right
dichotomy. An obvious example is Arthur Clarke's story 'The
Star', with its striking opening sentence: 'It is three thousand

light years from the Vatican.' Here we get two dichotomies at
once: science/religion and time/space. Although Asimov is
regarded as primarily a *scientific* sf writer, chiefly because he
has said so so frequently, his most popular stories are right-
hemisphere oriented. 'Nightfall' is loaded with night and madness. *The Foundation Trilogy* may superficially concern a scientific empire and Hari Seldon's powers of analytic thought; more
centrally, it is about the magic of belief in Seldon's thought.
The *I, Robot* stories lean heavily towards technology and logic,
with those Three Laws; but they are much more about the
human/alien dichotomy, whilst one of them (confusingly called
'Logic') is about subjectivism. Other robot stories of Asimov's
such as the novels *Caves of Steel* and *The Naked Sun*, feature a
subterranean world rather like Trantor in the *Foundation* series.
Subterranean cities are the stuff of the right hemisphere.

   Such celebrated madmen as Robert Sheckley and A.E.Van
Vogt all employ the technological and methodological attributes
of the sf genre cheekily or solemnly in a way which transforms
their writing into an entire gaudy celebration of left-handedness
and weird right-hemispherical cerebration; all space and eternity
is hardly enough for them – and I am convinced from lecturing
all over the world that Van Vogt and Sheckley are possibly the
two sf writers the world digs most. Neither are much discussed
in print, simply because their right-hemispherical lucubrations
do not lend themselves to verbalisation, just as the vocabulary of
music or art criticism presents its problems of transference and
translation.

   I should pursue this hemispherical business no further; it may
prove to be as false as phrenology – yet that is not to deny its
speculative worth. I feel that I'm 'getting warm', as children say
in Hunt the Thimble, and my own fiction has often Hunted the
Right Hemisphere. As Ornstein points out, we live in a predominantly Left Hemisphere culture, at least superficially. The
East offers a Right Hemisphere culture – or so we in the West
like to think, for the game of dichotomies is obscurely satisfying
and tickles both hemispheres.

   Science as a whole has been more prepared of late to
acknowledge the shadowy spatial side of the brain (hence such
popular books as Fritjof Capra's *The Tao of Physics*). Sf has

followed suit, and has showed itself since the sixties, after the *New Worlds* revolution, much readier to embrace both hemispheres – which is merely a trendy way of saying embracing all of life.

One of the heroes of this new attitude is Michael Moorcock, editor of the revolutionary *New Worlds*. Moorcock never gets his due; the fault is partly his because he is liable, like a petted dog, to bite the hand that pats him; but he is prodigious and prodigal, and to avoid Moorcock is to evade one of the central problems of science fiction: how can it be so stimulating, so clever, so all-seeing, and so trashy? Moorcock is all things to all chaps. His most renowned hero, Jerry Cornelius, is a typical product of the warring hemispheres.

Moreover, Moorcock has humour, and I am not sure where humour stands in the league table. It may be one of the great bridges between hemispheres, deriving its best effects from the conflicts between them. 'I'd give my right hand to be ambidextrous'; most typically Jewish humour; Irish jokes ('I was lucky that the ground was there to break my fall'); all such quips are bridges between two systems. There's an Oxford joke about the college which receives a large legacy from one of its most distinguished alumni. The members of the Senior Common Room are discussing how the money should be invested. The Bursar says, 'There's no problem; we invest it in land, as we have been doing for the last thousand years.' And the Oldest Member looks up from his corner and says, 'Yes, but don't forget that the last thousand years have been exceptional.' History is kicked into line with Timelessness, to form an hemispheric bridge.

My tentatively offered First Law of Thermodynamics of SF is that it gains power from bridging the divisions between hemispheres which our culture has emphasised, thus apparently diminishing the importance of both intellectual and intuitive (but actually celebrating their union).

Science fiction writers are the people who create stars – and planets – out of matchsticks.

The Hashish Club

Just as we sometimes become aware that we are in a gathering of people which consists, in effect, of few who are perceptually alive; just as we sometimes become aware – and this is the beginning of love – that we are in the presence of somebody whose thought and body can immensely enrich our own; so we sometimes wish for an awareness that transcends our own limited consciousness. The present becomes or prison. We have to escape, even if that escape means moving deeper into ourselves.

Means of escape are legion; life hath ten thousand several doors for men to take their exits, as Webster almost said. This anthology* concerns one particular exit: that baroque, mysterious doorway marked Drugs; and some particular people: those baroque, mysterious writers who have chosen to make their way through it, from Samuel Taylor Coleridge to William Burroughs.

For every writer who allies himself with a drug – for every Wilkie Collins quaffing down laudanum by the tumberful, for every Anna Kavan on snow for thirty-five years – there are many whom the alliance destroys. Writers probably have a better survival rate than other people, since they have their writing and the objectivity it requires to keep them on an even keel. Given an element of self-destruction in their natures, they utilise the drug to present some inner vision of the world – a vision which ordinary mortals without the fold are prompt to recognise as one more immensely convincing version of the truth.

And why not? For a third of every day of our lives, we are out of our minds, convinced utterly by the thousand charades of

* *The Hashish Club: An Anthology of Drug Literature*, edited by Peter Haining, 2 vols., Peter Owen, 1975.

sleep in which logic, time, our very selves, undergo distortions or annihilations which must make any surrealist grit his teeth with envy. Modern theories suggest that our dreams may be the brain's efforts to order the events of the day, as it comes off-line like a computer after a particular programme. I believe that, further, these witty distortions of thought-power are very much the cicatrices left by man's evolution from the animal, which will heal in a few million years, as we become fully human. If this is so, then what Sir Thomas Browne called 'the famous Nations of the dead' all dreamed more richly than we. Perhaps the present-day interest in the use of drugs can be accounted for by our trying to compensate for this unacknowledged loss at a time when evolution may be making one of its gear-shifts within us.

However that may be, drugs are as old as mankind itself. Which is to say (if guessing is not cheating) that drug-induced states were there at the birth of religion, art, and science, all of which spring from the same creative impulse.

Of course, a book entitled *The Hashish Club* has a great deal more romantic appeal than one entitled 'The Whisky Club', although we recognise that alcohol, tobacco, aspirin and so on are merely more socially acceptable drugs. As we can control, at least to some degree, the effects of alcohol, so with other drugs: LSD in particular is an accomplice, a symbiote, not an assassin. It seems that the brain on occasions secretes its own psychedelic chemicals, as an aid to perception.

Certain so-called psychotic states are known to be the result of such internal dosages. Recent researches indicate that schizophrenics suffer a much lower incidence of cancer than the rest of the population; what are they secreting? Or could it be that cancers originally developed to cure man's schizophrenic state? As these stories remind us, there is much we do well to be unsure about.

The stories work at doing directly what all forms of fiction do less directly: they allow the reader a freedom in charades in which logic, time, his very self, undergo a distortion or annihilation which otherwise he experiences only in sleep. Just to take the time element – the fall of the House of Atreus can be played out before us in a single evening, or the Fall of the House of Usher in a single hour; or, on the other hand, James Joyce's

Bloom enjoys a Dublin day which may take us a week to travel. In the cinema or on television, we can see the triumph and destruction of the Third Reich whilst smoking a couple of cigars. This element of time-distortion in art is one of its great unconscious attractions for us. In our art galleries, we find moments and scenes frozen for ever, much as

> The sweet, sad years, the melancholy years,
> Those of my life,

as one opium eater expressed it, become embalmed in our memory.

When Aldous Huxley first took mescalin, one morning in the spring of 1953, he found himself in a 'timeless bliss of seeing.' Experiencing a complete indifference to time, he says this: 'I could, of course, have looked at my watch; but my watch, I knew, was in another universe. My actual experience had been, was still, of an indefinite duration or alternatively of a perpetual present made up of one continually changing apocalypse.'

The time factor was banished. Could this be, I wonder, the predominant reason why we turn to drugs, that they lend us an illusory immortality?

If the clock in the mind is stilled which first started when man, alone among living things, discovered death, then other faculties awake, chief among which seems to be the visual sense. (Even beer can bring its hallucinations!)

'This is how one ought to see, how things really are,' exclaims Huxley from his trance. It is the cry of artists everywhere, seeking to convince their fellow men and women of the wonder of the world, of the lies of mundane life. Always at the basis of the cry lies an implicit condemnation of the way in which the world moves too fast. We must, says the artist, stop and stare, stop and dream, or stop and drowse.

Proust, speaking of Gérard de Nerval, who is represented in this volume, refers to the way in which one's life may be compressed into the few minutes before sleeping. Of these hypnoid visions, Proust says, 'Sometimes in the moment of falling asleep we see them, and try to seize and define them. Then we wake up and they are gone, we give up the pursuit, and before we can be sure of their nature we are asleep again as though the sight of them were forbidden to the waking mind. The inhabitants of these pictures are themselves of the stuff of dreams.'

And he goes on to quote from a poem of Nerval's:

> Puis une dame, à sa haute fenêtre,
> Blonde aux yeux noirs, en ses habits anciens . . .
> Que, dans une autre existence peut-être,
> J'ai dèjâ vue! – et dont je me souviens!*

There are many women, many life styles, which would suit us; ordinary waking life defeats them.

To conclude on a note of speculation. Drugs, by abolishing that enervating sense of time from our minds, give us the chance to touch on impossible things, as these stories show; we can move into the past, the future, or, as Nerval says, into other existences.

A research group in the Maryland Psychiatric Research Centre in the United States has recently discoverd that LSD can help people who are dying, particularly those who have an extreme fear of death. For some of these patients, the LSD trip proves extremely horrifying; but the importance of the experience lies with how a patient integrates it with his previous life-experiences. In effect, he receives a lesson in how to die (Huxley needed no such lesson, although he went out on a tide of LSD).

The brain under LSD is in some respects – for instance, as regards oxygenation – under similar circumstances to the brain approaching death. So the trip represents a physical as well as a spiritual lesson.

These stories also come from undiscovered territories within the mind. I wonder if, in throwing up their distorted and magnified images of life, they are not also bringing us word from the lurid worlds of death.

* A damsel at a casement high,
Fair-haired, dark-eyed, in antique shawl . . .
Who, in another life gone-by
Perchance I've seen before – and still recall!

1951: Yesterday's Festival of the Future

Nineteen fifty-one is now an ancient enigma which we decode with difficulty.

If today's generation could walk around the South Bank of 1951 today, as we can walk round Stonehenge, they would find themselves asking – as we do of Stonehenge – 'What was it a monument *to*?'

The South Bank Exhibition – unlike Stonehenge (presumably) and unlike its illustrious predecessor, the Great Exhibition of 1851 – was nothing less than a memorial to the future. The Skylon and the Dome of Discovery, architecturally non-functional, were structural expressions of a hope that the British would break through their psychosis of war and austerity into freer air.

We were hardly out of uniform in 1951. Indeed, we had started re-arming; army lorries still trundled through Britain's grey villages as in the forties. There was a war in the Far East which could at any time involve us all. Many of us were not long demobbed, and the talk of the time was still about the war, its heroisms, its shortages, its excitements. I turned up at the South Bank in my old demob mac; with its football buttons, belt, shoulder straps, it looked much like a uniform.

What I was after was a glimpse of the future. All the bright and flimsy architecture was great – anything different was great – but what I most wanted to see was Grey Walter's electronic tortoises. The electronic tortoises were animals begot between a new science, cybernetics, and a new technical development, automation (both labels coined during the forties). These chelonian hybrids were clumsy creatures of metal, not at all pre-possessing to look at, but they did something that no mechanical thing had done hitherto: they pottered about their cage and, when they were feeling hungry, returned to their power source and replenished their batteries of their own accord. Not only did they have feedback; inbuilt infra-red cells ensured that they did not bump into each other during their wanderings.

Suppose these creatures to be the first lumbering amphibians of the Devonian period, then the Apollo space rockets of the seventies are the ferocious allosaurs of the Jurassic; evolution among the servo mechanisms has been amazingly rapid, and one of the hallmarks of the past quarter-century.

Although I understood how the metal tortoises worked, I wanted to see them for myself — to feast my eyes on them, in that expressive phrase. So I did.

They were housed in the Dome of Discovery, squat, unlovely, but full of significance. They sat in their unlit tank, unmoving, gathering dust. A notice on the exhibit said OUT OF ORDER. More than I knew, it was the shape of things to come. The hibernation was not of technology but of British industry.

Under the Bovril advert in Piccadilly Circus there was at that time a dramatic sign which read EXPORT OR DIE. Some years after it was gone, an American friend who presumably felt nostalgic for it asked me, 'What happened to it?' 'We died,' I said. Despite the bravado of the Festival, Britain never quite recovered from the war, for reasons compounded of all manner of factors: psychological, socio-political, technological, and geographical. But in 1951 we were convinced we were convalescent; the Festival was our first walk out of hospital alone, getting a breath of fresh air.

The South Bank exhibition was laid out as an educational spread. There was a correct way to go round the exhibits, a specific way which would make everything clear. Lord Reith no doubt approved. Deviate from the page order of this mighty scrap book and, warned the catalogue, 'some of the chapters will appear mystifying and inconsequent.' My first wife and I were in London for a few hours only, had scrounged a day off work to come up, and were unable to take the proper route. As a nation, we were still used to discipline, but the long queues made recommended procedure impossible. Besides, being mystified was pleasurable.

The chaps who took the 'Elevator to Outer Space' with us

were mystified. They were mystified by the splendid working model of the solar system, which showed the planets with their full company of satellites. 'Coo, don't they come close,' one man said and, after a moment, 'That's us in the middle, the big one with the others going round it.' Copernicus had lived and died in vain. His friends contradicted him. 'No, it's not, because where's the moon, eh?' (Authentic 1951 dialogue, transcribed in my diary at the time.)

In the Transport Pavilion were cars with glass bodies, revealing their Morris Motors intestines, as well as a Cyclemaster. I was pleased to see that. I had just acquired a Cyclemaster, 'the magic wheel that wings your heel'. It fitted into the rear wheel of your bicycle and sped you along at fifteen miles an hour, making your turn-ups oily. Everyone thought everything was wonderful. The front of the Science Pavilion had stepped off a science fiction magazine cover. I bought a postcard of it. I still have it, together with some cuttings from the *Daily Telegraph* of the time, the headlines of which appealed to me. 'Pig Shoots Butcher', and my favourite, 'In Laughing Fit I Killed Her'. And there's a story about an Irish labourer who hid under his landlady's floorboards for three weeks because he couldn't pay the rent.

The science was well presented. It reinforced my feelings that technology and the Western way of thought shaping and shaped by it, was an integral part of life, not just one of its departments. Evidently the message did not get across on an effective scale; people still think of science as something apart – like religion, perhaps. It is a pity that the Exhibition could not have been permanent; the South Bank was more stimulating than the windy expanses of concrete which replaced it. The Land of Britain was a particularly striking exhibit, with a display designed by James Holland. It showed the history of the Earth in brief, dramatic form. Although it could offer nothing as overpowering as the typhoon you walked through in the Mitsubishi Tower at Expo 70 – unforgettable, that – I came away with one piece of knowledge which illustrates graphically the brevity of man's history. Following full-size models of Stone Age man doing their stuff with flints and antlers, was a Bronze Age group; fine-looking people, ornamented and bronzed (what else?). A notice told you that this was only two hundred and fifty generations ago.

It is a very brief period. Humanity does not evolve as rapidly as the electronic tortoises.

We had taken sandwiches to the exhibition to save expense. We ate them on a bench in light drizzle. It was only the weather that took our pleasures sadly – we enjoyed the tipping fountains, spilling gallons of water at random intervals. We took photographs with my father's Ensign camera, all of which turned out badly. Many Americans were there, photographing continually. In those days, you could tell Americans because they were healthier and wore at least two cameras to punctuate their broad stomachs.

Later in the afternoon, we took a water bus to the Battersea Pleasure Gardens, passing the fairly new power station on which I lavished what was then my best prose.

'No human hand had touched this devil-dedicated palace. Up and up it rose, unadorned, windowless and soulless, complete in its own surly strength, with four great chimneys capping it, chimneys like pillars supporting – nothing. Before it, dwarfed by it, yet dwarfing us, stood six cranes like skeleton vultures from an inter-stellar age, silent, black, unmoving.' At the Gardens, we watched a Punch-and-Judy show. And we admired the Piper and Lancaster kiosks, and the Emett railway to Oyster Creek and Far Twittering.

Then it was time to hurry for Paddington and the train home.

The fifties are remembered as a time of greyness, where the austerities of war were imposed on us without the mitigating drama of war. We had rationing, with 2d. a week lopped off the meat ration in 1951, clothes and sweet coupons, petrol restrictions, endless shortages. Another war raged in Korea, and many of us on 'Z' Reserve who had served in World War II were expecting to be called up again to fight the Communists in that miserable peninsula hanging from the frozen belly of Manchuria. As the Festival opened, the British Government sent a cruiser to cow Abadan; the Shah laughed and nationalised the oil industry. We were conscious of rapid changes but the threat of the H-bomb shrank our imaginations.

The cities of England 1951, not least its capital, were

dominated by gloomy nineteenth-century buildings and bomb sites. Today, we may be fond of Victorian architecture because it no longer overpowers us with its funereal-and-marzipan pomposity; we have diluted it with beautiful structures like the Vickers Building and Centre Point. I'm sure a trip in a time-machine to 1951 would re-awaken a hatred for the over-dressed pretensions of Victoriana. To it, and the rat-infested ruins created by the war, the clarity of the South Bank in '51 came like a bite of lemon at half-time.

Our response to the past is necessarily personal, for in a sense we re-create it in our own image, or recall only our own spoor through its jungles. Yet that decade, 1945-55, would surely get the vote for one of the dreariest decades in recent history.

I'm convinced that when we look at the ugly photographs of 1951 we see not only the war that threatened, the war that was over, and the war before that, but also the long war which had been England's peace, and which raised the meanest houses for those who did mostly essential work. We now have to decipher 1951 like Linear B, with its cryptic references to the once-living: George VI, Baden-Powell, Stalin, Tommy Handley, Aneurin Bevan, Trygve Lie, Gillie Potter, Klaus Fuchs, Farouk, George Orwell, Betty Grable, Smuts, my father. How should we call it back?

Best to cross ourselves, think of the phallic Skylon, and pass on.

Seeing

The Sower of the Systems: Some Paintings by G. F. Watts

Michael McNay at the *Guardian* invited me to write about an exhibition of paintings by G.F.Watts at the Whitechapel Art Gallery in 1974. It struck me in many ways as a depressing exhibition, not only because much of the art was pretentious, but because of an overwhelming sense that there are some aspects of Victorian art, only a century old, which render it as closed as an Egyptian tomb.

Yet Watts still haunts me. His more sentimental paintings are among the first I can recall looking at. Some of his canvases, those on cosmological or religious themes, retain great power. He was born in 1817 of a poor family and was largely self-taught; he rose to become the Grand Old Man of painting and died in 1904 revered as the English Titian. Yet his reputation has largely perished with him.

A case could be made for George Frederick Watts as a precursor of modern art, given a certain loading of the evidence. One seeks such intellectual aids to enjoyment when confronted by the fundamentally unenjoyable canvases ranged round the walls of the Whitechapel Art Gallery.

There was, for example, the way in which Watts could seize on random inspiration (the Inspiration of the Random, as he would no doubt have called it) – on patterns of light thrown on a ceiling – for the basis of his canvas, *The Sower of the Systems*, on the cracks and stains of a dirty plaster wall for the foundation of *Chaos*. His later techniques suggest a similar eagerness to escape from the academic – he left the Royal Academy Schools in disgust after only a week there. A visitor to Watts's studio complained, 'You paint with everything except the brush . . with rags, with nasty old bits of paper, with your thumb.' The one description we have of Turner's working methods is not dissimilar.

Well enough. Watts also espoused the didactic. One of his obituarists suggested that he could not paint; the greater trouble seems to be that he would preach. These days, we have learnt to forgive the former, not the latter.

His ambition was second to none, perhaps in the way of self-made men who taste success. He wished to paint big ideas, he wanted to be regarded as a thinker with a brush instead of a pen, he needed to express humanitarian principles in paint. To this end, his ambition was to decorate large buildings; the Houses of Parliament, prisons, Euston Station, or an even more grandiose (and imaginary) penitentiary he called The House of Life. Life is the biggest of all four-letter words, and this edifice, had it been built, would have served as a memorial to Victorianism as grand and dowdy as any of the great Life Insurance offices that march towards the City of London.

Throughout his life, Watts attempted to explore various modes of expression. Apart from the murals, classical subjects had their day (Orpheus and Eurydice at crisis point); so does naturalism (amazingly, studies of cricketers playing straight bats); so does the moral tale (*When Poverty Comes in the Door, Love Flies Out of the Window* – a study for which, with faceless angels and slum-dwellers, is the only cross between Blake and de Chirico I know); so does landscape (very flat, Egypt); so does – oh, dear! – humour (with titles like *The Cowl Maketh Not the Monk*, though it must be admitted that *Tasting the First Oyster or, BC* is the sole attempt to treat in pictorial form a subject many minds have dwelt upon); so does portraiture (Lady Holland upon a day bed, Cardinal Manning splendid in scarlet); but it is lofty sentiment that wins the day. The mind has its Euston Stations.

Here's *Progress* on a white charger. Here's *The Court of Death*, well populated. Here's Ariadne, sweating it out on Naxos. Here are Paolo and Francesca, whirling rather stiffly through all eternity. It's a bit like having to listen to lots of Elgar. Before your very eyes at the Whitechapel are paintings which, in cheap repro, made many grandparental homes uninhabitable to grandchildren: *Love and Life, Love and Death*,

Sic Transit and that beastly little *Hope* – one of the world's great bad pictures, like Millais's *Angelus* – of the maiden with bandaged eyes and broken lyre sitting on top of the globe. Chris Mullen's catalogue note is interesting. It tells us that (according to Mrs Watts) a man's life was given new purpose by contemplating it; and, after the Egyptian troops were defeated in the 1967 war, they were given reproductions of this painting. Rather a sly way of rubbing salt in the wound, I'd say.

Yet to walk round that never-realised House of Life, encountering all those massive canvases covered with paint of the colour and consistency of sacking, one might catch a glimpse of a quality of mind which had nothing to do with the cliché or anecdotalism or allegory. It is aloof, even brutal, expressing itself in symbols beyond symbolism. It surfaces here and there: in *The Sower of the Systems*, in *Mammon*, in *Endymion* (where, in a sweeping Blakeian composition, Endymion, prone in a swoon, is visited by Diana, descending from Heaven to scoop him into her arms) and in *Under a Dry Arch*.

Under a Dry Arch is, in one aspect, a painting of social consciousness, to be compared with the roughly contemporary paintings of down-and-outs in London by Luke Fildes, Doré, Egg, and others. It shows a woman, eyes closed in fatigue, resting under a stone arch. Phantasmally through the far end of the arch appears the outline of St Paul's. It is night. Watts's sorrow for the poor, and for suffering women, is evident. Yet the technique of.the painting, the sombre composition, lift it above sentimental realism and the tract. Misery and something unformed brood over the picture. The statement might be Goya's – here is an element of the human condition not to be alleviated by social reform, or by the shadowy Christian symbol in the background. At the same time, the woman's posture, the semi-subterranean environment, the sketchily rendered clothes of the figure, reminiscent almost of a shroud, put us in mind of an artist greater than Watts: Henry Moore, whose sketches of people sheltering in the underground system during the Blitz are etched indelibly in the memories of everyone who lived through those times.

This lowering 'something unformed' was presumably not recognised by many of Watts's contemporaries, who preferred –

or who we like to think preferred – pining children and simper-
ing dogs. It is beyond narrative and presumably – as Watts
himself tended to think – beyond expression. There are considerations apart from the financial why his House of Life was
never built; we have to honour Watts for the vision, even while
we laugh at it. He had something to express, but it remained
what it was, inchoate, and would not be housed.

Watts's contemporaries compared him with Titian, a comparison Watts encouraged by wearing a skull-cap and neat
beard like Titian's in the Uffizi portrait; they believed he was
achieving Great Art because the titles of his canvases claimed as
much: *Time, Death and Judgement, The Dweller of the
Innermost*, and that much-praised *Mammon*, of which it must
often have been said in sermons that it was better than any
sermon. Whistler blew that sort of pretentiousness when he
called his admirable painting of Irving as Philip of Spain,
Arrangement in Black No. 111.

For all that, Mammon sitting nursing his money bags in his
trumpery crown is a memorably nasty figure, bloated, a little
distorted, and with a hint of diseased skin-texture which Francis
Bacon was to bring to perfection two generations later. Watts
genuinely loathed Mammon-worship. He felt a strong kinship
with the poor, in a manner free from any ideology, and did much
good work in the East End of London. Unlike so many of his
contemporaries, he thought of his pictures as destined for somewhere other than the walls of the well-to-do; he helped organise
concerts for the poor, invited East Enders to his home, and
supported a drive to clear more open spaces in the capital for
recreation. In Watts's life, what we find sympathetic lies so close
to what we find intolerable. No other painter of Victorian times
arouses such mixed emotions.

Whitechapel has an impressive bronze of a man on a stallion
(a cast of it stands in Kensington Gardens). Watts cannot call it
simply 'Chap on Horse'. No, it has to be *Physical Energy*. How
typical of a man who doted on George Meredith's novels. One is
reminded of the unkind parody of Martin Tupper's best-selling
Proverbial Philosophy – 'If he cannot realise the Ideal, at least
he can idealise the Real.'

Small wonder that *The Times* in its obituary in 1904 referred to Watts as 'the most honoured and beloved of British artists', speaking approvingly of his high seriousness. Standing in the gallery surrounded by all those drab well-meaning canvases, painted in subfusc colours and generally lacking in precisely the detail that Blake or Samuel Palmer used to make actual the allegorical, one feels a violent aversion to a whole muffling pomp with which our Imperial ancestors used to fog the hollowness of their lives, spiritual and physical.

Yet Watts's virtues still manifest themselves. He was devoted to his work, that can be said. Unlike Millais and other contemporaries, he lived to paint lordly instead of painting to live like a lord. He took an inspirational approach to the actual job of painting, and his methods were spontaneous if not actually experimental.

Sometimes, putting aside shadows, he produces fine portraits of people. Lady Holland has been mentioned, and Manning. There's a lovely self-portrait at the age of seventeen, painted in 1834, where the brushwork, the easiness of manner, and the lightness of touch suggest the work of Lawrence or at least an earlier age, when Victorian plush had not yet suffocated Regency spirit. *Choosing* is a portrait of the youthful Ellen Terry smelling a camellia, a flower which has no scent. Watts was forty-seven when he married the actress, then only seventeen. They separated after a year together. Tension and sadness hang over this painting of a young woman with flowers; she looks away beyond the confines of the frame, at something no-one else can see.

Just occasionally in the pretentious paintings, ambition and execution marry. We catch an echo, sonorous and semi-terrifying, from that non-existent House of Life.

The Creation of Eve is one of the most splendid paintings of the 1890s – sumptuous, yet hard. The colour may be Titian's, but the image is entirely Watts's. In this first canvas of a trilogy on Eve, the female form erupts into existence like a mushroom cloud above Hiroshima: faceless, androgynous, puissant, even remorseless, yet gloriously female – a tower of flesh that will populate a world. It is almost unbelievable.

And *The Sower of the Systems* ... It never leaves the memory. It was painted in 1902, near the end of Watts's life.

Verging on abstraction, it seems more a pattern than a painting, a transmogrification of the mosaic of light the old man saw on his ceiling.* The Sower is barely glimpsed, just a titanic figure with an acid-green gown hunched about his waist, as much Reaper as Sower. Because his powerful shoulders are bent as he thrusts forwards into the blackness, the fossil night of uncreated space and time, so his head, if he has one, is hidden. In a fury of energy, he whirls about, scattering blazing solar systems from his fists. The whole enterprise is conveyed in a well-coordinated fury of paint.

With this picture, the first great painting of the twentieth century, Watts escapes beyond his usual confinement of words and poses. He becomes, like the mighty Turner, free of his time, a celebrant rather than a preacher.

The exhibition is well timed. It reminds us that we should give thanks to the Sower of the Systems that we are living in the awful 1970s rather than the unutterable 1870s. It also reminds us that even the most formidable of reputations have a touch of Sic Transit about them. It is given to few men, as it was to G.F. Watts, to be offered a baronetcy by Gladstone not once but twice; but it is hard to believe that massive critical acclaim will ever knock at his door a second time.

A few of his paintings may remain caviar for the few. He may be regarded as in a certain tradition that, at least in English art, goes back no further than the period when the flame of Enlightenment was guttering in its chased silver socket, and Henry Fuseli came leaping out of the Neo-Classical darkness. After him came Blake and de Loutherbourg and mighty Turner and Palmer and James Ward and Martin, all slightly deranged ('Martin, she fears, may go out of his mind, and she is afraid to speak to him' – Ralph Thomas reporting on Mrs John Martin), Richard Dadd, D.G. Rossetti, William Holman Hunt (who just

---

* But the old man had *trained* himself to see visions, on his ceiling and elsewhere. Watts was aware of the *'blottesque'* tradition, the originator of which was Alexander Cozens, whose *New Method of Assisting the Invention in Drawing Original Compositions of Landscape* influenced Romantic painters, including Victor Hugo. Like Watts, Hugo painted with whatever was at hand when the mood was on him – coffee grounds, soot, cigar ash. Hugo achieved the effects Watts sought, where, in his words, *'les aspects se dégagent pour se récomposer'* ('appearances dissolve and re-form themselves'). Hugo could have become a great painter; perhaps Watts had it in him to be a great writer.

occasionally, as in *The Hireling Shepherd*, achieves intense vision), the wilting Burne-Jones, Watts himself, down to more recent painters like Stanley Spencer and Michael Ayrton. Such men see what the rest of us do not see; they create myths, as well as recreating old myths; for this reason, they are often despised or remain obscure (like Blake) in their own lifetime.

We appreciate Fuseli more than any earlier generation could; we have inherited his passion for the inexplicable. Perhaps we could learn to appreciate Watts again, for in our century that brutal 'something unformed' has emerged farther from the darkness to which it belongs.

A permanent exhibition of Watts's work, including *The Sower of the Systems*, is staged in the Watts Gallery at Compton, near Guildford in Surrey.

The Fireby-Wireby Book

My maternal grandmother's home was in Peterborough, a prim house built of Fletton brick. It was dark and old-fashioned and had a damp cellar where Christmas puddings hung from beams to ripen. Upstairs was a forbidding picture which made the way to bed terrible: Sir Edward Poynter's *Faithful Unto Death*, showing the Roman centurion at Pompeii about to be engulfed by lava, while the population fled. Downstairs, on a shelf over the drawing-room door, was a fox in a glass case. The fox had trapped a small rabbit. It lifted its bloodied muzzle and snarled, showing its teeth.

The house was tranquil and well run. My grandmother had servants in those days. She was a farmer's daughter and, until the end of her long life, she liked to cook and laugh. I was sometimes sent there to stay with her. Peterborough was a beautiful city: I haunted the museum, the cathedral, and the market square, where live skinned eels were sold on market days. All is changed now.

My grandmother had a good collection of books. The one I cared about was the Fireby-Wireby Book. My bad manners were notorious, even at the age of six. I was known to burst into grandmother's house with the rest of the family and, before all the kissing and hugging and 'How-was-the-journey'-ing had been properly concluded, dash through into the drawing room to inflict on myself the alarming delights of the Fireby-Wireby Book.

The drawing room was a rather formal chamber at the back of the house, with large french windows which opened on to the lawn. To one side of the fireplace was a glass cabinet, glass on four sides, of a kind you nowadays see only in the V.&A., in which was imprisoned a collection of china objects which my grandmother cherished. I suppose they all went into the dustbin when the old lady died, and are probably worth a fortune now. The armchairs and the sofa were all very hard, and had antimacassars over the backs.

These details I mention to explain why I found the room formal. I could not enter the drawing room without someone calling, 'Now mind the china cabinet! Now mind the anti-macassars!' The room was designed not to accommodate but to quell children.

The flow of injunctions was merely a sign that they cared for me. The mild implied disapproval only made me feel secure. They knew very well I was doing nothing more dangerous than heading for the Fireby-Wireby Book.

It wasn't really called the Fireby-Wireby Book. It was called *Humors of History*, 160 Drawings in Color, by A.Moreland. The spelling of Humors and Color leads one to suspect an American influence. But it was a very English book, and the 160 drawings in color were reproduced from originals which had appeared in the *Morning Leader*, a properly English newspaper.

No date was given in the book. Internal evidence suggests publication in about 1905.

The pictures illustrate incidents in English history. Arthur Moreland, whoever he was, begins with the Phoenicians, 100 BC, trading with the Ancient Britons for lead and tin. Very Semitic the Phoenicians are, too, standing on the quayside, opening up a chest full of gee-gaws while the ancient Britons stream out of antiquated buildings in the background (conveniently labelled Tin Works and Lead Mine). The Brits wear tabby furs and look with naive astonishment at the cheap alarm clocks, umbrellas, mirrors, and pairs of braces they are being offered. Their physio-gnomies are characteristically Morelandish, with stiff reddish hair standing on end, snub noses, huge blunt teeth, and blue jowls or nasty ratty beards: in short, faces capable of expressing few but powerful emotions – rage, dismay, slyness, inebriation, illness, and, above all, fear.

Picture No. 2 shows the invention of the coracle in 99 BC. The ancient Brits are endeavouring to stay afloat while angling. Grimly, they smoke clay pipes while copies of *The Compleat Angler* topple overboard. A coastguard, telescope in hand, flings a life-belt to someone in difficulties. On the shore stands The

Angler's Rest, where survivors can refresh themselves. By
Picture No. 132, Moreland has got only as far as Bosworth
Field, where a manic Richard Crookback, sword in hand, runs
like fury for Market Bosworth Station (1 Mile by the signpost).
Three grinning Tudors bear down on him on horseback, while a
glum yokel looks on. With Picture No. 154, we have arrived at
Sir Isaac Newton, ghastly of face under a tree while the apple
cracks open on his bald pate. He writes with a quill pen; a lawn-
mower lies neglected on the grass behind him, while a boy in a
tricorne peers over the fence and sniggers at the incident. By the
last picture, No. 160, we have reached the present day, and a fat
financier smoking his cigar outside an enormous office block.
The history that interested Moreland was the early stuff. The
eighteenth century he could sneak over with scarcely a word,
and the nineteenth he found a dead loss. All satirists are conservative at heart.

Moreland's forte was anachronism. King Arthur, sleeves
rolled up, heaves at a winch, endeavouring to pull from the rocks
an Excalibur marked 'Made in Germany'. Egbert learns from a
ticker-tape machine that he has succeeded to the throne. Canute
stands miserably on his throne, drenched by the waves, in the
shadow of Brighton Pier. The Crusaders, off to the war, take
their golf clubs with them. Young Richard II smokes nervously
under the bulbous eyes of his uncles. Sir Francis Drake's game
of bowls takes place by the two large gas containers that fringe
Plymouth Hoe. Henry V receives his tennis balls via Carter
Paterson.

Comedy needs more than one string, and the fun of
anachronism soon wears off. But the greatest attraction for me
in the Fireby-Wireby Book was not the Humour, however spelt,
but the Horror.

Moreland's past is a forlorn place. Henry I lies in an ornate
chair, clutching his stomach. A waiter in a dinner jacket and a
minion in baggy trousers watch him detachedly, perhaps
repressing sadistic smiles. A mangy cat – all Moreland's cats are
mangy – champs on fish bones. On the messy dining table, wine
has been spilt, bones are everywhere. Henry, still wearing his
crown, dies of a surfeit of lampreys. His face is ghastly.

Another typical plate shows Vortigern in prison. He, too,

retains his crown. He sits on a rush bed, chained to the wall, a pitcher and a loaf of bread beside him. It is dark. The king clutches his gown to him and stares fearfully at Hengist and Horsa, who mock him through the bars of his cell window. Throughout the book, people are imprisoned, or being spied on.

And a third picture, illustrating trial by ordeal in the eleventh century. The accused has to pick up a red-hot poker and walk three paces with it. A bobby and various prelates look on, gloating, while the scruffy victim dithers in anguish. I believe it was from this picture that the book derived its name, the Fireby-Wireby Book. These were pictures that I dwelt upon long before I could read, or even speak properly.

Although Moreland was no Daumier, he had the skill of a Daumier in conveying economically impressions of poverty. Shops are always rat-infested. Offices bear aged bills and pictures of pugilists on their walls. Churches are damp. Private dwellings harbour plates in racks and screaming babes in rickety highchairs. Castles have rucked-up carpets, forbidding furniture, and slaveys giggling behind their hands in corners. Even the palaces boast little in the way of comfort beyond an upright piano beside the throne and a barometer in the passage; they are as prone to cracked mirrors, defunct cuckoo clocks, and old hat-racks as the lowest cottage in the land.

And the people are dreadful, well suited to the purgatories they inhabit. 'Hell is other people' was a precept close to A.Moreland's heart. Becket, propping up his Bible against a skull, reads over breakfast with a knowing leer. Queen Matilda is a bag of nerves in bombazine as she escapes over the ice, clinging to a knight's umbrella. William the Conqueror (in crown) grins sardonically as he shoots a subject's prize cow. Alfred merely screams with pain, flinging aside his book, as the formidable Mrs Gurth grabs him by the hair to point out the burning cakes. Boadicea is an early avatar of Old Mother Riley as, in bonnet and ratty fur, she rides her chariot against the Romans, imperiously waving an umbrella. The Princes in the Tower, playing marbles, are obviously juvenile delinquents, while there is every good reason to hang the six untrustworthy burghers of Calais.

The great fascination of the Fireby-Wireby Book was that it

carried a reminder, in my grandmother's cloistered house, that elemental forces were at large. Elsewhere in the house there were hints of predators and unexpected volcanic explosions. Arthur Moreland's Fireby-Wireby Book bore witness that such awfulness was part of the historic process.

Some swear by the illustrative powers of Tenniel or Lear or Beatrix Potter or E.H.Sheppard or Arthur Rackham. In my childhood, I had the benefit of the almost forgotten A.Moreland. He instilled in me a sense of the awfulness of history against which no amount of inspirational prose, read since, has prevailed.

SF Art: Strangeness with Beauty

A great stream of sf and fantasy magazines poured from American (and a few British) presses during the half-century between the twenties and the seventies. Illustration played a vital role in their format. The stream is a trickle now, which makes it high time that the general public discovered what a wealth of illustration is in danger of passing them by.

It may look strange at first – it was designed to look strange – but the pictures in the magazines derived naturally from the potential heritage of the past and from the immediate cultural environment.

The Industrial Revolution and the Napoleonic Wars, when the new powers of machinery gave a spur to man's ambitions, gave new impetus to art. An artistic history of the period could do worse than commence with Philip James de Loutherbourg (1740-1812). De Loutherbourg has yet to find a biographer, perhaps because he dared to work in more than one medium. His life links the Enlightenment, the Gothic Revival, and Romanticism. He was an artist and stage designer, famous for violent lighting effects. From designing a Covent Garden pantomime, *Omai*, based on Captain Cook's voyages, in 1785, de Loutherbourg went on to paint striking industrial scenes (such as Coalbrookdale, also treated by Turner) finally developing a forerunner of the cinema, the Eidophusikon, which featured moving pictures, ingenious optical effects, and, again, striking effects of light. These striking effects were translated into reality, when the Eidophusikon burned down early in the nineteenth century.

John Martin was imaginatively moved by both the Eidophusikon and by the great industrial enterprises, such as M.I.Brunel's tunnel under the Thames. His fantasy is an interpretation of reality. Recent years have seen restoration to favour of John Martin, once so internationally famed that the adjective 'martinien' was coined in France to describe anything on a grandiose scale. Later, he fell so far from popularity that his paintings were sold off at a few shillings per square yard. Engravings of his more terrifying paintings, such as *The Great Day of His Wrath*, once hung above the bedsides of innocent children – including the beds of the small Brontës. Water colours by Charlotte Brontë which depict scenes of the imaginary places she wrote about show Martin's influence; even the great J.M.W.Turner imitated him at one period.

Nightmares frequently inspired Martin's paintings. Henry Fuseli – whose most famous canvas is called, appropriately, *The Nightmare* – ate raw meat before retiring, in order to give himself bad dreams with which to populate his work. Some of his paintings show a perverse love of spatial disproportion and anomalies of size, which would make them ideal for science fantasy covers. There are a limited number of ways in which alien beings can be depicted; they can be different colours, different shapes, or different sizes. And such means were happily at the disposal of artists long before science fiction received its christening.

But the *science* in science fiction received its impetus from the growing technologies of the day. The first magazines of the nineteen twenties (*Amazing Stories* was published by Hugo Gernsback in 1926) were predominantly technophile in character; but there was no gainsaying the fact that early technologies presented a sooty face to the world. Good and bad rarely come in separate parcels. The excitement of the new has generally outweighed its disadvantages, at least for the young. The faster, the uglier, the noisier, the better. The romance of the first ungainly steam engines, crawling from the coal pits at twenty miles an hour, is echoed in the science fictional lust for bigger and better machines, machines like Frankenstein's monster which will eventually take over from mankind.

The earliest magazine sf is full of outrageous machines, all cogs and rivets and columns and winking lights and trailing cables, so that the characters are perpetually tripping through a gigantic Meccano landscape. But the relation to reality is not as remote as might be supposed. You invent futures by magnifying pasts. The outrageous futurist machines derive from a great age of invention, when diabolical engines proliferated – Bruton's drilling machine of the eighteen seventies, for example, would be perfectly at home in some subterranean horror planet designed by Harry Harrison or John Sladek.

The delight of the inventors lay in invention itself, not in the social consequences of the invention – what one might call the Frankenstein syndrome. Horrific experiments, like the attempts of a French surgeon to preserve the dead by electroplating them, are the stuff of sf, even when they take place in real life. The illustration of Dr Varlot's experiment which appeared in the *Scientific American* in 1891 is real Mad Scientist stuff, complete with Moronic Laboratory Assistant, and could serve as an *Amazing* cover (indeed, *mutatis mutandis*, it often did so serve!). To have one's dear ones electroplated by return post and at no great cost is not an unreasonable ambition; like much else which might, ironically or not, be termed Progress, the idea seems to encompass hope and fear in roughly equal proportions.

This mixture of hope and fear is often embodied in sf by taking something from everyday and placing it in a novel context, so that the message gets home. Among other things, H.G.Wells's *The War of the Worlds* features a colonisation war against the British not much different from the wars that Britain and other European powers were waging against Africans. When the technophile Gustave Eiffel erected his great iron tower in Paris in 1889 (while Wells was writing an early version of *The Time Machine*), it was an inspiration to technophiles everywhere – so much so that the tower appeared truncated on a *Wonder Stories* cover some years later as mining equipment on Pluto. The messages were different; the transportations were similar – and part of the new free-ranging powers granted to the popular mind by cheap newsprint, wider education, and the easier access to stimulation enjoyed by the new urban populations.

This infusion of fact and conjecture was hardly new; the Elizabethans had experienced something similar. The rate of infusion was new. Printing presses, railroads, telegraphs, steamships, began to link up the world; as arts as well as trade benefited from the acceleration. 'Is Little Nell dead yet?' asked the mid-century long-shoreman of New York, as the steamers docked with emigrants from Liverpool.

And the new sciences spread as rapidly. One particular Victorian heritage has left its mark on almost every page of this book: the awakening of the long dead past. Slowly, the evidence of the rocks was pieced together, the great dusty carpet of the past unrolled. As surely as the museums and zoos of the civilised world exhibited exotic specimens – rhinos, giraffes, ostriches, tigers – from the four imagined corners of the globe, so the palaeontologists began to resurrect whole new phyla of fantastic animals which had been extinct for centuries. How many thousands of centuries gradually became apparent.

This extended vision of the past became subsumed into the philosophical structure of evolution. Darwin, with those who worked before and after him, demonstrated that change was one of nature's great consistent principles. Imaginative writers like Wells – a pupil of Darwin's friend, Thomas Huxley – demonstrated that just as time had worked to place the mammal Man at the peak of creation, so that peak would give way to other great mountain chains still unborn in Earth's history.

These conceptions of Time and Change were utilised to provide science fiction's happiest hunting ground – the Future. It remains the last great unknown territory on the planet. Moreover, as writers were quick to see, evolutionary principles could be applied to other planets. They took over landscapes hitherto the preserve of mythology, religion, and astronomy. It is interesting to see that in sf, Mars has remained as it always was, the Red Planet, the planet of war, and Venus, the evening star, the planet of peace and gentleness. Old ideas die hard.

The great French writer Jules Verne conducted a four-decades-long romance with Geography, opening up his imagined territories with the aid of an atlas and with machines hardly ahead of his own time – with submarines which already had shadowy existence in scientific journals, with balloons, with propellor-powered dirigibles, with iron-clad steamers, with rockets fired from gigantic pieces of artillery.

Towards the end of the nineteenth century, rivalry between the Great Powers was intense. War was in the air. In his beautifully researched book, *Voices Prophesying War*, Professor I.F.Clarke shows how closely the science fictions of the last part of the century were related to the Imperial fears and intentions of Europe. We remember *The War of the Worlds* by reason of its superior imaginative power; but it was the tip of a large iceberg of militaristic literature. The fleets and the guns got bigger all the time. So did the paper armageddons. A French draughtsman, Albert Robida, devoted himself to chronicling *La Guerre du Vingtième Siècle*, illustrating it with his own graphic drawings of the armaments of the future. The first spaceships looked much like Robida's submarines, moving through vacuum rather than ocean.

The fin de siècle was much preoccupied with catastrophe and decline (*The Time Machine* is as much fin de siècle as Huysman's *La-Bas*) as with war. Artists like Beardsley, who set his stamp on the age, interpreted it without recourse to machines; he too finds his echo in such sf artists as Virgil Finlay and his imitators.

Although it may seem that science fiction occupies itself mainly with the novelties of its age, it is remarkable how easily it accommodates at the same time much that is shadowy in the human spirit.

Architecture of monumental scale and funereal intent awaken echoes in the thoroughfares of sf. The prisons of the Venetian Piranesi, the cemeteries of the great French revolutionary architect, Boullée, though never erected on this Earth, are reconstituted yearly in imaginative literature. Life has fortunately failed to live up to some art.

The designs for new cities and engineering projects on the grand scale, such as preoccupied John Martin and William Moseley, were destined never to come to fruition, like Professor Doxiadis's ecumenopolis in our own day. Yet they established themselves in the hearts of artists of different persuasions, as exemplified by Gustave Moreau's vast shadowy Eastern cities, where one might lose oneself and one's soul amid its erotic splendours. There are striking science fictional examples of such tower-ridden places. I think in particular of Hubert Rogers' great city, built under the seas of Venus, which formed the cover of a 1940s *Astounding*, to illustrate Henry Kuttner's *Fury*.

Kuttner's novel contains many touches of Decadence in its urban portrait; and it too is a mausoleum, symbolically imprisoning an immortal man. In the 1940s, Kuttner's city seemed no more inaccessible than did Moreau's in its day.

We need these grand visions. Like visions of utopia, they inspire us and keep alive in our daily lives the spark of greater things. But they are best confined to paper; they would, as Horace Walpole said, 'exhaust the Indies to realise', and exact too much in terms of simple human happiness, as we assume was the case with the pyramids of Egypt. The spaceships of Chris Foss awaken the same response: they are indeed superb: but the cost of the carpeting alone, supposing them to have carpets in those boulevard-like corridors, would ruin an average-sized solar system's economy for a millennium.

One of the grandest of all Piranesi's visions, a design for a monumental Roman harbour, contains most of the elements which appeal in sf art. It is archaeologically based, extrapolating from a grand past into a more grandiose future, with familiar elements added, enlarged, and reduplicated; it dwarfs the human figure; and it is in part ruinous. I have commented elsewhere on the attraction of ruins.

Speaking of the great Venetian's work, Horace Walpole said,

'Savage as Salvator Rosa, fierce as Michael Angelo, and exuberant as Rubens, he has imagined scenes that would startle geometry, and exhaust the Indies to realise. He piles palaces on bridges, and temples on palaces, and scales heaven with mountains of edifices. Yet what taste in his boldness! What grandeur in his wildness! What labour and thought both in his rashness and details!'

The name of Etienne-Louis Boullée is less well-known, but his work — for instance, the striking *Entrance to a Cemetery* — represents another element present in sf art, an impatience with the present, a wish to break with the past. We still gaze at the *Entrance to a Cemetery* and are amazed that it is late eighteenth century, for it is neither Palladian nor Baroque. By resorting to simple, even brutal, geometrical shapes which appoach the abstract, Boullée creates something which still stands as futuristic. As a final abstraction, none of Boullée's designs were ever built.

Ben Bova has said of science fiction that it is the modern movement. I believe that it may well come to be generally regarded as such in time. When it acquires its proper historian, he will have to pay attention to the architects of the imaginary who helped by their pictures to shape so many worlds.

The endless miscegenations of species revealed by evolution is perpetuated in sf illustration. Dinosaurs have been accorded pride of place, perhaps understandably. But one also meets vast land-going anemones, weapon-toting mantises, intellectual octopi, spinaches which do not stop at rape, and winged races which alone know the secrets of interstellar drive. Many such creatures are there merely to provide man with a menace (that legendary need); others take symbolic shape, like the lonely eagle-human visualised by the Belgian painter, Fernand Khnopff, just before the turn of the century. The concept of living on the Moon or another planet, as Jung has indicated, is itself a symbol of isolation. Often such meanings are used without thought in sf; they can be none the less moving for that.

As for those distant planets! The solar system was pillaged for picturesque versions of Dante's *Inferno*. It could be said that those versions were based on science. Their basis in reality was often remote.

One example will suffice. In 1917, the great Swedish astronomer Arrhenius published his findings on the planet Venus. His deductions were based in part on a belief in Laplace's Nebular Hypothesis, which provides a model for the solar system in which the outer planets are the oldest and the inner, Venus and Mercury, the youngest (thus the idea got about that Mars is an ageing world – a whisper of decay sf writers have never been able to resist). Basing his deductions entirely on what he could observe through his telescope, Arrhenius concluded that Venus was still in a Carboniferous age, with luxuriant vegetation growing in hot cloudy conditions. 'We must therefore conclude that everything on Venus is dripping wet,' he said. From this inspired – and totally incorrect – guess have sprung a thousand *Planet Stories* scenarios.

The inmost planet Mercury also provided striking locations. It was believed until the beginning of the seventies, when American probes made close fly-pasts of the planet, that Mercury's day was of the same length as her year — i.e. that she kept one face permanently towards the Sun as the Moon does towards the Earth. This supposition, in accord with the most rigorous astronomical observations of the day, gave the planet three different zones: a nightside, which was regarded as one of the coldest places in the solar system; a dayside, whereon streams of tin and zinc babbled down the ravaged and barren hillsides; and a twilight zone which girdled the planet, a band of habitability between the opposed desolations of extreme cold and extreme heat. Such dramatic locations served many a writer well.

But the solar system was never enough. Soon the paper spaceships were forging into the galaxy, into other galaxies. The planets the travellers found there were often bizarre, generally bleak. Stuck in a particularly bleak region of Italy, the poet Shelley — some of whose poetry is pervaded by science fiction imagery — complained that 'the imagination cannot find a home in it'. On the other hand, his wife Mary's monster instinctively sought the barren places of the globe, while the boisterous but melancholy imagination of the average sf writer is much at home in blighted surroundings. The illustrators follow suit. Where a far planet was not to hand, Earth itself could always be desolated, New York destroyed, the land of the Sphinx inundated by a new Flood. The atom bomb proved as adaptable as the Wrath of God and, luckily for the artists, there was no limit to man's ingenuity to man.

It would be easy to compile a volume of illustrations from more recent artists such as Ernst Fuchs (surely influenced by Moreau), Mati Klarwein, M.C.Escher, Carel Willink, and others who could rank as science fiction artists in their own right (we will come to Karel Thole later). But the sensibility is there in a previous generation; we have only to look at the haunted buildings of Georges de Chirico (who acknowledged a debt to Jules Verne), the distorted life-forms of Max Ernst, the jokey enigmas of Duchamp, the ambiguous objects of Yves Tanguy, or the barren landscapes of Oscar Dominguez and Salvador Dali, to see a thriving type of art which is akin in spirit to objectives the science fiction writers were moving towards. Science fiction, like surrealism, was once totally unacceptable to the multitude, looked down upon, misunderstood, regarded as mad.

The odd thing is that the writers and illustrators of the popular or pulp (the adjective refers to the constitution of the paper on which the magazines were printed) presses remained largely uninfluenced by the experiments of their own day. The fin de siècle, the art nouveau, yes; surrealism, expressionism, hardly at all.

The reason for this is to be found in the nature of the pulp operation. We shall not understand what we are looking at here until we understand the pulp jungle. Everything had to be done fast, cheap. *The Pulp Jungle* is in fact the title of a book by Frank Gruber, a writer who lived in New York and sold stories where he could, in the thirties when scores of magazines were published every month.

'A couple of days later I got a surprising call from Rogers Terrill. I had heard of these things happening, but up to this time no-one had ever called me.

It was Friday afternoon. They were going to press the next day, Saturday, and needed a fifty-five hundred word story to fill out the issue of *Operator*, no. 5. Could I write a fifty-five hundred word story overnight? I could, I solemnly assured Rogers.

I sat down at the typewriter. By eight o'clock I had created Captain John Vedders of Military Intelligence. All I had to do now was figure out how he could save the world . . .

By eight o'clock in the morning all fifty-five hundred words were down on paper, eighteen pages. There was no time to retype. I delivered the story at nine o'clock.'

If the work was scamped and hasty – and often not even read through by the equally hard-pressed, underpaid editors – it was not to be wondered at. Artists worked under similar pressures. The cover artists were kings because publishers knew that good covers sold the magazines, so the pay was slightly better; by luck and hard work, you could live well.

A popular artist like Virgil Finlay (1914-71), who made his

first appearance in print in 1935, commanded $100 per cover from *Weird Tales*. After the war, the pay for covers for *Famous Fantastic Mysteries* and *Fantastic Adventures* was $150; other publishers might pay slightly less. A full page drawing inside the magazine in black-and-white would earn considerably less — about $50. As the number of magazines dwindled and pages shrank from traditional pulp to digest size, rates went down instead of up, despite the artist's growing reputation, to $100 per cover or less, with a measly $10 for interior work.

Finlay was a painstaking craftsman. Limited in range, he overworked his few themes. Among the thousands of extant examples of his work, figures, gestures, patterns, inevitably repeat themselves. At his best, working with a thick sensuous line backed by stipple, he is highly effective. But his method required a lot of painstaking work, and he was a man who liked to give value for money and please his fans. The only answer was the answer found in sweatshops throughout the length and breadth of history: to slave away for longer hours. Finlay worked sixteen hours, seven days a week, and went without holidays. He was fortunate in having a loving wife who stood by him.

It goes without saying that such artists are unsung among the world's illustrators. There's no justice. Some illustrators had their own following; at least they were repaid by enthusiasm, that special devotion which is the living vein of science fiction (and much at odds with the cruel machines and disasters in which sf often revels). Rogers, Schneeman, the great Paul, Emsh, the starry-eyed Orban — these men were accustomed to seeing their every drawing scrutinised by the fans and generally applauded.

Some of the other names appear little known even within the field. I'm thinking of Henry Sharp, Gerard Quinn with his special colour sense, James Stark, the vigorous Rod Ruth, Leydenfrost, a small master of the macabre.

Obscure though these artists may be, their contribution to science fiction is immeasurable. Between them, they evolved a new idiom, a blend of smashing action, bizarre atmosphere and berserk objects, which stimulated a youthful reader just as much as the accompanying text. In many cases, they rose superior to the clichés inherent in the genre.

Elliot Dold was the greatest pattern-maker. He could so design a banal scene inside a spaceship that its claustrophobic obsessional intensity lifted the picture to a plane of its own, rather than remaining an appendage of the story. On the other hand, we have an illustrator like Vestal who remains strictly that, working in *Planet Stories* to present an all-action picture, and doing so brilliantly against an alien background, his scratchy line seeming to express something of the mystery of the circumstances as he packs the picture with detail that almost certainly is not in the story. In that last respect, he follows in the steps of the illustrious Paul.

Frank R. Paul is the first of the sf illustrators and, by general consensus, the greatest. Well. Howard Browne and Gerard Quinn are more subtle colourists; Emsh is immeasurably better at figure drawing; Schneeman and Rogers have more sublimity; Timmins is more of an *artist*; Brian Lewis is more versatile; many artists have a darker, deeper vision. Yet the crown does pass to Paul. Paul practically patented the genre of sf illustration.

He was a Gernsback discovery. Gernsback used Paul in his radio magazine before *Amazing Stories* was launched. He was a technophile, and his covers and interiors are filled with machines of all kinds, lovingly depicted, often with a female rotundity emerging from among the cogs and pistons. On the covers this is particularly noticeable; the manic technologies of other ages blush in apricot and viridian and pastel-blues.

Paul's approach seems rather pedestrian; his objective appears to be merely to translate as literally as possible the words of the writer into pictures, as if he were translating from one language into another. In Gernsback magazines, the illustrator was often anchored to the literal text, a line or two of which would be appended under an illustration in the old-fashioned way. Paul would probably have said with Gernsback that machines should take over the world; it is his machines that live, that radiate life. His human figures are limp and doll-like (though by the forties he had become much more proficient in depicting the human form): his aliens often seem perfunctory, never whimsical like Morey's or nightmarish like Leydenfrost's. Only his machines have the *élan vital*. Paul's creed was utilitarian. Functionalism roused his deepest responses.

Yet an almost mystical vision shines forth from his best covers. Here, in plodding Gernsbackian prose, is a description of one such cover: 'We see the men of the future, with atomic motors strapped to their backs, flying up swiftly to the sphere suspended in the air. The beams from power houses converging upon the sphere support it freely.' That is all. As Anthony Frewin said in his book, *One Hundred Years of Science Fiction Illustration*, 'Paul, when illustrating a story, created these monstrous galactic cities, alien landscapes, and mechanical Behemoths entirely himself – the descriptions contained in the stories were never much more specific than, for example, something like "shimmering towers rising into the clouds from a crystal-like terrain".' Thus Paul made amends for the inadequacies of the writers. In the cover Gernsback describes above, on the December 1932 issue of *Wonder Stories*, the sphere holds our attention, gleaming like an eyeball, an atom, an enigmatic artefact; everything else in the picture, even the flying figures, contributes to it. Paul thinks it is wonderful, and so do we. The whole is bathed in the warmest colours the Stellar Publishing Corporation could command. Such covers were masterpieces of their kind.

Paul's training as an architect helped. He summoned forth the science fiction city out of nothing, merging Byzantium, the local Odeon, and Durham Cathedral into a weird composite of skyscraper and stately pile. His attention to detail and his wide range of subjects provided a lasting example for the artists who followed or emulated him. He was rivalled, to my mind, only by Emsh in his productive years; but Emsh never showed much affection for architecture – Schomberg is his master there, Schomberg with his incomparable finish and shining surfaces.

The magazines went into a decline although, as I write in 1978, they are undergoing resurrection and, with the coming of *Isaac Asimov's Science Fiction Magazine*, Guccioni's ambitious *Omni, Galileo* and others, look like enjoying a new lease of life. It could be that their success in part reflects a revulsion on the part of the public to the increasing standardisation of paperback marketing. The paperbacks have opted for rocketships with everything and the noble art of astronomy reduced to a sort of trademark.

During the decline of the magazines, there was the brief-lived *Science Fiction Monthly* (1974-6), ever to be remembered, which was the first to place primary emphasis on the visual. It exhibited the work of many artists whose names and glory belong to the paperback field, such as Ian Miller, Hardy, Foss, Jones, Habberfield, the polished Pelham, Roger Dean, and Bruce Pennington. The magazine also encouraged the work of new artists, and must be in part honoured for what has happened since, an amazing proliferation of British fantastic painting.

This proliferation has brought us new kinds and shapes of books, such as Roger Dean's *Views*, Bruce Pennington's *Eschatus*, Patrick Woodroffe's lovely *Mytho-Poeikon*, and Harry Harrison's *Mechanismo*, with which the names of Dragon's World and Big 'O' Publishing are chiefly associated. Pierrot Publishing, the most ambitious new imprint, is bringing forth illustrated novels, the first of which was my *Brothers of the Head*, with fine illustrations by Ian Pollock, to be followed by volumes by Moorcock, Ballard, and Harrison. The illustrations for the latter's *Planet Story*, by Jim Burns, set new standards for the art. There is much to look forward to in this area with pleasure and excitement.

This new generation of artists, books, and publishers enjoys tremendous success and popularity, and has attracted imitators in the States. But in England at least we observe a positive response to the success. Commercialism is not always a foe of imagination and creativity; anti-commercialism is ultimately more deadly.

To conclude, I will call as evidence for this proposition the work of Thole, a Dutch artist living in Italy.

My friend Karel Thole deals with some extraordinary matters, yet is able to make them seem still more remarkable. A cat sits happily next to an old robot in a wheelchair. They have obviously known each other for a long while. There's that startling painting of an angel lying on the Earth with her eyes closed and hair trailing; before the angel's face is a sea of her blood; on the coasts of that scarlet sea stand men, pointing. They aren't pointing in horror; they are pointing out familiar landmarks to each other, commenting on the extreme delicacy of a nostril, the beauty of an eyebrow arch. That's the Thole touch.

Johann Zoffany: 'The Death
of Cook'. Oil on canvas, 1797.
To deepen the implications of
the tragedy, Zoffany adapts
familiar classical poses for his
chief protagonists. Cook's
murderer uses the pose of the
Discobolus, Cook of a dying
gladiator. Zoffany, who may
have met Cook, was aided in
his task by the fact that
Hawaiian chieftains wore
headgear much resembling
ancient Greek helmets.

Similar impulses are at work
in this poster for *Star Wars*.
The garments are at least Buck
Rogers Classical, whilst the
pose on a rocky plinth with
male dominating female is
traditional. Even the force
weapon has been made to
resemble a sword. We are
intended to be reminded of
chastity, virtue, courage, and
justice.

This remarkable cenotaph, never built, was designed by Etienne-Louis Boullée in 1784, and dedicated to the memory of Sir Isaac Newton. Its spherical form, cut by the skirt, is reminiscent of Saturn and is intended to express an Enlightenment view of the cosmos.

The *Startling Stories* cover (by Alex Schomburg) from the early fifties depicts, in foreground, a space machine (never built) which also owes a debt to Newton, and perhaps to Boullée. It, no less than the Boullée design, embodies an aspiration towards progress, in both cases a 'functional' form.

Another Boullée design from the end of the eighteenth century, this one for the entrance to a cemetery. With the population of cities rising, and high mortality rates, cemeteries demanded a new approach and a new technology. Boullée evidently had little patience with the bereaved: 'Temple de la mort' he cried, 'votre aspect doit glacer nos coeurs . . .'

More architecture of the imaginary, G. B. Piranesi's 'Monumental Roman Harbour', from the middle of the eighteenth century. Men have always dreamed of great cities; this one, utilising and recombining elements from classical architecture, is as overpowering as any. Nothing is left for its inhabitants but to stand about in conventional poses, admiring the view.

The Festival of Britain, 1951. Silhouettes of Henry Moore sculpture and a windmill in the Country pavilion. After a long war, the future had arrived: bold, bare, and, like all futures, somewhat lacking in detail.

'Captain Nemo remained motionless, as if petrified in mute ecstasy, leaning on a mossy stone. Was he dreaming of those generations long since disappeared?' In this illustration from an early French edition of Jules Verne's *20,000 Leagues Under the Sea*, the lost city of Atlantis is revealed in all its classical grandeur. Even if the city never existed, the myth is inextinguishable.

Humors of History, No. 21, The Burnt Cake Episode, AD 878. Alfred the Great is hiding from the Danes in the home of Gurth, a swineherd. Gurth's wife discovers the king has allowed her cakes to burn. Moreland's characters express a limited range of emotions, fear and anger prominent among them.

'I paint ideas not things,' said G. F. Watts, a British Symbolist painter highly regarded in his lifetime (he died in 1904) and almost totally neglected since. His canvas 'The Sower of the Systems', which does not reproduce well, is the first great painting of our century. This is his 'Mammon'.

Cultural totems in Georgia. Lounging on the balcony of the dacha mentioned in the text are Jon Stallworthy, Elaine Feinstein, the author, Charles Osborne (born to command) and E. A. Whitehead ('Gospodin White-hell'). This was May Day.

A last refuge of tranquillity: Samosir Island, in the middle of Lake Toba, in the middle of Sumatra. In this Batak village, the traditional wooden houses look no less beautiful for being re-roofed in corrugated iron.

Design for a Solar Energy Satellite by the Boeing Aerospace Company (detail from a painting by John J. Olson). A space shuttle rests on the assembly centre after its journey from Earth. The principle of necessity or imagined necessity is present behind even the most imaginative and abstract designs.

Ruination holds a profound message for science fiction writers. One ruin formed part of my dream world for many years, finally embodying itself in this Piranesi Veduta. The view shows the Roman mausoleum of St Helena, mother of Constantine; a humbler dwelling has been built in its embrace.

Such relationships suggest something much more extraordinary even than the superficial content implies. Many of the creatures and phenomena in Thole's paintings are pretty horrifying. But they rarely horrify the people in the pictures. The people accept the monstrous as an everyday event. Karel Thole is the master of the serene inferno.

And this is where I have an advantage in being able to view two sides of Mr Thole's art, the surrealist side and the science fiction side. For the surrealist side, Mr Thole numbers among his close relations, Max Ernst, Paul Delvaux, Salvador Dali and Carel Willink, the latter born in Amsterdam, like Thole. His art, like theirs, is to paint an unreal scene with fidelity. To this objective, Mr Thole brings gifts which are immediately apparent in any display of his work, in particular a fine colour sense and a delicacy which recalls the work of illustrators of mediaeval books of hours.

Representational although Mr Thole's paintings are, my belief is that he is painting abstracts. His abstractions include eroticism, horror, madness, remoteness, desolation, isolation, and catastrophe. These are not the sort of abstracts we expect to find conveyed through the medium of that exquisite sense of colour, that decorous brush.

They arrive via the other side of his art, the science fiction side. I give away no secrets here if I briefly detail Mr Thole's method of work. Since he is a busy and successful man, he has no time to read the novels for which he is asked to provide a cover. Instead, his publishers – Mondadori or whoever it may happen to be – send him a few lines of synopsis, outlining the theme of the book. Mr Thole makes his painting from the synopsis.

You know what André Breton said in his Surrealist Manifesto? 'The Marvellous is always beautiful, everything marvellous is beautiful. Nothing but the Marvellous is beautiful.' Breton's dictum applies to the way in which Mr Thole works, as well as to the paintings themselves.

What he does in fact is to free-associate. What is he free from? Basically from control-by-reason. He is programmed by the man from Mondadori, and he then proceeds according to Breton's definition of surrealism, which he said was pure psychic automatism. The work proceeds in the absence of rational thought, although the controlling expertise of long practice is present.

The result is a rare thing – a surrealist painter of great ability whose output is dictated by the world's science fiction writers. Or, not so much by them as by a sort of abstract of their imaginings.

Since I believe that science fiction writers – the writers of *fantascienza*, as the Italians gracefully call it – have sunk an oil-well into the collective unconscious with their machines, monsters, and logic-reversals, you can see why I consider that Karel Thole's work is more than merely decorative and why he is more than a cover artist. His serene infernos touch on a particular phase between waking and dreaming which scientists call the hypnoid state; in that state the world of every day blends with the world of the incredible.

The result is a personal mythology.

Like Magritte, Mr Thole enjoys pretending he is just a businessman. How much I prefer that to all the businessmen who pretend they are artists! But this particular businessman hates to part with his paintings.

I have quoted Breton; let me close by quoting another Honourable Ancestor, Francis Bacon, Lord Verulam, who says in his *Essays*, 'There is no excellent beauty that hath not some strangeness in the proportion.' And our best fantasy painters show us that the reverse is also true: There is no strangeness that hath not an excellent beauty in it.

The Film Tarkovsky Made

Something fugal by Bach on a dim organ; the screen brightens; we gaze on the riverain waters of Earth, in which sedges ripple continually. By the river banks, wild parsleys flower and seed. Kris Kelvin stands there, about to leave this strange but familiar planet. Young children play, plunging indoors to avoid a thundery rainstorm. Symbols of transience are all round us.

Throughout this beautiful film, *Solaris,** we are strikingly reminded that stability is achieved only by constant minor instability. There are shots of winter, of other seasons, of smoky bonfires in which Kelvin burns bits of his past, of a little bright twig fire made by a boy in the snow, of roaring traffic, of plants, and of Kelvin and his parents at different stages of their lives (Mosfilm must have the best make-up artists in the world). And, of course, the last heartbreaking scenes when the rain falls on the unheeding shoulders of the old man.

Mutability does not exist on the sterile world of the research satellite which men have put in orbit about the planet Solaris. In that respect, the satellite is in opposition to the planet, which is all mutability. Its vast flying tides, its slow crawling patterns, its indecipherable structures, are unimpeded by any hindrance; this is a water-world without coastlines. Over the ages, it has achieved its own sort of consciousness.

The power of Solaris is such that it can insert thought-made-flesh into the satellite, using as its vehicles images or memories from the minds of Earthmen there. When Kelvin arrives on the satellite, he is confronted in due course by a copy of his wife, who committed suicide some years before. These copies, too, are capable of change.

* *Solaris*, directed by Andrei Tarkovsky. A Mosfilm Studios Production in Scope and Colour. 165 minutes. With Donatas Banionis as Kris Kelvin and Natalya Bondarchuk as Hari. Based on the novel *Solaris* by Stanislav Lem.

I stress the theme of mutability because it is present but uninsistent, and capable of drawing powerful emotional responses from the viewer. But how far should we trust to the objectivity of science, how far to the subjectivity of our emotions? Or perhaps we should re-phrase the question this way: maybe the script writers designed an argument about science versus emotion; if so, the director, Tarkovsky, imprinted his own answer on every scene. He is for emotion.

His will be a widely acceptable answer; more and more we hear that we ought to trust to our intuitive feelings and not doubt personal experience, rather than being quelled by experts telling us what we feel. There are, I believe, intellectual reasons for conceding that this should be so. The trouble is that, in a popular medium like films, where emotion has always been made free of, objectivity and detachment have never had much of a showing; Madame Curie's work always played second fiddle to Miss Greer Garson's genteel sexuality. And in adapting Stanislav Lem's novel, Tarkovsky has played havoc with it as much as David Lean did with the intellectual structure of *Dr Zhivago* – a stunning cast of actors, some beautiful cinema, and a great love affair played out, not over a disrupted period of history, but a disrupted patch of psychology.

Having delivered myself of this sizeable objection to the film as adaptation, I am free to speak of its tremendous delights as film, to which end I will make no extended comparisons with Lem's fine novel (for that would be in itself an exercise in solaristics) and no comparisons at all with Kubrick's *2001*, for that would be an idle exercise.

To give an idea of what happens in the film: Tarkovsky presents a worried, bear-like Kelvin, sauntering about his parents' dacha on the eve of his departure for Solaris. He is a psychologist, and is going to see what has gone wrong on the space-station. An ex-astronaut, Burton, arrives at the dacha with a film about Solaris. Through his film, we gather a few basic details: that Solaris has been observed by Earthmen for many years, until solaristics has become a major study, and that now only three men out of eighty-five remain on the station. The problem seems to be how to make contact with the alien consciousness. As one of the experts says, man's knowledge is limited but thought is boundless (and that was the first platitude I noticed).

We are given a few oblique references before Kelvin leaves Earth. His moody estrangement from his loving parents, the death of his wife. 'I cannot let myself be guided by emotion,' he says. A horse trots about; perhaps it is the most alien creature in the film. The children are frightened by it, yet it is utterly gentle and dependent. There is also the curious metal box (a radio, a mess-tin?) which Kelvin carries about with him. The method of the film is to speak mainly in long-held takes, very carefully composed, yet always to leave much that is mysterious. The early shots in the house glow with interest as the humans move among chiaroscuro and fascinating objects.

Solaris. The wheel of the satellite moving above those cryptic waters, gonging out great bronze reflected rays from the sun as Kelvin's shuttle approaches. The spaceware is filmed with economic flair and penetration. In particular, the interior of the station, through whose unpredictable spatial configurations Kelvin cautiously moves, is and remains a brooding presence, observed with precision. Its smooth surfaces are draped with roughly laid coaxial cable, lights flicker where an electrical contact has broken, rubbish blows about curving corridors, while inexplicable draughts move across unexpected objects. Forced by the circumstantial evidence, we ourselves must prowl here with Kelvin, and face the unknown.

If we study the history of painting between the eighteenth and nineteenth centuries, we can observe the landscapes changing from the Picturesque to the Romantic; a place we are intended merely to dream at becomes a place in which we could walk. Under the powerful influence of geology and the advance of science generally, nineteenth-century painters were forced to examine rock, to re-think the character of rock and its effect on landscape, so that the generalised mountains of David and the Neo-Classicists give way to the obsessively observed strata of Turner and the young Millais. Something like the same momentous change affects us when we encounter the Solaris satellite for the first time; it shows the earlier spacecraft of, say, George Pal and the Wilcox of *Forbidden Planet* to be pale unrecapturable dreams of cosmic Neo-Classicism.

We meet Snauth and Sartorious, the only two survivors on the satellite. Kelvin's friend Gibaryan has committed suicide. Before dying, he left a visi-tape which explains that the 'guests' on the satellite are 'something to do with one's conscience'. We catch glimpses of the succubi and incubi which attend these doomed men: a little girl for Gibaryan, a fearsome dwarf for Sartorious. They are trapped in their pasts, perhaps not hating them enough.

Finally, Kelvin falls asleep in his comfortless room. When he awakes, morning has dawned. The rays of the sun light upon tawny hair, upon a splendid cheekbone, upon a pair of finely moulded lips. Kelvin has his own succubus now. A copy of his wife Hari awaits him. Escape from Earth is no escape – a point a less mature film might have laboured.

The scenes between Kelvin and Hari are superb, vibrating with anguish and physicality. Kelvin jettisons the first Hari by firing her out of the station in a spare shuttle, but another Hari soon materialises. Despite his objective mistrust of what she represents, and to the digust of Sartorious, Kelvin falls in love with Hari, and a several-sided debate ensues. The other men are annoyed by Kelvin's behaviour; they try to cope with their own baffling problems, and Sartorious complains that they have in fact achieved what was required of them and made contact with Solaris, although they don't recognise contact when they find it.

It is chilly Sartorious who announces, after experiments on his own 'guest', that the materialisations are made of neutrinos which remain stable only in Solaris's atmosphere. Whether this double error is committed in the original film or is a product of the subtitle-writer, your Russianless reviewer can but guess; what is possibly meant is that the guests are composed of neutrons rather than positrons, which hold stable in the planet's gravitational field. The implication is clear: Kelvin cannot take Hari with him back to Earth. Athough he later reaches an extreme point at which he rejects science, he is still subject to natural laws, implicitly accepting this when he tells Hari that they will live together and never leave the station. He has reversed his earlier position and is now entirely guided by emotion.

By this time, Hari has done considerable damage to herself, battling her way through steel doors and drinking liquid oxygen.

The damage is impermanent, her wounds transient. These scenes are alarming and well faked. Here at least the film has advantages over the novel, since we are involved in the suffering of an impressive female creature, the Hari of Natalya Bondarchuk, the sort of succubus men dream of. All the while, she – or Solaris – is learning what it is to be human, in a series of moving scenes. Hari admits to Sartorious that she may be a copy; 'But I am becoming human,' she says. The others, however, do not learn what it is to be inhuman, except indirectly, and this seems to weaken somewhat the grand theme of first alien-human encounter.

One says this reluctantly, for beyond doubt the cinema has never before made so superb an attempt to imagine that staple revelation of sf, the meeting of human and non-human. But because the learning is imposed on the copy instead of the humans, the central situation loses its fulcrum; solaristics are so much wasted time, since from now on the ocean can pretend to be human whenever it needs to, and thus baffle all human investigation. Solaris can never be comprehended, for it comprehends humanity.

Towards the end of the film, as this flaw reveals itself, one begins to notice platitudes creeping in. Are men really just objects for love? Will the new knowledge save mankind? Has life a meaning? So the men ask themselves. I should add that I have seen the film four times, once without subtitles; I preferred, was more profoundly stirred by, the version without subtitles – not only because the clichés did not get through but because the actors and the camerawork (by Vadim Yusov, who has worked with Tarkovsky previously) are so telling. The dialogue does not match the superb visuals: friends with Russian say there is much standard Sovexport philosophy. Unlike the novel, this is meant for the sensualist as well as the intellectual.

Before mediocrity can threaten to close in, the film is saved by a flood of new pictorial inspiration, such as Kelvin's hallucinations in his fever, when more than one Hari is present, and he dreams of his young mother, seen first chaste and Pre-Raphaelite, wrapped in a pink-and-white squared gown by a green brook, later bathing the symbolic dirt from her son's arms – and always looking hauntingly like Hari.

There is also the strange excursion into Breughel's paintings, when we linger over the details of a reproduction of his *Hunters in the Snow*. Perhaps we are to infer, always obliquely and never wholeheartedly, that the ocean is pleased to turn from water into the slightly more substantial form of snow we call flesh; if so, how astonishingly egocentric of us. Then the viewpoint moves on, over other Breughels (including his *Land of Cockaigne*, which one might think fairly apposite to Kelvin's case), and to more teasing mysteries. Aren't we all, in a platonic sense, copies of some greater thing?

Kelvin recovers from his fever. Hari has gone, leaving an unconvincing letter. He looks towards the circular window of his cabin. There lies that box (radio? mess-tin?) he has been carrying round. For the first time, we see it open. A green plant grows from it. This struck me as so banal, that I felt that the plentiful Earth symbols to which we had been treated were meant to be seen as failing at last, as ultimately meaningless; but that no doubt is too sophisticated a reading. However, it would lead logically to the final scene, which follows after Kelvin, gazing at the plant, admits it is time he left the station.

What can one say about the ending? Is it a spirited trick à la Philip K. Dick? Is it a literal illustration of a Jungian proposition concerning some oceanic consciousness? Or is it (as I believe) both of these things and a last lingering restatement of the film's theme, that there are varying degrees of reality and mutability? Whatever it is, it is certainly full of strength and pathos, making up abundantly for faltering towards the end, enhancing the human quality of the whole.

Solaris is a mysterious and abundant film. Although it has settled for becoming yet another great cinema love story, it still deals honourably with profound matters. There is no reason why it could or should make itself clear on them, provided it convinces us of their richness, and this it does richly.

Tarkovsky's *Andrej Rubelev* is also worth hunting down. Rubelev is a sixteenth-century icon painter. Like Kelvin, he had to make sense of chaos, the chaos caused by Mongol invaders. One episode concerns the moulding in the earth of a great church bell, which eventually rings true despite all doubts. In

Solaris Hari is that bell, sprung not from earth but ocean, lost eventually but worth the losing.

Well, the sense of loss is strong in Tarkovsky's epic. Yet one must close by emphasising its positive qualities. It bids fair to stand as the best sf film so far. References are made to both Tolstoi and Dostoevsky and perhaps much of its strength lies there – that Tarkovsky tries to deal with both man-in-society and man-in-relation-to-the-unknown, matters of interest to everyone, not simply sf readers. He may not be entirely successful in this endeavour, but of his power to conjure images illustrating his theme there is no doubt.

Kissingers Have
Long Ears

Millions of people have found *Star Trek* meaningful, and the reason is not far to seek. Despite the gadgets, the monsters and the plastic distances, the main attraction of the series lies in the fact that it provides reassurance disguised as challenge. Such double-think is one of the major triumphs of our age; we have learnt to speak out manfully without offending the sponsors.

The mock-challenge of *Star Trek* is, of course, the exploration of the universe. The real reassurance is, of course, that the Nice Guys from Earth can sort out any little problem that arises anywhere.

Things like *Star Trek* and *Star Wars* can easily kill off real science fiction, which seeks to open new realms of human experience and discovery to men's imagination. Whilst pretending to do this, *Star Trek* generally manages in fact to do the opposite and to conclude with a resounding cliché; as one or other plastic character says, 'Let's remember that the galaxy is too small for white men and green men to war together.' We never taste real blood because with this sort of thing we cannot leave our own milk bar.

The whole show is designed as a streamlined sedative. God is dead but the hull is airtight. The United States needed comfort in the sixties, and here it was in full colour and slow motion. For the Nice Guys are of course all American and, indeed, All-American.

In the real world, American diplomacy was suffering endless set-backs; all its good and less good intentions, all the hand-outs and hopes, all the military aids and props to tottering régimes, all the sob-stuff and sincerity, were meeting with the far harsher fates than they deserved, in Europe, in the Middle East, and of course in Asia. On the small screen, Captain Kirk and his chaps never missed a trick; know-how and a touch of the boot made politics an easy game to play among the stars.

I am proud to say that I did sit through some episodes in their entirety, occupying myself with the question, Is Kissinger based on Spock, or Spock on Kissinger?

Later, as animated cartoon, *Star Trek* was better. More like the wish-dream it really is. If the splendours of the universe and creation have to be debased, more fun to do it in animation, though my favourite cartoon nevertheless remains the Hanna-Barbera *Valley of the Dinosaurs*, even if that archetypal Hanna-Barbera family are all too reptilian and the dinosaurs all too human.

By the seventies, the war in Vietnam was drawing to its close, the *Star Treks* with live actors were things of the past, and the Arabs were about to clamp down sufficiently on fossil fuels so as to render further voyages of the uss *Enterprise* highly unlikely. *More* highly unlikely. So it is logical that when *Space 1999* comes along, it starts with a disaster.

Despite some very nice model-work, *Space 1999* is a bit of a disaster all through. If *Star Trek* is pabulum, then this British-made series is imitation pabulum, with characters even more puppet-like than many of its predecessors, such as *Thunderbirds*. The plots are riddled with inconsistencies. The series is presumably the tribute paid to *Star Trek*'s popular success: not a fake but a forgery of a fake.

It is sad that these two major series are not less lowbrow and that they fail to provide better excitements, entertainments, and insights for the people who enjoy them. British television has produced two superior series which are worth more attention.

The BBC's *Dr Who* series has been running for years, with rests in between serials. Currently, it is better than ever it was. The usual format is for a five- or six-part serial at peak Saturday early-evening viewing time. *Dr Who* can be enjoyed not only because it is inventive and exciting (and terrifies the daylights out of children who cannot resist watching), but because the direction, by Philip Hinchcliffe, is of almost the same level of professionalism as one would expect from the dramatisation of a classic novel (direction and camera-work in *Star Trek* were abominably amateur, emphasising the pure country-folk goodness of the crew). *Dr Who* has the common sense not to take its alien invasions too seriously; the scripts often crackle with witty remarks. Dr Who himself is one of a long line of English eccentrics who, like Sherlock Holmes, goes it alone and makes out where police and military are baffled.

Dr Who 'scapes whipping by being disarmingly unpretentious. The ITV series, *The Prisoner*, the brain-child of Patrick McGoohan, who plays the chief role of Number Six, is madly ambitious. It ran, I believe, to thirty-six episodes, was filmed in the mid-sixties, and is so tautly and sassily put together that even today it takes some keeping up with.

The Prisoner is the great paranoid drama of our time. Number Six has a vital secret which he refuses to divulge. He is held prisoner on an island by a power which could be Ours or Theirs which tries to break him, using futuristic attempts to crack his mind. Thus, the basic formula defies all box-office rules by proposing a double negative: at the end of each week, Number Six fails to escape, the Power fails to break him. Sets are very futuristic, dialogue clipped, everything stylised. Little explanation is forthcoming. Actors include such excellent performers as Leo McKern and Mary Morris. Some episodes were better than others. The best are unexcelled.

The Prisoner, unlike the other offerings, is adult drama. Will Spock, when we view him on the big screen, have grown up a little, instead of being a teenager's dream of school-teacher?

Spielberg: When the Mundane Breaks Down

We all need the appearance, or at least the hope, of something marvellous in our lives. Everything from the great religions to the least science fiction story reminds us that something marvellous is in fact within us.

In the cinema of the seventies, the films of Steven Spielberg, in particular *Duel*, *Jaws*, and *Close Encounters of the Third Kind*, have served as amazingly effective reminders of this understanding.

Duel (Paramount, 1972) is a non-science-fiction film displaying all the science fiction merits. It is Spielberg's first feature film; he was then in his early twenties. The script is by Richard Matheson.

Matheson made a sudden name for himself in the early fifties with a series of violent, poetic, and illogical short stories. In the mid-fifties, he started to work for television and the movies. From this period on spring the excellent *Incredible Shrinking Man*, and the various screen versions of his novel about vampires, *I am Legend*.

In *Duel*, the chief human character is Mann, played by the actor Dennis Weaver. The film is superbly mobile from first shot to last, with unobtrusively excellent editing and cutting and a neat musical score. It ranks with Clouzot's *The Wages of Fear* as one of the most suspenseful films ever made.

Mann leaves home and a sort of uneasy domesticity for a business appointment some distance away. He drives out of his garage in a red Plymouth saloon. As he gets through town, and the traffic thins, he encounters an articulated oil-tanker which he overtakes with some difficulty. The tanker challenges him. Soon it is clear that the tanker is out for his blood. The duel is between Mann and the tanker or, rather, between Mann-plus-Plymouth and the tanker. For many of the shots, we are caught with Mann in the fleeing car. The legend 'Flammable' looming on the back of the filthy old tanker is the codeword for an ingeniously constructed flow of terror which forces Mann to find extra reserves in himself when the car fails him.

The duel between the man and the tanker is an archetypal confrontation between Man and Thing, suggesting patterns that hark back to our origin as individuals and as a species. Some millions of years ago, sapiens won the battle against the automatic response, and so entered human existence; but that battle was only the first in a long war still raging. Through clever camerawork, we see Flammable as a living creature; shots from low by the Plymouth's hubcap looking back at the fuming pursuer emphasise its flexibility, its implacability. It is a monster, kin to one of Van Vogt's galactic weapons.

In *Jaws* (CIC, 1975), the most profitable movie in history until surpassed by *Star Wars* and *Close Encounters*, the situation is different, yet much the same. The alien environment is not the mountains but the ocean. The monster is not a machine but a giant fish – yet it requires only a little sophistication from the cinema-goer to know that this fish is really a machine. This is cleverly acknowledged in the best-remembered line in the film, when the ichthyologist says of the shark, 'All this machine does is swim and eat and make little sharks – and that's it!'

Spielberg ruthlessly simplified Peter Benchley's novel (also entitled *Jaws*) but he left in the conflict between the fish-watchers who want to close down the dangerous beaches, and the mayor of the resort who wants the tourists and their money. The most brilliant passages are not those where the shark is present but those where the possibility of his emergence is contrasted with the conventional holiday junketings on the beach, where families play unsuspectingly near the water and we, the audience, know that there's more to life than that. Just below the sunlit surface, as we children of the twentieth century are aware, terrible fanged things wait to strike.

Like *Duel* and *Close Encounters*, *Jaws* is extremely well put together (and perhaps we should pause a moment to marvel at any man who can create such enormous commercial successes and at the same time produce good work which does not rely for its appeal on violence or cynicism). *Duel* appears a simple mechanism, speaking directly to the adrenalin, one touch of which makes the whole world kin. Yet, although it is stripped-down simple, we still have room to wonder, if we want to be difficult, what are its central concerns.

First approach to the film is to say that it is about cars, and will appeal to non-motorists as well as drivers. This is the pragmatic approach. We can imagine the film moguls opening up Operation Duel by sitting round a table and asking themselves 'How can we make a film that is one long car-chase?' If they did so, then they came up with an amazingly effective answer to the question.

Or we may heighten our understanding by regarding this as a crypto-Marxist drama condemning the bourgeois way of life. The context is clear. The Plymouth functions as a mistress, according to the Vance Packard diagnosis of some years ago – remember it is scarlet in colour – and the central character escapes with her from an unsatisfactory bourgeois marriage. We begin with the car swinging out of one of those little surburban villas where The Family develops all its classic manias. The car's on the loose, but still lapped in a nursery middle-class environ-ment, with Mann snug in his seat for a slow downtown drive with traffic cops seeing that law and order is maintained, and radio belching out commercials. Our tame man sets out on a journey of re-orientation. In a way, his later difficulties with Flammable spring from his lacking a sense of commitment. He'd have kept out of trouble if he had concentrated; with a real objective he would have maintained speed and purpose. But he has no determination, his mistress is just an escape route, rather than an end in herself, to be enjoyed for her own sake.

But that interpretation can't be right. After all, Mann soon shows that he's a real man. Put to the test, he's full of the old pioneer spirit. Maybe the film eulogises middle-class virtues, showing how they can still rise supreme from California small towns when called upon. The antagonist is still destroyed.

Still, there is no doubt that Mann lacks determination; his resolve, when it emerges, is forced out of him by crisis. Maybe he lacks will-power. Maybe he's exploited by the machine, by consumer society. Ah, socio-economic meanings! Perhaps this is really a Communist film, full of veiled propaganda against

capitalism. Political levels of meaning are suggested more than
once, notably when Mann seeks co-operation from a middle-
aged couple in another car. They will not help him, trapped as
they are in their own lethal little machine which symbolises a
trivialisation of personal relationships, or, as the philosophers
Flanagan and Allen used to put it,

> The motor car is phoney –
> I'd rather have Shanks's pony . . .

We watch the death of personal relationships which
capitalism is classically supposed to bring about. A couple of
well-judged scenes involving the younger generation – kids
playing with war toys – show how the capitalist rot is setting in
early.

Or should our interpretation of *Duel* tend more towards the
mythopaeic? The duel itself – is it a duel at all, we ought to ask
ourselves, or a symbolic pursuit, reminiscent of The Hound of
Heaven? Spielberg's very name has mythic overtones (literally
Play-Mountain, suggesting Olympus and captious deities),
prompting us to empathise with Mann and hate the Flammable
tanker. Does the one embody Good, the other Evil, with Mann
as Mankind battling the Anti-Christ, the inhuman in man?
'Flammable' – there's a double clue: Flame is traditionally the
very signature of Hell, Mable a warped version of a (low)
woman's name.

Would it be as true to say, if we're really getting into the
realms of myth and symbol, that Mann is a mere passenger in
the story, as it were, that the two vehicles are the crux of the
matter? Reaction shots constantly cutting from Mann's worried
face to failing speedometer (when the radiator boils), emphasise
how alike are human and machine responses to a given situation. It becomes apparent to any critic on the make that
Plymouth and tanker, are really (a fine critical implement, that
word 'really': it passes unnoticed, like a dagger beneath a cloak)
are really *doppelgängers*, spreading havoc between them in the
hour of their consumation, and part of the same figure of
destruction – ply*mouth* suggesting the head, *tank* the body of the
figure? When a small zoo is broken up, writhing snakes suggest

the *intestines* of the figure. The story ends with the demise of one party, as end it must; it is not fanciful to see that the other party becomes *disembodied*, functionless, a Frankenstein without monster to pursue or be pursued by.

In the words of an Edward Thomas poem –

> He goes; I follow; no release
> Until he ceases. Then I also shall cease.

If we care to, we can accept *Duel* as a parable of the destructive nature of the automobile, a modern message aimed at the conservationists in the audience. Conversely, are we perhaps left with a commercial for the durability of Chrysler's Plymouth automobiles?

Being a critic is a hazardous profession . . .

But there are passages which support the anti-automobile reading. One of the most chilling incidents involves a school bus. While Mann is by the bus, he looks along the road towards the tunnel through which he will have to go. The oil tanker has turned back to await him under the arch of the tunnel; when it sees him looking, its headlights flare and die.

It's an unsettling moment. The Flammable is a monster, sentient. So I first thought; but maybe it merely sends a signal of recognition – like calling to like, as it were. Mayhem on the highway, where any number can play.

One last interpretation. You might like to buy this one. The uncheckable vehicle is an oil tanker, let us remember. The film is strictly a contemporary fable about oil, running unchecked over the good Earth like a weed, oil that *fata morgana* of our culture, luring Western man to destruction. Note that Mann is played by Dennis Weaver. Doesn't the very name Weaver suggest that a return to older values, hewing wood, potting, *weaving*, might bring about our salvation? If Weaver were less pushing, less eager to overtake all opposition, the world would be a better place. Mann succeeds finally in extirpating the dangerous weed by use of his one implement, the Plymouth. Plymouth what? Clearly, Plymouth *Hoe*, a simple garden instrument again suggesting older values (reinforced by the suggestion of piety via Plymouth Brethren). I find this interpretation the most persuasive of all, except for one detail – the film was made in 1972, before the oil crisis.

Which of all the interpretations do I put my metaphorical shirt on? I have a great deal of respect for my shirt. Though I can see that, in the sort of commercial conditions under which the film was conceived, some Paramount executive probably got the hots for a film that was one long car-chase from start to finish.

The other interpretations merely suggest themselves, not always implausibly but not definitively either. This ambiguity is an enrichment; the implications of the film – the freedom it gives us – is that it is not, say, a Marxist tract, or a hymn of praise or hate about traffic on our roads. The ambiguities open up naturally when Mann moves from the safety and banality of the known to the challenge and beauty of the unknown.

This is exactly what happens in *Close Encounters of the Third Kind*, (Columbia Pictures, 1978). In many ways, it is the archetypal confrontation between Man and Thing as expressed in *Duel*, but carried to a much higher pitch.

In both films, environment is important, even crucial; we travel away from home and familiar things towards the wilds; suburb gives way to frontier. The barren and inaccessible places may not in themselves be pleasurable, but Spielberg shows us the tensions apparently inevitable in a home environment.

The most brilliant aspect of *Close Encounters*, a film that presents us continually with things to admire, is possibly the way in which hum-drum every day life, family life, law and order, are dramatised as being maintained only at enormous psychic expense.* Here is Mann's uneasy domesticity spelt out. The ordinary has to be held in place almost by force – yet ultimately the extraordinary erupts from its midst; the mere presence of people with vision disrupts it, sending wives fleeing back to mother with frightened kids in the back of the station wagon whilst, in the kitchen, the centre of normality, something disruptively strange takes over.

The novel version of the film, also credited to Steven Spielberg, echoes in its paler way the point so powerfully made in the film.

* The same theme emerges in a recent brilliant Australian film, *The Last Wave* (1977), directed by Peter Weir.

Roy Neary, the chief character, is pulled by his wife into their bedroom.

' "I can't help you," she cried. "I don't understand."
"Neither do I."
"All this nonsense is turning this house upside down," she said.'

Neary's lack of understanding is one of the kind where wisdom begins – the sort of wisdom that almost literally 'turns houses upside down'.

This mysterious perception is embodied, in the film, in the striking image of the electronic toys coming to life in the middle of the night. The small boy wakes and looks at them in awe – for him, all this is natural and right because he has not yet been drawn into the grown-up conspiracy of believing that mundane life is the only life.

I use the word 'mundane' because it has a special connotation for sf readers. They are beyond mere realism; when they refer to someone as 'a mundane type', they put their finger on the enemy.

Not only is *Close Encounters* one of the most successful films ever made: it is a science fiction movie in its essentials as well as its trappings, in that in shows the mundane being ripped apart as a glorious vision of the unknown rises from it, lit like a thousand chandeliers and heading straight for the centre of the galaxy with us aboard.

Rarely has the unknown been portrayed so exultantly. Of course there is a touch of wish-fulfilment about those final sequences; it could have been avoided if we had been shown how Lacombe managed to persuade a previously sceptical government to adapt the five-note sequence discovered in India and so communicate peaceably with forces they had tried to destroy so shortly before – such a demonstration could have replaced the rather facile driving-about-and-escaping-from-the-military episode; nevertheless, the film demonstrates more triumphantly than has been the case before a human necessity for the alien.

Aliens are in a sense free, as once we believed the birds were free, to scud where they would, to fly where fancy takes them. Aliens do not obey all the painfully acquired rules that keep us marginally human. In the hatred of the unknown is a large component of envy.

The aliens in *Close Encounters* are Jungian creatures, having much in common with Prospero's Ariel. They fill the island with sweet noises and beautiful lights, mischief attends them. They are far from being the usual inhumanly rational monsters from the future, whose great swollen heads are empty of emotion. At last we have a convincing answer to H.G.Wells. The spirit also evolves.

It is remarkable that Spielberg made such a good movie, considering the remorseless nature of the publicity machine in which he was involved — yet less remarkable when we consider his fine past record with *Duel* and *Jaws*, both of which, under the skin, are elegant excursions into similar territory. What is really remarkable is the scale of the success, the popularity and admiration, with which *Close Encounters* has met. It appears that millions of people all round the world must experience a terrible rapture to contemplate the way in which their mundane lives could be torn apart and transfixed, transfigured, by the alien. Perhaps they are beginning to get the message.

Rough Justices

Sleazo Inputs
I Have Known

Speaking with the decorum of his age, Horace Walpole declared
that the world is a comedy to those that think, a tragedy to those
that feel. There may have been truth in the aphorism at the time,
but the world has rattled on since then, acquiring a more
exquisite complexity, and becoming both tragedy and comedy,
inseparably mixed.

One of the many delights of Dr Christopher Evans's book* is
that the author perceives comedy and tragedy together. His
twentieth-century cults are crazy, illogical, and built round
ideas which should be confined to sf magazines – yet they
mirror faithfully the illusion we feel the world to be.

Some examples. A good half of the book is taken up by an
examination of L.Ron Hubbard's Dianetics, later reborn as
Scientology, with its jargon of Clears, processing, and Operating
Theatres. Then come ufology and ufolatry; the Aetherius
Society, gallantly swarming up mountains to give a heave for the
Spiritual in the galactic battle now raging round us; the Process,
hip guys who believe in Jehovah, Satan, and Lucifer; various
nice chaps who place faith in Black Boxes of various kinds –
such as George De la Warr, whose laboratories in Oxford were
fashionable in the fifties – the Hieronymous Machines, the Dean
Drives; Ted Serios, who photographs thought; Dr Wilhelm
Reich and his sexy old Orgone Box; the mystics who act as bell-
hops between the East and mystic West, such as Gurdjieff and
Ouspenski, the Subud clan, Lobsang 'Third Eye' Rampa, and
sundry swamis; those who believe that Tolkein's Frodo lives;
and the pundit of prehistoric inter stellar travel, Erich von
Daniken, whose question 'Was God an astronaut?' has proved
irresistible to many millions of people.

About the only cult that Dr Evans omits is the Knights of St

* *Cults of Unreason*, by Dr Christopher Evans, George Harrap, 1973.

Fantony! Even then, its founder, Eric Jones, gets a mention as the builder of a Hieronymus machine.

It will probably not escape the notice of readers that all these cults thrive on theories dreamed up by E.E.Smith and John Russell Fearn in the pulps of the thirties, or embody science-fictionalised versions of earlier and less swinging theological ideas, or actually incorporate sf machines of mysterious functional value, from the E-meter, through Dynamisers, oscilloclasts, and flying saucers, to the currently vouched-for Toomin Alpha Pacer.

Of course it has not escaped Dr Evans's notice either. Those who have heard him talk at conventions or read his articles in *New Worlds* when that magazine was drumming up a storm, will know that he knows his science fiction. They will also know that he has his own theories about parallels between living brains and computers and their dreaming states.

His chapters on Scientology are boldly headed 'The Science Fiction Religion', and chronicle the evolution of L.Ron Hubbard from a writer of pulp fantasy to the High Priest of his own religion, showing how Scientology's emphasis has changed from psychiatric activities to more pietistic ones – and not only because the Clears predicted by Dianetics in its early days either failed to materialise or turned up to embarrass the founder. This history has many dramatic moments, for instance when the Church of Scientology sued the MP for East Grinstead, Geoffrey Johnson Smith, and the case went to the High Court. After a lengthy hearing, it was decided that Mr Johnson had said nothing defamatory, and the case was dismissed, with the Scientologists having to pay costs – some £70,000. In fact, the Scientologists made rather a good showing in court.

John W. Campbell and A. E. Van Vogt put in guest appearances in these chapters; Campbell launched Dianetics in *Astounding* and took the cure himself; Dr Evans notes that Campbell began as a pulp writer like Hubbard. It would have been interesting – though no part of his brief – if he had also mentioned that extremely successful author, Arthur C.Clarke, whose beginnings were in pulp magazines, and whose writing has often shown an engagement with the religious as well as the technological, notably in *Childhood's End* and *2001*.

Legitimate sf writers have steered remarkably clear of flying saucers, although the discs used to appear on covers of sf magazines, in an understandable editorial bid to raise circulations. Dr Evans also comments that sf writers are more hardheaded than some fans. One cannot imagine that any sf writer worth his salt would muff a meeting with real Venusians to the extent that George Adamski (*Flying Saucers Have Landed*) did. After the publication of *Gulliver's Travels*, Jonathan Swift wrote gleefully to his friend Pope to tell him of an Irish bishop who had read the book and claimed that he didn't believe a word of it. As a reviewer of over fifty books on flying saucers, this critic can say much the same thing.

It would be a pity to run through *Cults of Unreason* chapter by chapter; the book demands to be read. Here and there, Dr Evans plainly has his favourites, like Lobsang Rampa, who scores high for imagination and local colour, and George De la Warr, who would gain an alpha in anyone's charisma stakes. Like L.Ron Hubbard, De la Warr made a brave showing in the courts, although costs also went against him.

But Evans remains constantly interesting, his tone never lapsing into the style of journalistic paste-up books (*Lunatic Fringes of Today*, *Great Mysteries of Small Religions*, etc.). Freakiness seems to interest Dr Evans less than what makes the cults tick. Here one regrets that he devotes no space to Charles Manson, who founded his own cult and has become something of a minor cult-figure. The whole tawdry Manson affair is recounted by Ed Sanders in *The Family**** with great gusto and secret formula English. Mr Sanders points out how Manson's 'sleazo inputs', as he picturesquely calls them, include a dose of Scientology and a big helping of Robert Heinlein's *Stranger in a Strange Land*. Manson also believed in a variant of the old Hollow Earth theory, an sf delusion if ever there was one.

There are two more complaints, both minor. Firstly, it is odd to list and discuss Ron Hubbard's writings without mentioning his stories about Ole Doc Methuselah,† which contain what one imagines must have been Hubbard's previsions, nineteen-forties style, of the Church of Scientology of California.

* *The Family*, by Ed Sanders, Longman, 1971.
† *Ole Doc Methuselah*, by L.Ron Hubbard, Daw Books, 1972.

Old Doc is an immortal galactic medico who travels round the galaxy clobbering disease and graft, aided by his multi-armed slave, Hippocrates. He is a Soldier of Light and a member of that élite organisation, the Universal Medical Society, which ceaselessly patrols the universe. 'Saluting no government, collecting no fees, permitting no infringement, the UMS became dreaded and revered as the Soldiers of Light, and under the symbols of the crossed ray rods impinged their will upon the governments of space under a code of their own more rigorous than any code of laws.' Ron eventually went on to found that big Health Service in the skies – the days of Auditing, The Org Book, Suppressive Persons, the Ethics Officers, and Ron's ship mysteriously sailing round the Med, are presaged in the Old Doc stories.

My second complaint concerns Dr Evans's treatment of Ouspenski. For once, the author's sympathy with cranks deserts him, and he speaks of P.D.Ouspenski's writing as 'among the most obscure and humourless works ever penned by man.' Not so. He should try Kant and Nietzsche. Quite a lot of Ouspenski's work is highly readable, if not actually a bundle of fun. *In Search of the Miraculous** is as bumpy and enjoyable a ride as its title suggests; one sees a nut cult through the eyes of the chief nut.

It's true that Ouspenski goes in for strange parallels between, for instance, food, music and chemistry, and one soon has enough discussion of food octaves, and such elucidation as 'The note sol 48 by uniting with "carbon" 12 present in the organism passes into nitrogen 24 – la 24.' The importance of Ouspenski is that he tried to incorporate what he understood as science into what he understood as religion; and it is this comparatively early striving for union which is a common factor in all the later cults under survey.

In his fiction, Ouspenski does better than in his non-fiction. 'The Strange Life of Ivan Osokin'† is an interesting tale of time-reversal and human alternatives, while the two long stories in

---

* *In Search of the Miraculous*, by P.D.Ouspenski, Routledge & Kegan Paul, 1955.

† *The Strange Life of Ivan Osokin*, by P.D.Ouspenski, Faber Paperback, 1971.

*Talks with a Devil** are highly imaginative and reveal a nice sly sense of humour, related to the Absurdist school.

The cultist search for an equation between religion and science is one that many of us find funny; and of course, the goofier of these cults are nothing but comic. It is to Dr Evans's credit that he finds them not only comic but worth study. He is for rather than against Scientology. Even the Aetherians chatting up Master Jesus on Venus raise in him only a tolerant smile, rather than rage at man's idiocy.

Not so long ago, it was widely believed that science and scientific thought might banish religion entirely, and that people would then lead rational lives; one sometimes sees a faint hope of this kind gleaming through the clouds of H.G.Wells's pessimism. We understand better now that unmitigated rationality is merely another variety of madness, and that religious impulses are deeply rooted in our natures. Indeed, the religious impulse is probably part of the creative impulse; stamp out religious feeling and you stamp out the arts and sciences.

This impasse is both tragic and comic. Legit science allows us no reason to deduce that there is an Afterlife in any form; we have to turn to vaudeville science, the science of prestidigitation, of Gernsback and Campbell, of radionics and psionics, for hope of pie in the sky. On the other hand, the legit religions shift their ground uneasily and are wary of offering pie anywhere. So the sermon has given way to the astrology column. When God drops out of touch with the twentieth century, sleazo inputs give you a better buzz.

Dr Evans appears to regard the cults as a number of life-rafts, some less buoyant than others, floating in a sea of doubt. This is a too generous view of things. The cultists are generally kidding themselves that they and only they are the saved, the ones in possession of truth. To maintain a position of doubt is a braver thing. The cultists have their equivalent in the tribes who follow Pacific cargo cults, where poor benighted natives pray to the big white birds that roar overhead to drop largesse, or at least wristwatches, upon them. The poor benighted natives of the West pray similarly to black boxes or UFOs or reflexophones for

---

* *Talks with a Devil*, by P.D.Ouspenski, edited by J.G.Bennett, Turnstone Press, 1972.

hope of similar technological largesse. It is noticeable that many of Dr Evans's cults employ clique words for some sort of fluid or vague emission, from ectoplasm to orgone, odyle, and telepathy; thus one gets a suck at the twin teats of Nature and Science at one and the same time.

Dr Evans does not moralise. We draw our own moral from his entertaining book. To each his own, but my moral would be: let's keep sf in paperbacks where it belongs; once it seeps into the world outside, it can be dangerous. The Process is a truer example of sf coming true than Verne's famous submarine ever was.

The basic imaginative donné of the pulps to which Hubbard, Campbell, E.E.Smith, Van Vogt, Heinlein, and the others contributed was a pretty primitive bit of power-fantasy: that Man (rarely Woman) has various God-like abilities. In the knockabout farces of their pulp universe, Man always won through by force; Galactic Law replaced ethics. That was entertainment. When it becomes religion, as it did with Charles Manson — watch out, the sleazo priests pack blasters, the Soldiers of Light tote lasers, and the infinite is full of crap.

It Catechised from Outer Space: Politics in SF

As long as publishers, readers, and some writers continue to treat science fiction as if it were a watertight compartment of reading matter, then critics must expatiate upon the delights and disappointments which seem most characteristic of it. On the one hand, the more effective sf writers frequently derive strength from a sense of the somewhat hastily thrown-up traditions of the genre, while thrusting beyond its conventions; on the other hand, less ambitious writers are often ingenious in wringing new significance – or at least new twists – from established formulas. The variety of current novels suggests that there is still plenty of vitality in those formulas.

The most thoughtful, if not ultimately the most successful, novel is Ursula Le Guin's *The Dispossessed* (Victor Gollancz) which has much to say about human societies, while telling the story of a man divided between two worlds.

The planet Urras is Earth-like, and most of its nations flourish under a mild form of capitalism. Annares, on which our attention is mainly focused, is the moon of Urras; it has been marginally colonised by the mother world. The colony is independent and has survived, enduring a sparse existence, for one hundred and seventy years. There is little contact with the parent planet; mutual suspicion holds the two worlds apart. The Urrasi are Odonists, Odonism being a mixture of anarchy and non-authoritarian communism, with male-female equality.

Although this is predominantly a political novel, and the parallels with our real world are apparent, Ms Le Guin is too subtle to make Annares stand for (say) our Moon or Mars, or Urras for (say) colonial America or Lenin's Soviet Union. Her cultures are their own thing – as they were in *Left Hand of Darkness* some years ago – and do not 'stand' for something else. She originates rather than imitates.

The central figure is an Annarean called Shevek (all Annarean names are computer-given, consist of six letters, and have no male-female connotations – which is unhelpful for lazy readers). Shevek is a sort of physicist-Solzhenitsyn mistrusted by his own people and invited to go to Urras to collect a valuable award for his contributions towards a General Temporal Theory. He does go, and so becomes the first colonial to return to the native world. There he suffers all the temptations of capitalist society, such as easy living, drink, and being teased by an attractive girl who does not actually wish to go to bed with him. Grappling with her at a party, he spurts semen down her dress; the sense of disgrace he feels moves him towards finding his real self and helping to ferment revolution on Urras, as well as perfecting his theory.

Nobody establishes more effectively their imaginary milieus, ecological and social, than Le Guin. She employs some felicitous touches, such as the famine which threatens to overwhelm Annares, that fauna-free world, or Shevek's delight in bird-song when he arrives on Urras, only to believe later in his disillusion that the birds are singing *This is my Propertee-tee* (shades of Auden!). Nor is Annares held up as a utopia; its imperfections are revealed little by little. In many ways, *The Dispossessed* is a model of what a politically aware sf novel should be.

It is the model-like quality of the book which tells against entering fully into its virtues. Like a Zoffany conversation piece, the characters are caught transfixed in a curious waxy light, more the subject of tableaux vivants than living subjects.

One admires the way in which that seminal scene at the party is designed to form a central pivot of the novel, when we as readers, like Shevek, change our opinion of Urras and foresee what he must do. The almost biblical weight given to the wasted semen is entirely apposite to the frugal systems of Annares, while much of Urras's meretriciousness is embodied in the girl's careless, 'Really! Now I'll have to change my dress.' And yet . . . the scene has not enough dramatic force, the party is too tame, to crystallise the reactions supposed to emerge from it. The theory, in fact, operates the characters rather than deriving from them. *The Dispossessed* is a considerable novel; and yet it is peculiarly joyless, and one sneaks away from its worthy bulk with some relief.

Another novel which operates beyond the orbit of conventional sf is Barry Malzberg's *Beyond Apollo* (Faber, 1974) which won the first John W.Campbell Memorial Award, to the consternation of those sf fans who live or die by the old rules.

Malzberg's central character is Harry M. Evans, telling his own story, or being unable to tell it. He records his madness while incarcerated in an institution, trying to recall why the flight to Venus failed. Evans is the survivor of the two-man crew. The captain died. The institute would like to find out why. So would Evans.

The clinical neurologist, a man called Forrest, tries to get at the truth.

'He stops, takes out his handkerchief, wipes his forehead. "Excuse me," he says. "We're all under consummate strain here. Caused to no small degree by you."

"I'm sorry."

"Do you realise that hundreds of people, this entire facility, have been mobilised for you? Hundreds of thousands of dollars are being spent to give you the best of care, and in return – "

"I'm truly appreciative," I say. I mean this. I have nothing against the institution; the program has always tried to take care of its own. "You know that."

"What happened?", he says. "Tell me, what happened?"

"What happened where?", I ask mildly, inquiring, curious. "I don't understand what you mean."

"What happened on the *ship*?" Forrest puts the handkerchief away, leans towards me. "This can't go on indefinitely, you know," he points out. "We're going to have to take drastic action. We have as much respect for you as anyone could, but we have to get at that information and we know you have it . . ." '

Thousands of dollars will not purchase the truth, not even when Evans is so keen to cooperate. Did he bugger the captain or murder him? Is Venus populated by telepathic green lizards?

Evans's attempts to recall are at once touching, macabre, and wildly funny.

In lesser hands, Malzberg's theme might have degenerated into an allegory about the relationship of Truth, or into a sort of cosmic whodonewhat. Instead, it is an acute study of a baffled state of mind, nicely organised and written with wit. It seems — but we can never distinguish between subjective and objective — that the captain and Evans played a game on the Venus journey. Evans had to guess the real underlying reason for the flight, and explain it in not more than fifty words; in return, he would have been told about the captain's sex life. 'There is no truth which cannot be given in fifty words; the truth is always concise,' says the captain.

Evans never guesses correctly; the institute never understands. The understanding lies in the novel itself, in its mosaic of pain and desperation and comedy.

All of which is so refreshingly far from the usual jingoistic tosh that sf writers write about space travel that I'm tempted to think *Beyond Apollo* the most original and pleasing sf novel of the last five years.

Of course, the pursuit of originality can lead downhill. It is hard to imagine a more unimaginable idea than the one round which *Worlds Apart* (Gollancz 1974) is built. Richard Cowper, who knows better, has invented a story about a drab little schoolmaster called George Cringe who takes refuge from a drab marriage by writing an sf story set on a distant planet concerning two characters called Zil Bryn and Orgypp. Meanwhile, on a distant planet, Zil Bryn (married to a lady called Orgypp) is writing something called *Shorge Gringe's Pilgrimage*, which takes place on an imaginary planet called Urth. Fearful symmetry indeed!

Some pure genre pieces, by respecting the field in which (and to some extent by courtesy of which) they exist, yield peculiar satisfactions. It is easy to laugh at the space civilisation story, with brave humans swaggering among the alien-ridden stars; such things are what highbrows imagine lowbrows most enjoy in sf — with some justification. But a good space adventure contains its own beefy pleasures. You can't help liking *The Halcyon Drift* (Dent 1974), by a young British author, Brian Stableford.

A spaceship with a secret aboard has crashed on an unknown planet in the eponymous Drift, and several nasty characters are after it. All traditional fare, with a breezily cynical hero called Grainger who is nice to aliens, and a planet with a creepy metamorphic life system. What makes the tale is the fun the author has with its telling, and the really beautiful articulated spaceship he invents.

When imagination fails, an sf writer can always turn into a sort of science-scaremonger, rifling the scientific journals for sensational scare stories of the future; there is no shortage of them. Over-populated and over-polluted worlds have become part of the sf reader's staple diet. Not that diet is exactly the word for *The Sheep Look Up* (Dent 1974), a highly emetic novel by John Brunner. With dreary relish and pedestrian thoroughness, he offers us a year in a future United States, where his characters undergo biliousness, blepharitis, bronchitis, brucellosis ('they say it brings on abortion'), conjunctivitis, diarrhoea, dysentery, enteritis, gangrene, haemorrhoids, hepatitis, impetigo, jaundice, leukemia, pellagra, pharyngitis, salpingitis, septicemia, thrush, trachoma, urticaria, venereal diseases (assorted), weeping sores, and whitlows, not to mention plain old lice, fleas, flies, boils, sties, vomiting, and facial tics. All on account of the profit motive.

If you get that far, you will see where our civilisation has landed itself: 'Those that haven't been shot went insane, those that aren't insane mostly have one of the three or four killer diseases that are rife . . .' Not that this message is not rubbed in on every page. The know-all father figure who appears in several of Brunner's novels is here called Austin Train; he surfaces towards the end and delivers an explanation to the nation on television of how things went wrong. Even the tough television cameraman weeps. But you can hear Cassandra sniggering. Brunner writes about the USA but lives in Somerset.

It is a pity that the book is such a disaster, since the theme of the exploitation of life under political economic systems is plainly one that can be appropriately handled in science fictional terms, as Frederik Pohl demonstrated some while ago. Unfortunately, Brunner has chosen an old-fashioned method of demonstration, called Piling on the Agony. The result is absurd rather than moving. And the weakness of taking a narrowly political viewpoint to the question can be seen when *The Sheep Look Up* is compared with *The Dispossessed*: the people of Annares believe themselves to have built a utopia, whereas they are incarcerated in their own fear of public opinion. Le Guin suggests that we exploit ourselves, whereas Brunner suggests that the US should burn, as if that would solve the world's problems, rather than adding to them.

The underlying concern in *The Dream Millennium* (Michael Joseph 1974) is, as in *The Sheep Look Up*, with the collapse of urban civilisation. The author, James White, generally uses a background of galactic scope. This novel is a tightly controlled story of a starship leaving a horrible dystopian Earth for some possible colony world. It's a slow ship, taking a thousand years to reach its destination; the colonists lie in chilly suspended animation below decks, while two members of the crew are woken by the ship every century or so to check that all systems are still operative.

White makes of his ship an eerie place; it grows senile while the personnel remain unageing. Ekeing out their half-life, the colonists dream in their caskets. And what are the troublesome dreams, shot through with death, from which all sleepers suffer? Well, the answer to that, when it comes, is a bit lame – and surprisingly ignores contemporary theories of sleep and dream, from which a more meaningful dénouement might have sprung.

Nevertheless, this is a thoroughly absorbing story, and White's most mature piece yet, partly because his glimpses of our urban society – grittily futuristic and violent, with private vigilante groups taking the law into their own hands – are nastily truthful. Unarmed citizens are called Sheep. Under the traditional story line lie images of death and frustration, the more impressive for being understated. A brief note on the jacket reveals that White lives in Andersonstown, Belfast; he knows what he is writing about.

The Flight into Tomorrow

As long as there is no general agreement on what does or does
not constitute science fiction, there can be no agreement as to
what 'pure' science fiction is, although the term is frequently
used. But Charles Harness's *The Paradox Men* must come close
to anybody's idea of one kind of pure science fiction: the wild
and imaginative kind which juggles amusedly with many
scientific concepts.

Before this imaginative play is dismissed as fantasy – or
perhaps 'fancy', in S.T.Coleridge's definition – it is wise to consider how Harness has been moved by the tremendous challenge
of Einstein's theories of Relativity. The American philosopher,
Henry LeRoy Finch, says of Einstein's imagination that it
'reformed our conception of the universe'. The original formula-
tion of the Special Theory of Relativity involved an
imaginative feat unparalleled in human thought ... When asked
many years later how he had come to formulate this theory, Einstein is said to have replied: 'By refusing to accept an axiom'.*

The magazine sf writers of the thirties and forties were fired
by this defiance of intellectual frontiers. They came,
paradoxically, to feel that one was being most true to the spirit
of science by upsetting all its established laws which, like stones,
might conceal a real truth beneath them. In the same way,
another influential thinker of the age, Sigmund Freud, generated
disciples who were moved to scrutinise words and actions for
their concealed motives, often turning meaning upside down in
the process.

This contemporary preoccupation which 'calls all in doubt'
extended to questioning some of the basic tenets upon which
Western civilisation is based. Two such tenets are questioned.

* Henry LeRoy Finch: Introduction to *Conversation with Einstein*, by Alexander
Nosekowski, USA, 1970.

First, Harness contradicts the conventional idea of civilisation as a neat progression. To this end, he employs the theory of Arnold Toynbee, whose multi-volume *A Study of History* was then highly fashionable, that civilisation was not the continual if faltering upward march as depicted by H.G.Wells in his book, *The Outline of History*, and by many other historiographers before and since, but rather cyclic in nature, somewhat as proposed by Oswald Spengler, each civilisation containing the seeds of its eventual decline. Harness proposes a spaceship which will act as a bridge between Western civilisation and its successor civilisation, setting the main action of the novel in the heady days of Western decadence, when Imperatrix Juana-Maria of the House of Chatham-Perez rules over the Western Hemisphere.

The second basic tenet brought to question is the Aristotelian logic on which our rational thinking has been based since the Renaissance. The Greeks formulated a concise way of handling concepts in which the answer at each stage of an argument was negative or positive (Yes or No); as long as this problem is settled at each stage, the deductive series can continue ever onwards. With the immensely greater information-flow about us today, we require more ways of solving problems (intuition must play its part, for instance); Harness's non-Aristotelians are simply people who use new deductive processes. Nowadays, we might call them lateral thinkers. The challenge to Aristotelian logic was a popular one in the science fiction magazines when Harness was writing; it helped reinforce the idea, derived from Einstein, that anything was possible in an impossible universe. It is most notably enshrined in A.E.Van Vogt's two novels and titles, *The World of Null-A* and *The Pawns of Null-A*.

Incorporating all these elements of change, the novel is itself about a world of change, in which eventually all men become brothers.

Some years ago, I categorised this novel and others like it — such as the Van Vogt titles already mentioned — as Widescreen Baroque. The label remains adequate. Despite the intellectual background sketched above, *The Paradox Men* is far from being a work of cerebration; indeed, it is a fast-paced pursuit story. Its style is exuberant rather than fine, sometimes dropping into extravagance – which is one definition of baroque. Widescreen Baroque requires at least the whole solar system for its setting, with space- and preferably time-travel as accessories, and a complex plot with mysteries and lost identities and a world to ransome. Perspectives between Possible and Impossible must be foreshortened dramatically; great hopes must mingle with terrible destruction. Ideally, the characters involved should have short names and short lives.

All these conditions are fulfilled by Harness's novel. The hero, Alar the Thief, is a secret master, a traveller through many dimensions, a cryptogram in the riddle of his culture, and he dies before the conclusion of the novel.

Most Widescreen Baroque novels are ultimately frivolous. Under all the swashbuckle, there is a pleasing seriousness about *The Paradox Men*, a seriousness having nothing to do with the ideas of Toynbee or Einstein, which act in part as window-dressing. For all the surrealist effects – of which the plunge into the raging heart of the sun is the most spectacular – for all the derring-do and costume drama, Harness is saying something about life. Though his statement is never set directly into words, it is far from vague; on the contrary, it is clear and concise. That living is vital is hardly a profound message, yet it was profound and immediate enough to move the great Elizabethan and Jacobean dramatists. Their feeling for 'this sensible warm motion' was most aptly expressed when set against torture and death, and Harness's lively figures move against that same dark foil: 'The Thief knelt without a word and gently gathered Raven's body into his arms. The body of the older man seemed curiously shrivelled and small. Only now did Alar realise what stature the bare fact of being alive contributed to flesh and bone.' (But Alar himself will undergo death and transfiguration.)

And the woman Keiris, who loves Alar, endures as much suffering as Webster's Duchess of Malfi, and surely discovers that 'death hath ten thousand several doors for men to take their exits'. This is very much a neo-Jacobean novel, right down to the profusion of grand gestures and adjectives.

Because of the prejudice against science fiction, it has seemed at periods of its existence to be almost an underground movement.

The publishing history of *The Paradox Men* is tortuous for this reason.

It was first published under the title *Flight Into Yesterday* in the sf magazine *Startling Stories*, Vol. 19, No. 2, for May 1949. Four years later, it appeared in hardcover, after which Ace Books of New York reprinted it in paperback under its present (and to my mind superior) title. That was in 1955.

At the beginning of the sixties, the publishers Faber and Faber asked one or two devotees of science fiction to choose a title hitherto unobtainable in Great Britain: Faber would publish these titles with introductions by their mentors. Edmund Crispin introduced Cyril Kornbluth's *The Syndic*. C.S.Lewis was to have introduced Kepler's *Somnium*, but became too ill to do so. Robert Conquest and Kingsley Amis also had their favourites, Amis's being Budrys's *Rogue Moon* – but for some reason these two choices never materialised. I chose *The Paradox Men*. It was published by Faber on 1 October 1964, in its first hardcover edition. It was reprinted in paperback by Four Square. In 1976, Harry Harrison and I reintroduced the novel to the public as a title in our SF Master Series, published by New English Library.

Charles Harness was born in Texas in 1915. He is also known for a short mystic novel, *The Rose*, again on a theme of death and transfiguration, and for a fantastic novel, *The Ring of Ritornel*, which employs the same theme against a galactic background, with eternity represented as a recurrent cycle of cosmic death and rebirth. Each of Harness's infrequent but highly individual novels enjoys a coterie reputation. In the case of *The Paradox Men*, there is every reason to believe that that reputation will continue to grow.

Burroughs: Less Lucid than Lucian

It is hard to believe that Edgar Rice Burroughs actually existed, so much of a phenomenon is he, so perfectly does he conform to the great Best-Seller Success Story myth. Almost a quarter-century after his death, he is the centre of a cult (ERBdom), has a town named after his most famous character (Tarzania), and still enjoys record sales (well over one hundred million copies to date).

Reasons for all this are clear in the trilogy of novels – well, actually, they were serials in the grand old pulps – collected in *The Moon Maid*, and published in Britain by Tom Stacey for the first time in 1972.

Almost two thousand years ago, Lucian of Samosata used the moon journey for satirical purposes; Burroughs fills the craters with blood. A spaceship heading for Mars has to land on the Moon, and finds the lunar interior inhabited. The spaceship contains our hero, Julian, and our villain, Orthis; they and their descendants, who always bear the same name, remain at odds throughout the book, over twenty generations, until death and marriage finally heal the breach.

The three dominant species on the Moon are the U-gas of Laythe, who are much like good white Earthmen, and supply the eponymous romance; the degenerate and brutal Kalkars, who war with everyone and therefore most possess ERB's imagination; and the ferocious and centaur-like beings, the Va-gas, into whose hands Julian initially falls. These three species survive by eating each other.

Eventually, Laythe is destroyed and the Kalkars, led by Orthis, invade and conquer Earth. This is in the second book, in which Earthmen are reduced to semi-urban peasantry under the brutish oppression. They revolt, with little more than minor success. In the third book, set many generations later, the Yanks

– as Earthmen are called – have become very much Red Indian tribes; Julian 20th bears the title the 'Red Hawk', and so on. By now, the Kalkars, who have intermarried with Earth women, have been driven to the western ocean, the Pacific. In the end, they are entirely defeated.

The sweep of the whole thing is attractive, and the first two books are particularly good by Burroughs's standards. The burning of Laythe, with the inhabitants casting themselves into a crater in their despair, is a fine bit of animated John Martin. And the nastiness of Kalkar rule is well-conveyed (although unfortunately this version is abridged and not the original magazine version, so that some inconsistencies show through).

Of course, such science as there is is pure hogwash, with rays being stored in tanks and a deadly weapon 'generating radio-activity at any desired vibratory rate'. It matters not. The important thing for ERB and his devotees is a loathing of urban culture (he had a bad time and endless bad jobs in Chicago before being rescued by John Carter and Tarzan) and a mystical obsession with land, purity of blood, courage, leadership, and rape – not necessarily in that order.

All Burroughs's books, and *The Moon Maid* is no exception, ring small variations on these themes. Here as usual are women dragged away by their hair, sentries being killed bare-handed, endless blood-letting, and inferior races breeding like rabbits. ERB often sounds like something Leslie Fiedler invented to prove his case against American letters. Let me not seem to imply that it is not all highly enjoyable for an adolescent imagination, but one does eventually get anxious about all that sword-play between two chaps while the beloved of one of them looks on, holding a torch so that they can see better.

Kingsley Amis, in a smallish foreword, praises ERB for writing 'a *story* without embellishments or self-indulgent psychologisings'. Yes, well, but ... nobody was more self-indulgent than ERB. That's what the fans love him for. And the self-indulgence means that it all grows repetitive.

ERB's influence on magazine sf was extensive – greater than Wells's and less benevolent, greater than Lovecraft's and less disastrous. Since a whole central part of sf became more intellectual and questioning, the Burroughs syndrome has broken

out anew into s-&-s, as its devotees call Sword-and-Sorcery —
another urban escape route which bears the name Burroughs
over its main exit. Better to have Burroughs than his imitators,
no doubt.

He possessed a barbaric imagination. The gross simplification
of having Julian and Orthis survive through generations would
sink anything approaching Literature. But it serves for Myth,
besides according well with ERB's hazy notions of reincarna-
tion and heredity. Such idiocies he often turns into strengths.

His remorseless worlds, with their grotesque cultures, their
war-obsessed warriors, their steel-muscled heroes, and their
women ever cowering before obnoxious intentions, do touch on
a genuine lode of feeling. ERB was a railroad cop and an
assistant in Sears Roebuck before making good with the first
Barsoom novel in 1912. How common his brutal fantasies are to
all cops, store assistants, and other respectable citizens, has been
proved by the realities we have soldiered through since that date.

'Yes, well, but . . .'

*The Craft of Science Fiction** is what I call a 'Yes, well, but . . .' book. It consists of an introduction and fifteen chapters by known sf writers, and is designed to instruct 'people who want to start writing – or keep on writing – science fiction and science fantasy'. Or so the blurb says. Myself, I believe that *keeping on writing* sf is a different kettle of fish from beginning to write, but we will let that one go.

This volume is full of sweeping statements. The experienced writer or critic is going to catch himself nodding and saying, 'Yes, well, but . . . ' an uncomfortable number of times. A beginner should find chunks of it helpful; maybe a beginner should have reviewed it.

Reginald Bretnor is to be congratulated on his title: his book does attempt to define the craft, rather than the art. The intention is moderately work-a-day. All the same, one's heart sinks, and has every right to sink, when we find an editor trotting forth jaundiced and incorrect judgements against every form of fiction which does not conform to what he personally enjoys. Eclecticism is a virtue in editors; prejudice is never a virtue in anyone.

'I have already spoken of the difference between the sf world of chance and the as-always world of mainstream fiction. Both, of course, differ from the world as currently accepted or acceptable scientific assumptions show it to be, the sf world because it allows more latitude, the world of mainstream fiction because it remains decades or even centuries behind today's realities.'

This is not correct. Likewise, remarks about 'the remnants of

* Edited by Reginald Bretnor, Harper & Row, 1976.

the New Wave, that |sic| attempt to inflict on science fiction the
hysterical illogic characterising so much of this century's
"intellectual" writing', make us shake our heads sympatheti-
cally. Not only is the statement in error, it is expressed in a form
which indicates a withholding of any attempt to understand a
movement which shows much in common with the difficulties
experienced in all of the arts this century.

So one approaches the body of the book in a jaundiced way,
armed against similar belts of ignorance. However, the contributors are successful writers and, perhaps for that reason,
bring a greater liberality to their task than their editor. One
doesn't always concur, but one respects their points of view.

For instance, Poul Anderson, in the first chapter, 'Star-flights
and Fantasies', would probably be in agreement with Bretnor's
basic position; yet he merely remarks that 'the opinion is
dominant (in académe) that a protagonist's principal activity
should be introspection ... Of recent years, a certain amount of
science fiction has been based on this theory.' Yes, too much, I'd
say. We can agree there. In a book on *the art* of science fiction,
one could go into the whys and wherefores of the preoccupation
with introspection, and the answers would have to connect with
the changed nature of our societies over the past half-century, as
well as merely with the hysteria and illogic of New Wavers.

In the shadow of the introduction, Anderson seems a little
pale. And that Verne enjoyed 'exuberant optimism' is surely
incorrect, a simplistic view of rather a complex man. Anderson's
discussion of sf sagas will interest many, and never more than
when he turns to his own *Tau Zero*.

Hal Clement writes on 'Hard Sciences and Tough
Technologies'. His tone is firm. He prefers sf to be scientific, and
is the ablest man to say how it should and should not be done;
after all, this is the author of *Mission of Gravity*. Of course, the
paradox is that the affection we feel for that novel (as opposed to
the respect) does not rest on its admitted virtues of scientific
exposition, but upon values not unknown in the rest of literature:
an heroic quest, atmosphere, and the relationship between man
and alien. All the same, this chapter would genuinely help a new
writer; the remarks on 'psionics' should particularly be taken to
heart.

Clement depends rather heavily on truisms. Norman Spinrad is much more fresh and amusing; perhaps the subject of 'Rubber Sciences' gives more scope for humour. At any rate, this was the point at which I began positively to enjoy the book. Spinrad is acute and funny on FTL drive, a prime and all-pervasive bit of rubber science, and many of his rules for writing are of the Shavian order of humour (i.e., the truth is unexpected, consequently witty); like, his Rule Three of Rubber Sciences: 'you are not Albert Einstein – know when to stop explaining'. This rule could be carried a lot further. Many sf novels are themselves explanations which never stop, reducing all life to a diagram; instead of celebrating life in all its unkempt beauty, they transfix it.

In his zippy way, Spinrad questions much that sf takes for granted – a habit of thought beginner-writers should acquire if they wish to make themselves unpopular. For instance, he condemns 'future histories', and points out that hard sf suffers a built-in shortcoming: 'characters in hard science fiction stories have mid-twentieth-century consciousness, no matter how far out their bodies are in space and time'. Such comments could be much developed, but Spinrad sticks successfully to his Rule Three.

Alan Nourse talks about 'Extrapolations and Quantum Jumps'. He begins by stating that the construction of a science fiction story depends on certain factors that are common to any kind of fiction at all. That is too obvious to require stating, until one realises, wearily, that there may still be some who regard the remark as – is 'challenging' the word? He goes on to say that an sf story must contain a premise, just like *Romeo and Juliet*, *Ghosts*, *Who Goes There*, and *Nightfall* (to name but four World Masterpieces). Nourse labels the premises of these pieces, respectively, as 'Great Love defies even death'; 'the sins of the fathers are visited on the children'; 'things are not always what they seem to be'; and 'blind superstition can overcome reason and lead to disaster'.

While Shakespeare's name is being dropped, it may be said that the last two of Nourse's four premises apply with equal effect to, respectively, *Othello*, and *Julius Caesar*. So the premise is not the main raison d'être of science fiction, and, supposing that we should be dim enough not to know from experience that 'things are not always what they seem', then we would set about reading *Othello* rather than *Who Goes There?*, since Shakespeare got his version of the premise down in writing first, and much more effectively.

On the whole, Nourse's is a nice solid expository piece, which says something of interest about *Dune*, *Half-Past Human*, and other novels. Nourse falls into an error several other contributors cannot resist, of using their own writings as examples. The result is generally a bit mawkish (Anderson shows it can be done well).

As usual, Theodore Sturgeon, who writes on 'Future Writers in a Future World', is going his own way. Unlike all the other contributors, he believes that what a reader is most attuned to are those things closest to personal experience: love, pain, greed, laughter, hope, 'and above all loneliness'. I go along with that, but hands up those who thought that what the average sf reader was most attuned to was those soggy old pulp plots. The way in which Sturgeon adheres still to those tenets that made his fiction so vividly memorable – so nourishing among the thin diets of wonder – three decades ago is commendable.

So many of the best things in the Sturgeon piece are implicit rather than explicit; after all, it is a shame to read his non-fiction when much of his fiction is so charged, loaded, in a way to which articles can never aspire. It goes without saying that this is still an enjoyable contribution. Note the marvellous little vision of Hannibal crossing the Alps by hang-glider. Sturgeon and Spinrad, alone of this august company, convey something of true creativity. Maybe you can't learn it or teach it.

Perhaps the best (most functional) article comes next: Jerry Pournelle, 'On The Construction of Believable Societies'. It is a fine, positive article which deserves to be widely reprinted. Much of what Pournelle says is new; and often that which is not new has rarely been stated so succinctly. An example: 'Characters in (historical fiction) act from one of two classes of motive: 1) motivations similar to those which work in our own society, and 2) those peculiar to those times. It will be as true for sf as for historicals.' Pournelle then develops this promising theme in rigorous fashion. This rigour, by the way, is saved from excess by Pournelle's recognition that it takes all sorts to make a world, or even another world; while explaining in lucid detail how to construct a credible social order, he exempts the humourists and satirists, recognising that their purpose is different and meaningful. Writers are far more likely to be able to accept Pournelle's advice because he shows an implicit understanding of the (historically recent) many-sidedness of the science fiction genre. He understands also that some writers write to arouse emotions; they are also let off his hook (although it's true that his example here is Harlan Ellison, who does not so much arouse as give off in buckets emotions).

We cannot escape some questions even if their answers do not directly affect our plot, says Pournelle in a striking aside. He makes sf seem the relevant literature we all, in drunken moments, hope it is. He instructs his audience to study. That must surely be correct. This essay is itself a notable product of careful study. (Yes, well, but, why didn't the man deal with *utopias*, for god's sake?)

Frank Herbert can't quite follow that. His impressionistic piece on 'Men on Other Planets' is not so searching, and again here is the embarrassment of a writer holding up his own writing for example. I found much here I could not learn from, since I could not understand it. 'Any reader of science fiction turning to page one of a new story has an implicit understanding that the function of what he is about to read will extend far beyond physical descriptions.' That is beyond me. My simplicity is rammed home to me again on the following page, when Herbert asks, 'Were you really surprised when Charlton Heston discovered the remains of the Statue of Liberty on the Planet of the Apes?' Well, yes, I must admit I was very surprised, and moreover much admired the surrealist appearance of it in the sand, canted at an angle. I do not know what Herbert means when he claims that it would have been more interesting if Heston had discovered a toilet bowl or a Landon button. I don't even know what a Landon button is. What was needed in those final seconds of film was a universally accepted symbol which even the benighted foreigner could identify, and most people on the planet readily recognise both the Statue of Liberty and its significance (the same significance which, wrenched dramati-

cally out of context, surely gives the film much more clout than
Herbert allows).

Yes, well, but . . . I liked what Herbert told me about conjecture as a literary tool, but would have regarded the Statue of
Liberty as a good example of same.

We are still less than halfway through the book and this
review grows longer than the book as a whole perhaps deserves.
Katherine MacLean has a spirited piece on 'Alien Minds and
Nonhuman Intelligences'. As we would expect, it is stimulating,
delivering some sharp matters of fact as well as being in itself
imaginative – for instance when MacLean sees van Vogt's *Black
Destroyer* as an ecology story published before ecology was
known to intellectuals, or discusses the cold germ as a possible
factor in human evolution. Beginners might pick up creative
clues here, chiefly by the induction coil method. All the same,
should not such an article include the obvious statement that,
when pitching his scene in the Unknown, a writer perforce pop-
ulates it to a great extent with creatures from his psyche, even if
they play the rather hackneyed roles of nasty aliens, nice aliens,
gods, monsters, or little green men? The whole book is apt to
treat creation as a sort of Erector-builder set, as if all bits came
out of encyclopaedias and none out of your head. Surely a
greater proportion of sf than of ordinary literature does come
'out of the head'. If you compare those great modern
masterpieces, Anthony Powell's twelve-volume *Dance to the
Music of Time* with John Norman's *Tarnsman of Gor* series
(okay, I know it's a fool thing to do), you can see that the former
is built up from the activities of characters very similar to people
Powell knows or knew 'in real life'. Perforce Norman drags
much of his material from his psyche. I should add that I see
nothing against either method in the correct place, though
obviously the latter method depends heavily on one's having a
fairly interesting psyche – whereas all Powell needed for raw
material was a fairly interesting social life.

To press on. James Gunn presents an innocuous discussion of
'Heroes, Heroines, Villains: The Characters of Science Fiction'.
He perceives that sf often uses attitudes rather than characters,
yet does not probe deeply enough into this distinction. He skirts
nervously round Ballard's work. (In most of the essays one

senses a strong preference for the good ole home-cooking like Gernsback and Campbell used to make it, a dread of garlic and spices; Gunn, for example, does not find it at all awful that stories are now 'being written in the styles of Burroughs, Asimov, or Heinlein'.)

Similar emanations rise even more strongly from Larry Niven's 'The Words of Science Fiction', a disconnected piece about 'gnurrs coming from the voodvork out'* and similar expressions. Niven does not give the impression of having read much sf or, beyond sf, anything but Dante, Heinlein and Mickey Spillane, not necessarily in that order. All the same, his piece would be useful for a beginner in its corralling of a lot of titbits about things most of us do instinctively. Unfortunately, constant references to the works of Niven are embarrassing.

Jack Williamson's piece has lots of good advice for cautious worthy little prigs of rookie writers, like 'A good story idea must pass several tests. It should be original, but not too far out . . . It must interest the audience . . . ' etc. It is chiefly notable for Williamson's poignant honesty in confessing that he prefers his novelette, *With Folded Hands*, to the novel, *The Humanoids*, which John Campbell made him write. What a slave mentality Campbell's authors showed! Williamson, incidentally, is one author who, with Anderson, talks acceptably about his own writing. Which brings us to John Brunner, who, in 'The Science Fiction Novel', remarkably stays away from his own material and produces a clear, workmanlike piece which has been thoughtfully designed for its specified audience. 'A short story is cast . . . a novel is assembled . . . ' I like it; it may not be one hundred per cent true – what is? – but it hath pith and gives you something to think about.

Brunner has an ingenious piece of jugglery to the effect that there are only three plots; he then justifies the argument with some brio. These are his three plots: Boy Meets Girl, The Little Tailor, and Man Learns Lesson. (Someone else in the book – I've lost the reference – says almost the same thing.) Yes, well, but . . . what about Man Fails to Learn Lesson? Is that not a favourite plot, from *Frankenstein* onwards? In any case, it is

---

* Esoteric but affectionate reference to a memorable phrase coined by the editor in his story-telling days.

interesting to reflect that these three or four or twelve basic plots
have little reference to the diversity of story. I mean, to which of
these three basic plots does Van Vogt's *Black Destroyer* afore-
mentioned belong?

Perhaps the best advice for a beginner in the whole
book is Brunner's: 'Set down the events in the story in the
order in which the reader benefits by learning of them.' All
this presupposes is a writer who can penetrate to the heart
of such advice and use it.

'With the Eyes of a Demon' is the title of Harlan Ellison's
advice on writing a television script. Ellison thinks writers
should 'write in *all* forms, should not limit themselves, should
constantly strive to enlarge the scope of their abilities'. Such
dogmatism is confused. Some writers may take pride in *not*
dropping their pants for the television mammon, in not writing
film criticisms, in not catering to the preferences of editor A or
B; *and* they may enlarge the scope of their abilities by so limiting
themselves. To refuse to write of things in which he does not
believe, like an all-white Earth or FTL travel or telepathy, a
writer re-asserts his own moral faith and brings that strength to
bear on the things on which he can write with conviction.
Ellison's piece is deeply confused. He quotes Cyril Connolly's
heroic statement, 'The true function of a writer is to produce a
masterpiece' (from Connolly, that dilettante! – he should bloody
well talk!), yet, contrary-wise, most of Ellison's noisy energy is
devoted to spelling demotically out how ya gotta leave the hero
in the most dreadful straits by the time of the commercial break,
whether story-logic demands it or not, and engaging in other
processes Ellison baldly admits are artistically corrupt. Hardly a
procedure likely to produce masterpieces – or anything but
noisy hack writers.

Having soldiered on through all the hectoring, it is a relief to
come to Frederik Pohl's calm piece, 'The Science Fiction
Professional'. I doubt if anyone can ever become as professional
as Pohl, even with Pohl as instructor – and, in his mouth,
'professional' is a good word. Wit and common sense make this
a fine piece for any tyro – or even for old hands who may get
discouraged; 'Any manuscript can be bounced a few times.
Editors make mistakes. Maybe they're wrong and it's really

good. Or maybe the ones who bounced it are right and it's awful; the next editor might make a mistake in your favour and buy it.' Good stuff, if slightly enervating.

Perhaps it is no more than sensible that a book calling itself carefully 'The Craft' and not 'The Art of Science Fiction' should exhibit little deep feeling about *being a writer*. Yet a few assumptions crop up several times which are inimical to a writer's role in society. Ellison seems to think it is a matter of putting one over on someone – the viewer, the producer, anyone; Williamson and others preach that you must please the editor; Spinrad says 'All fiction is lies.'; Brunner says, 'Telling the truth is forbidden to writers of fiction.'

These careless attitudes are damaging to any author. They need to be refuted.

The writer's position it barely tenable; he lives always among conflicting forces, internal and external. As Sturgeon hints, loneliness is his foe – and his ally. I cannot see how a writer can exist for long as a creative writer unless he tries to tell the truth, and goes on digging through the lies of his own life until he throws up a bit of it, and then maybe a bit more, and a bit more, until truth is his habit and his god. This must be what Yeats meant in that poem Willis McNelly is so fond of quoting:

> Now that my ladder's gone,
> I must lie down where all the ladders start,
> In the foul rag-and-bone shop of my heart.

Any sort of writer must come to terms with what is in himself, for there he sees written the image of all humanity. It is a harrowing experience. He has much to accept, much to reject, and his experience, when transferred to paper, is not for editors to meddle with.

Instead of waving the tattered old banners of fandom, the editor of this volume should have taken his job seriously and told would-be writers that writing is a hard but marvellous job, because honest writers come face to face with pettiness as well as grandeur, because honest writers fail most of the time and know it, because honest writers secretly prefer suicide to another novel like the last one, and because dishonest writers are the rich

ones with weekend places in the Bahamas and mistresses in
Monte Carlo.

To be honest, our much-loved sf banners sometimes get in the
way of the truth. 'There is nothing intrinsic to sf that [sic] limits
it either in its scope or potential literary quality,' trumpets
Bretnor. Yes, well, but . . .

The Universe as Coal-Scuttle

The basic premise behind these two books* is a simple, indeed a Victorian one: that everything about us is put there for Man's use, like all the convenient objects on the island of Swiss Family Robinson. Only the scale of the premise has been changed, and the degree of exploitation involved. Here, Man (never, somehow, Woman) is again the centre of the universe, and the universe is a coal-scuttle.

Mr Berry is a Fellow of the Royal Astronomical Society, a journalist, and science populariser, as both dust jackets inform us. In *The Next Ten Thousand Years*, he popularises the views of Professor Freeman J.Dyson, of the Institute for Advanced Study in Princeton, who had developed an ambitious scheme for securing virtually limitless energy resources, together with the limitless technological development which that implies. Continuous economic growth, product of unchecked population, will motivate Dyson's scheme.

Dyson's name is already enshrined in a phrase embodying his engineering dream, the Dyson Sphere. A Dyson Sphere, briefly, is an artificial biosphere which surrounds a star and is composed of debris from a demolished planet. As Berry puts it, 'If it is true, as I have argued, that there is no natural limit to technological growth, then it is evident that we will eventually be compelled to dismantle the gigantic planet Jupiter in order to construct a Dyson Sphere around our Sun.' Compelled is good. After all, Jupiter is of no economic value at present, Berry argues. The Sphere will consist of millions of planetoids up to whole-Earth-sized planets (Jupiter's mass is sufficient to build thirty-eight

* *The Next Ten Thousand Years: A Vision of Man's Future in the Universe*, by Adrian Berry, Jonathan Cape, 1974.
The Iron Sun: Crossing the Universe Through Black Holes, by Adrian Berry, Jonathan Cape, 1977.

worlds as big as Earth), revolving round the Sun in Earth's orbit. Fusion motors, roaring through Jupiter's atmosphere, will have converted its hydrogen to iron and heavier elements.

The danger in all this, we are told, is that breaking up Jupiter releases huge amounts of energy, much of it in the form of lethal short-wave radiation. This could be guarded against. All that is needed – and here we are indebted to the quick thinking of Iain K.M.Nicholson, the Lecturer in Astronomy at Hatfield Polytechnic Observatory – is to pepper Mercury, which is 'intolerably hot' anyway, with some well-chosen hydrogen bombs, thus launching it into Jupiter's orbit, where it can be broken up and formed into 'a sort of mini-Dyson Sphere' round the gas-giant, to act as a shield between us and the armageddon going on beyond.

Fortunately, 'the actual building of planets will present no great complication'. Not that mankind is going to be satisfied with our piddling solar system for long. The galaxies lie ahead. We can learn to blow up the stars themselves – Berry shows how in under four pages. 'Entire star clusters might be dammed and controlled.'

We have come a long way since a somewhat similarly titled book was published in 1955, two years before the first space satellite went into orbit. This was Sir George Thomson's *The Foreseeable Future*, in which he says, 'The conception of a satellite station should not be dismissed as wholly fantastic, though it bristles with technical difficulties.' Space-travel has changed many things in two decades, not least the neoteric ape's estimate of its own importance.

In case we should ask not only *Can we* but *Should we* blow the heavens apart, Berry provides a chapter entitled 'The God of Spinoza'. This god is a much simpler being than the previous incumbent, who was forever pottering around uttering ethical questions which nobody could solve. 'His sole interest is in the advancement of intelligence, by which I mean technological achievement.' A meaningful switch of pronouns, one may think. Has space-travel changed this too, that God is now interested only in intelligence, and intelligence means only know-how? But we ourselves, Berry tells us, are 'a machine species'. Machines in a machine universe destined to be ruled by machines, with GNP as the Holy Ghost.

As a sort of science fiction, such brain-storming is something to be enjoyed for the breadth and bleakness of its vision. As factual speculation, it is too carelessly littered with assumptions as unchallenged as Jupiter itself. To claim that mankind's development is inexorable and rapid is to contradict the observation that almost everyone (present company excepted) is stupid and averse to change. It is incorrect to assume that infants cannot tell us very much that is of value, although it depends on one's values in the first place.

Francis Bacon is called on to give some sort of philosophical respectability to all the uncheckable technological development. Great man though Bacon was, electronics and nuclear energy are not *direct* results of his writings, as Berry claims. There were intermediate stages, with much struggle and hard work involved. Nor are we *direct* descendants of blue-green algae. Again, there were intermediate stages. Words and concepts have been misused here. Before we start dismantling the stars, we need to find out which end of the monkey-wrench is which.

The Iron Sun is not a different kettle of fish, merely a bigger kettle. Jupiter and Mercury – and presumably Saturn and Venus and the Moon – having been consumed in order to keep the home fires burning, black holes are next in the firing line.

The first duty of a reviewer is to summarise, with as straight a face as possible, the volume before him.

In this book, Mr Berry suggests that we – well, Man – build our own black holes in space and pop through them, to materialise elsewhere in the universe. He gives reasons why such a course of action is necessary.

This modest proposal is set out with an attractive innocence and a care for the stupidest reader which would melt a heart of titanium. The stars are millions of times further from us than the most distant of our planets, Mr Berry explains. All history shows that it is desirable to get there as soon as possible and develop them in the way that we have already developed Tasmania, Bikini, Coney Island, and other remote places. The problem is to get there in the first place.

It costs money. However, it has been estimated that the

wealth of the human race, the gross world product, was about five trillion US dollars in 1974 and, assuming an annual rate of three percent, we can readily understand that a citizen of the year 2215 will probably be about a thousand times richer than his counterpart today, and thus well able to invest in black holes, or anything else that catches his fancy.

Although there are no natural laws governing increasing wealth, space-travel is different. When it comes to buzzing through space, one bangs one's head on the wretched Alfred Einstein's Special Theory of Relativity, which postulates many foolish things. For instance, if you set out in a spaceship during the middle of the Carboniferous Age (to get away from all that anthracite, let's say) and travelled here and there at the speed of light for a hundred years, you would return to Earth only to find that you had missed the dinosaurs entirely, and probably hit the Angevins instead. Also, at such speeds – according to this same Einstein – you would contract until you were a mere photographic image of infinite mass.

If we are to move freely round the universe and not become a nation of photographic images, we need a better way of doing things. Fortunately, Mr Berry has found a loophole in Einstein's equations (I knew it, I knew it!) The equations forbid faster-than-light travel only in *this* universe; the small print says nothing about taking short cuts through other universes – and this is what we must do.

Black holes defy topology. A black hole is three times as massive as the sun; the matter has collapsed in on itself; light cannot escape from its surface, and so it is called a black hole. (In fact, latest news suggests that there are black holes scudding about the place no bigger than my head, but I cite the example Mr Berry uses.) After more patient exposition, we understand that black holes are rotating very fast, say one thousand times per second, so that they naturally suffer from equatorial bulge. Ordinary black holes are useless to an astronaut, but a Kerr black hole, properly navigated, will take him through an Einstein-Rosen bridge (which we may liken to Edgar Allen Poe's famous maelstrom) into another part of the universe. There's a hole in the middle of a black hole, like the hole in an LP. Physics says there must be.

The navigation problems involved are tricky, but nothing that a 2215 pocket calculator will be unable to handle.

It is at this point that Mr Berry gets into his stride, or, to put it in his own words, 'I now come to a proposal which may, at a first consideration, be regarded as raving insanity.' Second and third considerations do not much alter the picture, for Mr Berry suggests that we build a large fleet of robot spaceships, which will act as ramjets and – with the aid of huge magnetic fields – gather together interstellar dust (waiting around for the asking) and build our own black hole just a convenient light year away from the solar system.

The robot fleet then buzzes through the centre of this home-made hole and builds a second hole of the same mass as the first. By buzzing through that, they find themselves back in the vicinity of the sun once more. *Voila!*

It may be difficult, even in the year 2215, when everyone is rich, to persuade politicians to support this enterprising project. Of course, we may all be Communists by then – a prospect Berry does not entertain – in which case politicians will decide for themselves without inviting our opinion. We are treated to an imaginary dialogue between a democratic politician (Commissioner Bandwagon) and an administrator of the twin-hole project (Dr Black) in which the commissioner is crushed by Black's rhetoric: 'We are giving humanity the chance to colonise millions of habitable but uninhabited planets . . .'

Black clearly does not visualise that those millions of planets might be inhabited by space-going Aliens just as greedy as Man, and that those Aliens might pour gleefully through his home-made holes much as the Boche and the Frogs were supposed to pour through any hypothetical Channel Tunnel, and shovel Earth up into their alien coal-scuttle.

This splendidly imaginative book is going to take the bread out of the mouths of science fiction writers. It cannot otherwise do great harm, whereas his earlier work, proposing that we mine Jupiter, is hardly the kind of volume one would want to fall into the hands of Rio Tinto Zinc.

Herman Kahn, another thinker not unduly rattled by the grandiose, has called his new book more modestly *The Next 200*

*Years.** We might expect this to be less ambitious than *The Next Ten Thousand Years*, and so it turns out.

With the assistance of the staff of the Hudson Institute, futurologist Kahn has produced a sort of 'Guinness Book of Hedged Bets'. Were colonisation in space to prove technologically feasible as well as achieving economic viability, then it could conceivably lead to a massive migration of population. Developing nations will have to make many difficult decisions in complex situations. New off-shore oil-drillings will be defeats in the eyes of some people but victories or reasonable compromises for others. If the Arctic ice caps melted, this would substantially raise the level of the oceans; on the other hand, a warmer average temperature might bring huge agricultural areas in Canada and Siberia into production. And one speculation that really did amaze me: 'Of primary importance to mankind is the maintenance of reasonable proportions in the chemical constituents of the biosphere.' You mean we'll still need *air* to breathe?

They are nothing if not realists at the Hudson Institute, and for those fatheads among us who believed that utopia was about to be declared, a fatherly warning is given: 'The future may well hold in store not only the familiar "four horsemen" (war, famine, plague and civil disorder), but *more modern catastrophes as well*' (my hysterics).

This is ominous, particularly since it follows a table – Table 17, 1985 Technological Crises – which includes a number of remarkable hazards such as, listed under *7, Bizarre Issues,* 'Life and death or other control of "outlaw" societies which have not yet committed any traditional crime.' Does he mean Wales or the Penthouse Club?

The trouble with books such as these is that they treat the universe as if it were their coal-scuttle. In the light of such thinking, human beings shrink into Man (and it is shrinkage, despite the capital letter), and Man into GNP. The schemes are okay purely as science fiction, when they possibly awaken imaginative fires within the breasts of young engineers, etc. It is when they escape into the real world that they do damage. The situation is

* *The Next 200 Years: A Scenario for America and the World,* by Herman Kahn, William Brown and Leon Martel, Associated Business Programmes, 1977.

analogous to that regarding such architects of the imaginary as Piranesi and Boullée (see 'SF Art: Strangeness with Beauty'). Piranesi's *Carceri* turned to stone as Newgate Prison; Boullée's geometrical shapes, never realised in his lifetime, inspired Speer and Hitler when they were drawing up their plans for 'The Next Thousand Years', and so became embodied in the criminal architecture of the Third Reich and Stalin's USSR.

It must not be thought that such megalomaniac schemes are a monopoly of the West. Whilst the Hudson Institute seeks to turn the Amazon Basin into a series of Great Lakes, Russian engineers seek to make their Arctic-emptying rivers flow south. The Russian visionary, Vasili Zakharchenko, in his book *Beyond the Dawn* (Moscow 1970, published in Russian) outlines a scheme to dam the Bering Straits, possibly by a series of thermonuclear explosions, concluding by saying: 'The only thing in the way of success is capitalism; already Lenin saw this when he spoke of the disagreement among capitalist countries over the Channel Tunnel.'

The greed and malaise of the West – and by no means only the West – can be summarised in four words: We consume too much. Or, better still, conserving one letter, I consume too much. The last thing we need is to gulp other planets down into our maw.

Moreover, such a vainglorious scheme would merely increase the politicising of our lives, exacting as it would all sorts of corporate needs at present merely dormant in society. With that politicising goes an increasingly vain search for political solutions to what is a fairly simple spiritual dilemma. Science and politics unfortunately advance hand-in-hand through whatever is the predominant power structure; the more we look for political and scientific remedies to our condition, the more difficult becomes the lot of the individual. Without the individual, the rest is nothing.

This World

California, Where They Drink Buck Rogers

I look up from the menu to the waitress, who wears hot-pants and white calf-length boots, and an attitude halfway between ingratiating and impatient.

'What's a Buck Rogers?'

'You know what a Shirley Temple is?'

'No.'

'Well, a Buck Rogers is a Shirley Temple with Coke in it instead of 7-Up.'

So you ask a silly question. These researches into Californian drink take place in Luigi's, Imperial Beach, San Diego, 'The City of Motion'. Nice joint. Evading Buck Rogers, we buy beer and play pool. A few days later, a man is shot dead on Luigi's doorstep, when leaving with someone else's wife.

A couple of weeks before, another guy gets himself shot in the Saddle, a doubtful little bar by the tracks of the San Diego and Arizona Eastern Railroad. Again a woman involved; she always kept a gun in her bra. Just a little one.

San Diego is a navy town. As we left, the mothball fleet over towards Coronado was being rigged with pretty lights for Christmas. The Mexican border is a few miles down the road and some old frontier traditions survive. We were staying at a writer friend's house. From his windows, you can see the sinful lights of Tijuana twinkling through the night.

The radar plane endlessly circling sea and land is looking not for wily Mexicans but angry Russians. Wetback patrols wait up in the barren hills. America is relaxed but alert.

There are advantages in having Mexico so close. A lot of good flaming food can easily be consumed. Tijuana is a handy place – 'The Most Visited City in the World' – in which to get laid or boozed. The Mexicans also benefit. Right next to the 'Hiltom' Hotels and Go-Go Girls, are used-car and used-house lots. If your house gets in the way of yet another new highway project, you jack it up on wheels and roll it south of the border; some guy will set it up in the desert, its plumbing forlornly trailing.

Our friend, heterosexual to a fault, takes us to several Tijuana girlie shows. The 'Sans Souci' is a wow, presenting a preview of next year's attractions. Great floorshow. The tables are arranged about a raised floor, so that you gaze up from your Mexicali beer into serried ranks of dancing crotches.

In San Diego, there is the 'Bali-Hai', a glamour place with Polynesian dancers and a lot of genuine high spirits. Whisky-sours are good, almost as good as in New York. The centre of San Diego is attractive, with bay to one side, zoo and airport to the other – planes sweep in lower than the restaurant floor of the El Cortez Hotel. Indoors, everywhere, everything is amazingly clean to British eyes. Never any cigarette stubs in the urinals. And a high standard of graffiti: 'Mickey Mouse – One Black who Made It', 'Jesus Sucks', 'Just because your breath stinks of ape-shit, you needn't think you're Tarzan'. Always this obses-sion with personalities.

I give a talk at the State College. Immediate American friendliness and wit. Immediate payment of cheque, too, con-current with vote of thanks. When did that happen over here? We retire to a drinking house (what, south of the border, is termed a 'cockteleria') for heavy schooners of light beer, while the students in the party order milk and decide whether to have a double-deck hamburger, a budgetburger – an ordinary burger re-labelled to make you ashamed of being a cheapskate – a giant steerburger, or a half-giant steerburger. They then relax and talk about dodging the Vietnam draft; patriotic talk, *outré* to an older generation. For the first time, I recollect that the States is at war. It has done this navy town no harm.

We flash back to Imperial Beach, through National City ('Mile of Cars', it boasts, and 'New Olds Are Here'), through Chula Vista, through Palm City, past the Aztec Furniture Company, past the Gay Nineties Car Wash, the Howdy Folks Motel, and Greenwood's, the World's Largest Mausoleum – done in Eastern Orthodox style, with just a hint of Moghul. It must be okay to die here. Compared with being poor. Better dust than bust.

As we stop for gas at a filling station, I jump out for the pleasure of picking up instant conversation from the folks in the next car; after the Irish, the Californians are the readiest people to talk. I pick a guy who wants to talk about tunny-fishing off Florida. He makes it sound like fun. He's just back from Yucatan, I think he says. 'Say, aren't you a Britisher? I'd know that accent a mile off. You know a city called Bradford? You do? Give my regards to Bradford — it's a great city.' Bradford. Chalk it up to good old yankee enthusiasm to like Bradford.

Next day we walk into The Swamp at the back of Harry's place. The frogs arf at us, falling uneasily silent when we try to track them. Harry shows us a crack in the dirt which snakes away northwards into the grass and peters out beneath our boots. 'Know what this is? The tail end of the San Andreas Fault.' 'Did you know it was here when you bought the place?' 'It was miles further north then.' It's fun. It adds life.

We see humming birds in the garden, despite December, before we go to shop. We drive everywhere, shop everywhere. Everything's new and unnecessary and shines. Take-away shops, hot-rod drive-in movies, freeways, San Diego is a desert of low urban sprawl punctuated by neon signs, glaring lights, billboards, drive-in pay-first motels, and tumbling tumbleweed. Restaurants have no locks, stay open twenty-four hours a day. Time has been cancelled, direction abolished. Under pressure from the automobile, everything's accessible, but desolation has replaced destination. Just keep driving, you're okay. The oil's still jetting out of the earth, isn't it?

You can't walk to the new shopping complex, Fashion Valley in Mission Valley. What a haven of nursery excess it is! How many kinds of salt alone do the supermarkets sell? Here's Artificial Butter Salt for your popcorn, Margarita Salt for your tequila. Garlic salt, onion salt, apple salt, pretzel salt. Here are three-ring pretzels and single-ring pretzels, 'the Only Pretzels Made to Music'. We buy beef sticks, hot sticks, beef jerky in 79-cent packs. I smoke a rum-soaked mentholated tipped cigarillo. Everything is just dandy. Tomorrow, dinner with Ray Bradbury in LA. My cup runneth over. Luckily it's disposable, like everything else. At a nearby used-car lot, the sign says encouragingly, 'Stupid Buyer On Duty'.

There are Tiepolos and things in the Fine Arts Gallery, and Mexican blankets down the road. But on the whole these are culture-free people. It's all present tense. No sf title on the racks of the Pickwick book-store more than three months old. But a new and genuine native culture is growing up, based on nostalgia, one of the growth industries. All of Dick Tracy in one bargain volume. The songs of Alice Faye. Currier and Ives repros. The reign of La Guardia. Xavier Cugat Hits. Vintage Superman. The pulps are being canonised, like Beowulf and Sir Gawaine. 'I'm up to my neck in a knee-high culture,' Harry cries.

It's easy to tuck away English intimations of doom. Californian air is infectious. The guy with the Chevy next to us stows six half-gallon bottles of brandy in his boot and drives off. As he goes, I see his bumper-sticker, a hand clutching what looks like a brick but is in fact a can. It is issued by ALCOA, big hereabouts, and reads: 'Yes We Can.' The message has more than local applications.

Modest Atmosphere with Monsters

[An essay for voices. Scene: Trieste. An international cast, some of them well known, sit at assorted tables on the terrace of the Grand Hotel et de la Ville. Music plays.]

Oh, but wouldn't you say that Italian – at least to English ears – is a somewhat salacious language? Even an innocent word, the word for 'ice cream', say: isn't there a whisper of corrupt sexual practices in the word '*gelati*'?

In-built linguistic salacity? It's a new theory to me, but there could be something in it. Half-a-dozen miles away, over the frontier in proletarian Jugoslavia, ice cream becomes '*sladoled*'. You'd never want to practise sladoled, would you? It must be far more reprehensible than gelatio: a capital offence, no less.

There can't be much gelati going on in Trieste. It's too down-to-earth. In spite of the Roman amphitheatre and the picture-postcard Venetian castle, Trieste's glory lies in its banks and its dockyards.

I must send mother a postcard. Remind me. Let's have a drink.

Let's have some wine, strip the soul entirely of its camouflage. I can't take any other Italian drinks whatever – little shallow things they are! They suggest Italy doesn't take its drinking with a proper seriousness.

Trieste is a good drinking town. The old Austrian tradition still lingers. That's what makes it such a practical place, just the opposite to Miramare, up the road. The blending of cultures generally produces something prosaic.

Like Andalusian gipsies, you mean?

For Christ's sake, shut him up or he'll be on about Svevo and

Joyce next. You know what he said about *Fahrenheit 451* this morning? 'It is in its essence philosophical.'

First time I've heard science fiction mentioned today. This is supposed to be a science fiction festival. Remember that line in *Dr Strangelove* where the President of the United States says in a shocked voice, 'Gentlemen, you can't fight here – this is the War Room!'?

The Italian term for science fiction is pretty: '*Fantascienza*'. Don't you like it?

Wow, I'm so flaked! I must go take a shower. I've been walking around town filming all morning. Trieste is just the craziest place round all those little back streets – the old city is an absolute maze. Smells just great! At that, I guess it's better than the stink of gasoline fumes in the main streets. You don't wonder they don't have so many tourists.

The lack of tourists suits me well. I'd come here for a holiday, even. I like the place, the strange political atmosphere and the old Viennese buildings and everything. What a place to make a thriller film! Do you know, just the far side of the Piazza della Unità, there's a mammoth hotel, a block wide, and it's all shut down! What a setting that would make for a bit of nastiness, the camera prowling up and down those vacant corridors ... The city's too prosaic to be sinister, but, my God, it's unique! Look at the Adriatic, right on our doorstep! – see that white boat moored against the mole called *Audacity*? She's from Venice. She stops here overnight before heading south for Dubrovnik, Kotor, and the Piraeus. I was on her once, several years ago, heading for the Greek Island, with a girl I was very much in love with. Those were the days! We boarded the vessel at Venice but we came ashore here in Trieste for dinner that night. She married a motor-racing driver in the end. [*Sings*] I met her down in Italy ...

My wife's four grandparents are of four different nationalities. That sort of mixture is by no means uncommon. My own father came from Montenegro and was shot by Nazis in the war.

Ye Gods, did you see that? That little bugger in the Fiat nearly ran into the trolley-car!

It's a way of keeping the old muscles flexed. You must keep the muscles flexed. I shall be fifty next year but I'm in as good

a shape as a man of thirty-five because I keep the old muscles
flexed. Exercise every morning, moderation in smoking, drinking
and sexual activity. Not that releasing semen is by any means
harmful. Those spontaneous pelvic movements – they're all
exercise, aren't they? They all help keep the stomach muscles
flexed. You may say it's a simple philosophy, but I'd race you
upstairs any day! Not that I'm afraid of growing old. I'm not, I
just want to keep my responses alert.

Call the waiter over. We have time for another round of beer
before we head for another round of films at the castle.

Wasn't that little Jugoslav animated film *Pauk* just lush?!

You know, the setting here is very nice but just outside Oslo
we've now got a brand new Arts Centre, all very well equipped.
They made a few damned-fool mistakes, of course. When they
sort them out, it will be a really great creative centre. We ought
to hold a proper sf film festival there, with panels of real artists
and writers. Show proper avant-garde sf films like Goddard's
Weekend and *Zabriskie Point*. The world's all science fictional
now you don't have to call in the hacks any more. It's a style, a
vocabulary, you see, not a form analogous to a . . . I don't know,
to a plum-pudding!

Everyone likes monsters. What's wrong with monsters, my
life? That's what the audience loves up at the castle, whatever
you highbrows give the prizes to! Monsters! Horror! My
company is now planning to make a round dozen monster-
horror films for world markets, and you bet they'll do a bomb! I
bet you you'd be glad to write the script for one if the old
moolah was good enough? How'd you *like* to write the script for
one?

King Kong is the best monster film ever made, and the best sf
film after Whale's version of *Frankenstein*. Probably its appeal
lies in the way it's so open to a Freudian interpretation.

After this, we go down to the Jugoslav Film Festival in Pula.
Maybe we meet Grandi there. We hope so – he's a real great
man and a fine director. He planned to come to Trieste but his
wife . . . a very pretty and beautiful lady – Swiss, but you'd
never guess it. She has a strong will, so she wears the trousers
when she wears anything at all.

Hey, sweetheart, why didn't you come to the Retrospective

this afternoon? They were showing an excellent copy of
Nosferatu.

You know, I fell asleep directly after lunch, I was so tired!
And when I woke up, I said to myself that I must have a swim
before anything. And it was so warm and so beautiful in the sea!
I simply longed to swim underwater, but, you see, I'm just afraid
that my contact lenses might float away and be lost.

Are all Italians as friendly and pleasant as the ones in Trieste?

You can't generalise from Trieste. Trieste isn't Italy. It can
never forget it was once Austria-Hungary's main sea-port. That
was really Trieste's heyday – ever since then, it has been a bone
of contention between rival countries up to no good. It suffers
from chronic distortions of history and geography.

Sure, sure, that's what makes Trieste the ideal place in which
to hold an annual Science Fiction Film Festival. No matter how
shoddy some of the films may be, I still get a charge sitting in
that immense courtyard up in the castle, watching the horrors
chase themselves across the wide screen.

It's a pretty setting.

It's a gigantic setting! On the first year of the festival, the
moon rose above the battlements on the first night and went into
semi-eclipse, to hang for an hour blood-red above the screen.
Superb stage management! But what I mean is – look, take this
week so far. As you might expect in Trieste, unreason sleeps
uneasily. Didn't you feel it stir in that silly Japanese monster
film? Monsters making that well-known monster noise ... And
in that semi-documentary, *Errinerungen*, with the solemn
teutonic voices asking if God was an astronaut, plus a friendly
word from Wernher von Braun.

Yes, how did he get in there?

And all the other national forms of an international malaise.
The Gladiators, with its melancholy Swedes working their war-
computers. That Anglo-American thing, with the guy having his
limbs amputated one by one ... And that black bit of Polish
humour, with the stark ugly houses in the sick half-light. The
Balkan versions of Edgar Alan Poe, that animated film about
the prisoner turning into a spider ... The world's nightmares
were homing in on Trieste.

Everyone always looks back as much as forward.

Let's not talk about the films. I'm half-afraid they'll devour us. Showings at ten in the morning and nine-thirty at night and things in between and the Retrospective every day at five, my life! Where did reality go?

At least we've managed to punctuate the showings with a few al fresco meals up in the hills.

Marvellous! But the meals aren't real either . . .

Oh no? They're beginning to show on my waistline! But sure, I know what you mean. After a couple of days of this intensive course, you see everything that happens as potential fodder for the screen, drained of spontaneity, with meaning translated into image, gesture into pattern. One's senses are sink-or-swimming, I guess.

Well, I find I can't even talk meaningfully. Is what I say true or not true? I mean, do I believe what I'm saying half the time? Maybe it's lack of sleep, or too much drink, or something. Perhaps it's meeting so many people and talking to so many of them all at once. That's not natural, is it? Your character gets crunched down to a mere hub.

Odd the way everyone has different opinions, yet they don't clash so much as just glide by each other. We have the Italian love of oratory to thank for that.

Have another campari-soda.

It's lovely up at Opicina. That marvellous view of the bay. Really lovely . . .

It was just a little chilly when *we* were there. But the lime trees smelt beautiful.

I tell you this, the Austrian ladies used to spend the summer there. Practising gelatio, no doubt. That same longing for the happy past goes on here more intensely than elsewhere; you hear them say it all the while – 'If only we could have back the days of Austria-Hungary! After all, Franz Josef was a very enlightened man. Many races were united under him, contentedly in the main.

You'd not be likely to hear that from Serbs and Croats.

The Triestini are pretty comic about the Jugoslavs, 'our friends across the border . . .'. Tito is a gentleman – they say it always. He could walk in and take Trieste if he wanted; the government in Rome won't lift a finger. Rome sometimes sounds more like an enemy than Belgrade.

Do you know anything about how this city is run? Until the late fifties, it was a sort of free zone, governed by British and Americans. Now it's a bit of Italy – the bit farthest east. A postscript. Where Trieste stops, the Communist world begins, right? It's a big port, it's stacked with marine insurance offices, from Lloyd's Triestino down, and yet all shipping must be registered in Genoa. I asked why. The answer was, 'It's the politics of Rome.'!

I've lived here now since three years – my little villa's above Miramare – and I prefer the Triestini to the pure Italians. The Triestini are more phlegmatic and less showy. Is that the right word? Yes, showy! Making a show. Watch the favouritism shown to the Italian judge, watch their polished bad manners at the cold buffet as the vultures descend with many a soft '*Scusi*', while they smudge their over-charged plates against the back of your evening dress. Britishers would be too stiff for that. And they gobble every last remnant. The women soigné, hawkish, hungry; the men plump in their satiny suits, never satisfied, drinking always to next year's free bonanzas.

All nationalities are plain awful when you come to think of it. Imagine this binge taking place in England, in some inhospitable place like Brighton – so much better organised, so much less . . . pardon me . . . fun. I admire the generosity of the Italians, their innocent delight in giving gifts and surprises and footing your enormous bar bill, switching all their 'Noes' unexpectedly into 'Yeses', like Russians in reverse. In love-making the women here are capricious but generous.

A woman a night? That's what you call sexual obesity!

Ah, making obese of yourself!

They eat pretty well in Trieste. Though it's kinda odd the way the city aquarium is tacked on to the city fish market. Which gets the live stuff first?

I admire the way they co-exist with the Jugoslavs. There's a strong minority of Croats and Slovenes in the city, I gather. Have you seen those shops by the Grand Canal devoted almost solely to selling goods to Jugoslavs? I bought this shirt there! Not bad, is it?

This city may be invaded by the Jugoslavs, but when you move across the frontier, you find Jugoslavia invaded by

Italians! The Triestini drive over to buy cheap meat and cheap petrol. It pays the car-hire firms to cross the border and fill their tanks with Istra-Benz or Yugo-petrol. Nobody knows or cares which country is which any more, and maybe it's better that way. Slav vowels precede Italian endings, and you get three new dinara back in your change for your *mille* lira note.

They set us a good example, world-wide. That's not the sort of mix I like to see. Co-existence. Mind if I move over to your tables, darling, and mix it a bit with you? Your smile is so very international.

You are correct, it's a mix-up down there. Not counting the thousands of Germans sunning themselves on the beaches. The coastal strip below here was Venetian for centuries, then it was Austrian, then a free territory, then the fascists ran it, then it was a special zone administered by British and Americans, then it went to Tito. I think I've got the order right. Why don't I write a novel set in these parts?

How the hell's my film ever going to win an award? The projector broke down. So they showed it at two fifteen and of course nobody turned up! Siesta time, goddam it.

The Berlin Festival is beautifully run. But you don't get the nice family atmosphere you have here.

Hey, take a look at that boy, strolling along with that big plastic water pistol! There he goes, squirting himself to keep cool as he trots along! Lovely! Local colour!

It's beautiful over the frontier, driving down to Piran, umbrella pines, cypresses, villas with their sprawling vines. Italy must have looked that way in the thirties, before she sank under Lambrettas, transistor radios, and adverts for aperitifs. Piran's prettier than Miramare, any day.

Linguistically, it's a nightmare. The people don't know what language they're talking! We tried out our patchy Serbo-Croat on them and even that doesn't work properly, because they're Slovenes, speaking some benighted idiom of their own, like Croatian but different. What language do they dream in, do you wonder?

Stick to music, that's my motto. I have a Bechstein in my villa, a real pre-war Bechstein, and I play three hours every day. Three hours without fail. Some days I speak with no-one.

Sad old Trieste ... No, it isn't really sad. Just stolid and fantastic and grandly stranded. It is the centrepiece of its own dreams – as we all are.

The trick is to wake up occasionally. I don't go for mysticism – besides, the Adriatic's wrong for it.

The Triestini are just so clapped out by all the switches of régime that all they want is a long materialist sleep. And who's to blame them?

What does our Hungarian lady-friend think? Isn't there a slight somnambulism about her?

It's the climate just. In Trieste they have maybe a little too much of climate as of political events. Also, the lady had a little brush-up with the German film producer just last afternoon. He sneaked into her room on a pretext, locked the door and sprang on her with a revolting cry. She fought, he struggled, trying to bear her successfully down. But she gave forth a few hearty yells and he got frightened and ran off.

You mean that little German guy with the mandala and the side-whiskers? He tried to rape Jedmilla?

Maybe not rape her exactly. She seemed mainly indignant at the element of the unexpected in his manner – and her complaint to me after was, 'He also was such a small man!'

She's a fine figure of a girl. She motored down here in her Porsche from Bucharest non-stop. I mean Budapest. They say sexual mores are pretty free and easy in Hungary nowadays. [*Sings*] Yellow tigers in the jungles of her eyes ...

Summink has to make up for other forms of oppression and suppression. These Eastern European countries take science fiction more serious than us. They see it as a crafty way of conveying contemporary truth.

So do we. Nobody pretends 1984's in the future. It's a state of mind. We like it. It's an enjoyment. All suffering is an enjoyment. The pain of present day living is our own invention. We want regimentation and pollution and nuclear war. We volunteer for it, we are disposed towards it, as towards cancer and stomach ulcers – or aren't ulcers fashionable any more?

Guys only want World War III to happen because it will at least resolve their impossible personal problems. It's a secret we all share that a war a little way down the road is rejuvenating.

On other planets, Communist writers can build allegories of today, of suppression and psyche-distortion. Some Russian science fiction writers have recently been criticised for doing just that.

See what I was saying about opinions gliding by each other? Nobody is in contact any more. It's the special Trieste thing, not to be able to tell the trivial from the vital, not to distinguish between rape or seduction, between truth or *fantascienza*.

I got a shoe mended yesterday by a cobbler in a twelfth-century hole in the wall. Is that what you'd call reality?

Down over the border in Jugland, they're drinking drinks called things like Pleskovac made in something called Alko Factory. Isn't that 1984 made manifest?

You're thinking in purely literary terms. That's not reality, whatever it is. It's just an act of translation. The real thing – look, yes, I'll tell you the real thing. The difference between Trieste and its neighbours. Cross the border – it's just down that road, past the watermelon stalls. Instantly, you start seeing war-wounds and scars and hunchbacks. And a few miles further down the coast, Tito's old Partisans bask by the sea or are lowered in – amputees lying like seals on the rocks, *sans* legs, *sans* arms. This part of the world's all scar tissue. Lacking the privileges of history.

Mama mia, that's just another version of the past. Have a little more campari? Just one?

Yeah, *grappa's* more like the truth than *fantascienza*. It's stupid to pretend that life's all scar tissue, even in Trieste.

Let's organise an expedition tomorrow to go down and see those Partisans. We could have a swim at the same time.

They say the Adriatic has a major pollution problem.

That's just what the Triestini tell you. They like to be in the fashion.

Cultural Totems in the Soviet Union

Our flight had scarcely left Heathrow before the air hostess on the Japan Air Lines plane was announcing (but of course we could have mis-heard), 'Your pilot on the flight is Captain Kamikazi.' Charles and I got up immediately to leave. The jokes, together with the persistent kamikazi atmosphere of Communism which gave the jokes edge, helped our whole trip maintain constant flying-speed.

Now that we are back on the capitalist ground, our fortnight in the Soviet Union becomes a more complex experience than it appeared at the time: something to be unravelled with care, as enjoyment succumbs to analysis. We were five cultural totems (or tokens) in the hopeful 1977 détente following the Helsinki agreement, pawns in the schizophrenic dumb-show which the USSR acts out with the West; while the script was running, however, our personal enjoyment and fascination were uppermost. Our hosts were alert to keep us happy, and Charles Osborne, Elaine Feinstein, Jon Stallworthy, Ted Whitehead and I made a good team, working together without friction.

We were guests of the Soviet Writers' Union. We owe them thanks for much amazement.

For two or three days after our return to England, I remained in a daze, re-living the details of our tour. At home, the familiar lowers one's threshold of awareness; abroad, novelty raises that threshold. For this recovery of pristine attentions, one endures the discomforts of travel. Air tastes strange, fresh sounds entice the ear, gestures and faces suggest alternative histories, food requires a new palate, sleep has a different consistency. Just to walk into a hotel foyer becomes a particular event – naturally so when there are hotels like Moscow's *Ukraine*, built in the Stalinist Gothic of the fifties and resembling a slavonic Gormenghast.

We were escorted to many of the recognised tourist sights. It would have been heresy to visit Moscow and not investigate the Kremlin, which is an eyeful with its fresh-licked lollipop domes, its acres of new gold paint. Everywhere in the Soviet Union, the standard of restoration is high and expense no object. The most striking example is Leningrad itself, which, during the siege of nine hundred days, was heavily bombarded, and one third of its population wiped out. The Stroganof Palace, the Winter Palace, the countless other beautiful buildings, have been returned to their former glory. Leningrad is beyond description; the city of Peter, the Nazi killing-ground, is now a tourist target and a national shrine, to which the message of service to the state forms an obbligato.

One day we drove out to Zagorsk, a monastic centre some distance from Moscow on the road to Yaroslavl. Zagorsk too is impeccably restored. It clustering churches and domes, new-painted, might be toys for a Czar's children. Under light snow it must look like a dream, a child's dream. Pilgrims crowded to Zagorsk, lighting candles and praying at shrines, a non-stop performance every day from seven a.m. to seven p.m., we were told. In the main church, a communion service was in progress at eleven a.m. on a working day, packed with a congregation mainly composed of old women and their progeny, all delivering up to God the electric wail of Eastern Orthodoxy.

At each of the other churches in the complex, guides told the usual stories one hears in churches – tales of blood and massacre, siege, cannonade, starvation and severed heads.

After the churches, we walked round Zagorsk Museum (or Cabinet, as they insisted). This contains many antique delights, chief among them being the collection of ikons; from a mist of gold, angular figures stare out, wide-eyed, at the wicked modern world. Then came lunch, which we took with an archbishop. Archbishop Vladimir of Dimitrov, the Rector of the Theological Seminary.

He was a striking man, almost too good to be true. We talked with him as an enormous lunch went down, accompanied by vodka, wine and mineral water; well, the meal had its limits – no butter with the caviar, because this was Wednesday and a day of fasting, hic. We said to His Excellence that we came from a nominally Christian country in which only eight per cent of the people went to church; here we were in an officially atheist country – what sort of equation did he have to make between Church and State?

The Archbishop's blue eyes remained twinkling, his beard unruffled. He said he regarded atheism itself as a kind of belief; so there was less difference between the two sides than might be imagined. Besides, the State gave Zagorsk its land rent free.

No mention of how broad the lands had been that the Church owned before the Revolution; nor were we impolite enough to raise that issue. But I remembered lovely monasteries in Serbia, where the monks whined to us in French, after the official guides had gone, that their lands had been stolen, and that they themselves existed only on sufferance. Communism, taking to itself religious trappings, remains the enemy of religion.

The trip to Zagorsk enabled us to see the outskirts of Moscow. London shrinks, Moscow grows. The population is now something like eight million, and a thousand new arrivals flock in every day, looking for work – 'more philologists than there are navvies,' commented one guide shrewdly. Ancient wooden villages fall under the bulldozer, giving way to complexes of massive concrete blocks – not a bad exchange, from what we saw of the shabby old Czarist towns. But the great piles of splintered timber, with machines prowling round them like dogs round dungheaps, indicate the ruthlessness of the process.

The day after the excursion to Zagorsk, we flew to Georgia, accompanied by our retinue of interpreters and journalists, and passed over the Caucasus in daylight. Below lay the mountains, sharp as teeth, ploughed deep in snow, where Shamyl, Imam of Daghestan, once defied Czar Nicholas and his armies. By a peculiar accident of Russian geography, the first east-west mountain range to stem the cold influences of the Pole runs this far south; the Urals, in their north-south orientation, are very badly planned.

South of the Caucasus, the climate changes, and the population. We landed in a warm and fragrant land, where the acacias which shade the pavements of the Georgian capital, Tbilisi, were coming into blossom. This human-scale city has pleasant side streets and not too much heroic statuary. The eyes that meet yours are darker, more ready to exchange gaze for gaze. I was there two days before realising – owing to some accident of idiocy – that we were in the city known historically as Tiflis. (I once made a similar mistake about Koper, hating it until discovering that it was the fabled Capodistria. What's in a name? The essence of romantic association.)

The hotel in Tbilisi at which to stay is decidedly not the Intourist where greetings were always surly, but the smiling new Iveria, overlooking the Kura River. The hotels from Titograd to the Black Sea are built by architects trained on mausoleum-designs. The Iveria is no exception. It contains vast acres of Slavonic marble halls of no obvious function which terminate in wardrobe-sized toilets, pushed against an entanglement of restaurants and snack bars. But there are compensations. The Georgians are a carefree lot, and the Iveria's main restaurant at night is a lively place in which to eat. The iced mango juice is as superb in its way as the champagne.

As usual in Soviet hotels, one's keys are lodged with the floor-ladies, a convenient arrangement which precludes waiting at main reception. Throughout our stay, these matrons were in general both cheerful and helpful. In the Iveria, they are particularly to be commended.

Let me mention two of them. Floor-ladies are usually of advanced age, to avoid arousing the Adam in their male guests. But one of them on the seventh floor was a well-built woman in her late thirties with a radiant smile and a word or two of English. One night late, going cheerfully up to my room after a very Georgian evening, I blew her a goodnight kiss as I climbed the stairs. To my astonishment, she returned it warmly. Intourist verily hath changed its image.

And the other lady. She was quite aged and round. She wore glasses and dyed her hair with henna, a prevalent Georgian fashion. On our last morning in Tbilisi, we had to rise early. I came clomping down the marble stairs with my bags at five a.m. The lady was asleep on a couch on her desk. I could not avoid rousing her. As I waited for the lift, she reached for her spectacles, smiled at me, and launched into a speech in Russian about the glories of English literature, and in particular about her enjoyment of John Galsworthy and his Saga of the

Forsythes. It takes a severe effort of will, not to mention a Monty Python sense of humour, to imagine a similar kind of ceremony happening in a London hotel.

Our Georgian excursions had a slight atmosphere of shaggydog about them. At one point, our motor calvacade, swelled by Georgian officials (always referred to as 'writers'), picked up the mayor of the district we were passing through. He was a neat man in a sharp suit with a witty air about him; Italian in appearance. At his behest, we stopped in a village to look round the private garden of an old man who had recently died. It was a shady little nook, and we lingered among the flowering shrubs, wondering when we were going to be asked to plant a tree with a golden spade. That was in the village where we also visited an ancient cathedral, scene through the years of considerable worship, piety and bloodshed, not necessarily in that order. The name escapes me; all I have at that point in my notebook is a reminder to send a collection of Ben Travers plays to a mutual friend. Ah yes, here we are: Mtskheta, ancient capital of Georgia, on the Georgian Military Highway. Mentioned by Strabon, Pliny and Plutarch.

Further along the route, we stopped at an open-air museum. The mayor walked with us while we strolled among flowering bushes in long grass, regarding old blocks of stone. The stones had been gathered from here and there, were unnamed, presumably unnamable. Having formed a part of someone's past, they were precious. A cuckoo called. I caught a darting green lizard. Only its tail escaped.

Later, we visited an ancient church on a hill where ghastly things had happened throughout the centuries. I failed to note its name. It probably began with a V or a Z. We climbed about, politely admiring the views. The Georgian writers stood about the hillside, smoking, in striking poses.

We sat hemmed in in the back of the big black Chaika cars, sweaty scrotum pressed against sweaty thigh, bumping along, and there, closing around us unexpectedly, was this large dusty town in a valley – Gori, birthplace of J.Stalin.

The hut in which Stalin was born remains intact. It is about the same size as our kitchen. A glass pavilion protects it from the elements. One peers at the tiny room, the worn furniture, poverty made concrete; preserved things accumulate a waiting quality like holiness; is this how Deity must always begin? Behind Stalin's hut stands Stalin's museum. This is the only Stalin museum in the USSR, the guides point out. Or in the rest of the world, we mutter.

Six large chambers are set out with the history of Stalin's life. He nearly made the priesthood. One of the big nearlys of history. Documents, portraits, manifestoes . . . We are obscurely stirred. The Russian interpreters, unsure of their ideological ground, move at a brisker pace than suits the Georgian guide; after all, Local Boy Made Good. Local guide wants us to enjoy everything.

Among the public clutter is a glass case containing more personal items. A portrait of Stalin's mother. Photographs of the son who was killed by the Nazis, the son who became a hopeless drunk. 'Why is there no picture of Svetlana?' I ask. 'She is no longer a citizen of the USSR, so we do not have her picture.'

In the next room are photographs of Churchill and Roosevelt, dressed for Yalta. Uncle Joe smiles and sucks at his pipe. Depression sets in. History is sufferable, faked history insufferable. No pictures of Beria, Yagoda, or Yezhov. I recall Svetlana's words in her book: 'My father was the centre of a black circle . . . People vanished like shadows in the night . . .'

At the end of that drive lay the spa of Borzomi, set in the hills and sub-Alpine scenery, and not so far from the frontier with Turkey. We wonder if we could make it on foot, supposing the worst came to the worst. On the way I regale Anatoli Melnikov and the lady from *Literaturna Gazeta* with the story of how Stalin, during the Great Patriotic War (sometimes known as World War II), would come and rouse his schoolgirl daughter at dead of night, and how together they would walk across the courtyards of the Kremlin to a small chapel where American musicals, forbidden to the Soviet people, were shown. With the two figures went an armed escort, an armoured car rumbling slowly behind them. It was such a beautiful tale, their attendance was so acute, that I began to embroider. Stalin's favourite star was Betty Grable. She made him smile. He saw *Springtime in the Rockies* over and over again. He was once overheard by Molotov, humming one of the film's trivial songs to himself.

'How strange it is that Mr Aldiss should know and tell us such things,' says the *Literaturna Gazeta* lady. 'It's a fairy tale,' says Melnikov stoutly. 'Besides, Stalin would need no protection inside the Kremlin – it was then a well-defended fortress.' 'He was nervous,' I say, politely avoiding the word 'paranoid'. I explain further, 'Svetlana is my age; but our childhoods were very different.' The others fall silent. There is no way in which our thoughts can be made known.

We remained in the seclusion of Borzomi spa over May Day. Our dacha stood in beautiful woods, the leaves of the ash trees trembling against our very windows. Food was brought in to us in vans, carried by old women through a rear service entrance, and served on fine china. All was calm: the privacy was extreme, for torture or meditation. Internal doors were of the old-fashioned double kind, *vrata*. Windows were deep set and also double. Night filtered in through the surrounding trees. A full moon dawdled among shoulders of mountain, a ruin was impaled in floodlight on a nearby hillside. We slept two to a room. Ted Whitehead snored.

Our hosts did not wish us to view the May Day parades. One by one, towns as we travelled dwindled in size and importance: Moscow, Tbilisi, Gori, Borzomi; and in each we saw all the signs of preparation for the great day manifesting themselves – banners, slogans, red flags, portraits of Lenin and Breznev, platforms being erected. We said we wanted to see the missiles. No, they did not have missiles any more. Only people. No parades, only demonstrations.

There was a television set in our dacha. I switched on and there were the parades. Moscow on one channel, Tbilisi on another. Oodles of people. No missiles. Slogans. Speeches. Inspirational music. Hands waving. Interviews with outstanding workers. Flaxen-haired children. Old men with medals. Interminable.

We let our friends know that we knew we were in Borzomi because of its remoteness as well as its beauty. They denied it. Later, others told us that we had been taken to Borzomi because it was pleasanter than Tbilisi on May Day, for in Tbilisi the streets were roped off, and we would have to stay in our hotel and be bored. We never knew the truth of it. I remembered a past May Day in Belgrade, when my wife and I had been roped in among friendly crowds, and of individuals who had laughed at the passing Jugoslav army and said, 'Note particularly the Russian uniforms and the American lorries!'

Most probably we were kept away from Tbilisi, not because of missiles, but because the town gave itself over to drunkenness. The Soviet Union is hot on law and order. The next night, also a holiday, all restaurants and bars were closed and the Iveria was practically under siege, with tough-looking guys guarding the lifts.

This question of May Day worried our friends until the end; it would have been so much easier to have been frank, but local customs die hard. As we were driving to the airport on the last day, one of our interpreters suddenly explained that the Georgians had done what they believed to be best for our comfort. And so, I believe, they did – in a devious way.

Most of the Georgian 'sights' arranged for us were engagingly amateur. I could have borne up under such standard old-style delights as a hydro-electric plant, a new dam, or even a bicycle factory; but no doubt the Soviets have decided wearily that Western observers only laugh at such things. Instead, we got another ruinous church – at the site of which something awful had happened – a second-rate painter whose work was not hung in the National Gallery because he had once been lured into abstraction, and a strange little theatre at which we were assured John Osborne was about to appear. He didn't.

Another of these 'sights' was a visit to a Pioneer Palace in the centre of Tbilisi itself. We arrived after an excellent meal and were in jovial mood. The Palace catered for twelve thousand children and provided them with such out-of-school pleasures as sports, dancing, chess, puppet theatre, and music, including classical and jazz. Also internationalism and patriotism. Literary and scientific interests were catered for, and careers directed. After a long introduction, a fetching fourteen-year-old girl rose to make us a short speech in English. She said that the children were fortunate to have five hundred teachers. We wanted to ask if sexual instruction and contraception were taught, but at this point even Whitehead was overcome by uncharacteristic bashfulness.

We were taken on a tour of the Palace, which had its unexpected pleasures, including a room full of mechanical dolls and automata, many of them made in Paris, which collectively must have been worth a fortune. We were ushered into a large airy baroque hall. As we seated ourselves on a row of gilt chairs at one end, a traditional Georgian orchestra assembled at the other – and then in poured the dancers! The Pioneer children put on a half-hour show for us, singing and dancing with sharp sparrow-like movements, all in lavish colour. Their standard was high and it was as pleasing as unexpected. So did pashas entertain their guests.

Tbilisi was made for such brief excursions. One morning, we ambled down a hill to inspect a working church in which something deplorable had occurred, and to see the graves of Stalin's mother and the poet Gribiedof. The Judas trees were in blossom, smelling sweetly; the air was hot; we bought mineral water, postcards, maps and photos of Stalin from a stall, while the guide explained how Gribiedof had been appointed Russian ambassador in Teheran, where, in 1829, he was murdered by Muslim extremists in the pay of the British. This was territory over which, in Britain's hey-day, the Great Game was played. Now, on the shabby doorways of Tbilisi's side-streets, you see the name Zorro scrawled in chalk. Dangerous games still go on.

Where our Georgian hosts excelled was in hospitality. They drove us out to a state farm (not to be confused with a collective farm), and explained how their HQ had been a palace belonging to a cousin of Czar Nicholas; we took a stroll in the cousin's park before going into the cousin's palace for a three-hour meal which was washed down with vodka, cognac, and two sorts of wine. After that, we climbed back into our black cars. We never saw a tractor, a field, or a worker.

In this connection, I had better describe our breakfast in the secluded dacha in Borzomi spa. These were the foods that the women brought in and arranged upon the gleaming mahogany table: cold sturgeon, blinis, two sorts of caviar, buckwheat, hatchapuri (a Georgian delicacy like a hot paratha filled with cheese), sour cream, two sorts of cottage cheese, a delicious meat stew called hashi, spring onions, radish, bread and butter, tarhuna (Georgian grasses resembling parsley), mineral water, pear water, tea and coffee, fruit and nuts.

In the Hotel Iveria in Tbilisi, we made another remarkable breakfast. We had been celebrating a belated May Day in the Foreign Currency bar on the previous evening, and arrived for breakfast in a Never Again, Older and Wiser mood. I was there first, with Anatoli Melnikov. As we began a modest snack of mango juice, eggs, bread, and tea, we noticed two young Georgians at a nearby table, drinking cheerfully to the pop of champagne corks. Than which, I always maintain, setting aside Beethoven's Choral Symphony, there is no more inspiring sound. The Georgians saw our smiles and, lo and behold, a complimentary bottle of champagne arrived on our table.

'Must we?' I asked. 'Should we send them one in return?'

'No, no,' said Anatoli. 'Or we shall have an escalation.'

Like dutiful chaps – we were both in a foreign state – we sipped the champagne. Pretty good. Reviving. Elaine appeared. We told her: 'You must help us out.' Elaine had already proved herself sound on the drinks problem, and we had high hopes of finishing our quota without too much damage, particularly when one of the other interpreters, Vladimir Skorodenko, arrived. But then a second bottle of champers materialised.

Come the fourth bottle, we were getting into the swing of things At ten o'clock, we were supposed to be off for a drive, but by then a party was in full swing. All of our group has assembled at the breakfast table, and to each a fresh bottle of champers was delivered. After a consultation with Charles, I nipped off to my room, fetching souvenirs to present to our two Georgian hosts. When I returned, they had joined our table, which was now a-chink with champagne bottles and surrounded by waitresses of cheerfully Byzantine cast who were kept busy filling glasses. Everyone was looking pleased with life.

I had brought along some Silver Jubilee medallions in plastic cases. I presented one each to the Georgians, with a speech of thanks. I raised my glass and offered a toast. 'God Save the Queen!' All drank. It was our finest hour. When was a British sovereign last toasted in Georgia!

It must be said that the Georgians responded gallantly. Their toast was: 'To your three great Englishmen, Turner, James Aldrich, and Newton!'

At each meeting with writers in various towns, the procedure was the same. On entering their club (or Hall of Friendship in the case of Tbilisi), we were introduced, after which all would gather formally round a large table. The talk would be serious (though alleviated considerably, it must be said in parenthesis, by the presence of vodka, cognac, and mineral water on the table) until it was time to make a move for lunch, when conversation would continue more relaxedly and personally. This proved an agreeable way of getting to know people and becoming conversant with local problems, traditions and drinks.

The Georgians have a tradition of toasting under the direction of a *tamadar*, the most honoured person present. In Tbilisi our self-appointed *tamadar* was the novelist Nodar Dimbarza, a rugged man who would have been equally at home in the Maquis or a Rowlandson print. Toasts give everyone a chance to address the table, whilst eliminating the obligation to conduct aimless conversation with the person sitting next to you. A Georgian meal is a riotous affair, once experienced never forgotten.

In all meetings, there were doubtless chaps present who had no love for the opposing side but who were told to make themselves affable. No great understanding was generated between us. We all had our beliefs. Our most pointless moment came in our first meeting, when we were at the offices of the *Literaturna Gazeta* in Moscow. Stallworthy said that East-West understanding could be furthered by increasingly free facilities for tourism. The Chief Editor, A.Chakovsky, replied with a ten-minute oration, an extremely imaginative interpretation of world history since the Revolution. According to him, relationships had been fine between the Soviet Union and the rest of the world until Winston Churchill made his infamous Fulton speech. Then the rot set in.

The other Russians present took Chakovsky's remarks with straight faces. Chakovsky then walked out. Elsewhere, Churchill's Fulton speech was mentioned with disfavour. Memories are long in the East, as well as distorted.

When we met the Leningrad writers – we were more

experienced by then – we sensed that they genuinely welcomed us. In all discussions, each member of our team had something particular to contribute – Elaine Feinstein with her knowledge of Russian poets and poetry, Jon Stallworthy with his knowledge of publishing as well as literature, Charles Osborne with his musical knowledge and unflappable command of cultural mores, and perhaps especially Ted Whitehead ('Gospodin Whitehell'), whose indignation with religion and the nuclear family gave him a clear line of approach to many arguments. And there were insights into both English and Russian literature which Vladimir Skorodenko was always able to provide.

The strangers who faced us across the tables were often introduced as critics. They might have been truck drivers for all I knew; many looked suspiciously unlike, say, David Daiches, and radiated little in the way of cultivation. What sort of criticism is allowed to these critics and officials whose unions are housed in grand old palaces? I returned home knowing nothing of Soviet literature, except what I learned from Elaine, though with my admiration intact for *Gulag Archipelago*, Solzhenitsyn's mighty record of our century.

My role as science fiction writer was useful in our discussions. Osborne held forth about a Canadian poet called Purdy; I had never heard of him. The Russians asked me about Simak. 'Who?' asked Osborne. There were cultural gulfs on our own side as well as between us and the Russians. But poets, with all due respect, are plentiful; a science fiction writer has scarcity value. When we discussed Simak, both sides were interested; the witty lady present, the poet Rimma Kazakova, knew her science fiction and agreed that Simak had begun to repeat himself. His work in the forties was fresh – now the old themes looked threadbare. Two of our interpreters joined in smartly with comments on other stories of Simak's which they had enjoyed: we discussed *City*.

The man with most apparent responsibility for our road show was Melnikov; he had met Osborne previously on a cultural tour in Australia and had also worked as interpreter at the UN in New York. He and I easily established a relationship because of our love of science fiction. Skorodenko is secretary of the All-Union State Library for Foreign Literature; he too had translated science fiction and enjoyed it. Our third interpreter, Victor Pogostin, was a journalist and a Hemingway fan.

The business of being interpreted is intolerable to some people, yet it is a technique which can be mastered. It gives one time to think and be amusing. Victor worked with us, not against us, and proved an excellent interpreter. Whatever other contacts we failed to make – contacts as distinct from expressions of goodwill – we got through to our three travelling companions. The tour would not have been what it was without them. Wherever we met writers, they expressed interest in science fiction and commented on how widely it was enjoyed in the Soviet Union. It is valued there more than here, despite our honourable traditions in the medium from Mary Shelley through Wells to the present, and for one reason in particular. The excitements of science fiction make it readily accessible to the young; at the same time, its content befits it to be a painless purveyor of facts – or of course of socialist propaganda. To use it for such purposes is to treat science fiction in a utilitarian way, debasing it. But, as one of the Leningrad writers said, we shall never understand literary matters in the Soviet Union until we understand that Russia has a long tradition of educational, pedagogical, and non-commercial literature (which has been debased by the purposes of the totalitarian state). It is into this tradition that science fiction fits in the USSR. Inter-stellar voyages always end on Marxist planets. In the United States, by contrast, popular sf springs from the commercial Gernsbackian tradition, with a flimsy educational veneer overlaid. Never the twain shall meet. The only Western sf translated into Russian are stories and novels, such as Pohl and Kornbluth's *The Space Merchants*, which criticise their own culture.

Russian science fiction has to operate within well-defined limits. Generally speaking, it is utopian in tone and the future of the world or the universe must be purely Communist; as men evolve, they naturally foreswear decadent capitalism. Foregone conclusions replace speculation. So even truck-drivers can write it, since stylistic grace is not required. Ingredients of horror and sex which spice much of our science fiction are not to be found in prescriptions for Soviet sf. Which must be why their readers show such eagerness for capitalist excitements.

In this area we come upon one of the cruxes we never resolved. Censorship. Much Anglo-American science fiction is junk, wish-fulfilment about barbarians in rocketships, or evil princesses who enslave galaxies. We could well live without it; then the more ambitious reaches of science fiction might be better received. But, after all, we in the West have settled for an open system; if you can get it into print, okay, the rest is up to the guy with the spare buck in his pocket. He must decide. In the Soviet Union, they order these things differently. They have no equivalent to *Metal Shagbags of Bor*, no gutter-press. They have censorship instead. The ordinary citizen has no power of decision.

The Leningrad writers were prepared to discuss the question of censorship. With Whitehead's prompting, they talked about how much — or rather how little — sexual relations were a permissible subject for a novel. Taking a deep breath, one of them told us that *Literaturna Gazeta* had just published an article declaring that journalists led novelists in airing such matters as the problems of unmarried mothers, and that novelists should be bolder. Everything is served up as a 'problem'; 'problem' is a word you frequently hear in East Europe.

Optimism is public, pessimism private. As long as an official cult of optimism prevails, it is difficult to see how serious social questions can be discussed with honesty, if they can be discussed at all. After only a fortnight's trip, it would be absurd to make sweeping judgements on subjects as complex as politics and literature; the Soviets must solve their own internal problems, just as Britain must solve its problems, however much we may hope for co-operation from the USA, West Germany, or the IMF. One does, in some of the unspoken things we encountered, catch a glimpse of a monstrous being, bound hand and foot, struggling to express itself. In such circumstances, the creature may not be open to rational arguments; and I believe that the best thing our group of five achieved was to make it clear that we spoke for ourselves and often disagreed with each other without being afraid of disagreement.

My experience as a cultural totem in the USSR has at least brought my stereotypes up to date. As the Soviets think of England as still swathed in Dickensian fog, I had thought of

Moscow as a grey place full of hordes swathed in shapeless coats, à la fifties newsreels. At the Tananka Theatre, where we talked with the distinguished producer Lubimov, the crowd was dressed much like an English one. The sprawling centre of Moscow (capitalist land-rates would have made for more compactness) proclaims itself the heart of an empire; one cannot help contrasting it with the poverty of Poland.

We met no dissidents. It proved very difficult to meet friends. Three friends in particular I wanted to see; but they never appeared and I could get no word of or to them, although I had written to them and given their names to the Arts Council beforehand. Only one old friend and colleague showed up at our hotel.

One could easily drone on about seeing fights, drunks and prostitutes on the Moscow streets. The same things may be encountered over here, although we do not pretend they do not exist; such debating points are petty. The imperfections of all societies may be ascribed to the fact that human beings have enjoyed only a brief tenure of the Earth and have a lot to learn, over the next few million years, about the relationship of the individual with society and the state. Those of us who, amid the storms of our dark and primitive century, enjoy the fortune of a civilised constitution are few. We don't know our fortune, and allow enemies to tunnel away at it. If, in addition, we have the privilege to pursue art – that fragile but perpetual cream on the milk – our fortune is doubled, and must be doubly secured.

I hope to return to Leningrad. The Kirov Ballet Theatre is restored to all its Czarist glory (the Soviet Union, like the West, is in the grip of nostalgia and loves all manifestations of the past). We saw a new ballet of *Hamlet* with music by Shervinski, powerfully performed – though Hamlet without that majestic flow of words is reduced to a mixed-up teenager, as humans without free speech become robots. Without tongues, Gertrude and Claudius turn out rather well, heroine and hero of the piece.

Of course we had a canter through the Hermitage. One needs a week there, on roller-skates. The Impressionists are particularly recommended. That room full of golden Gauguins . . .

And in Moscow, there is the Trechykov Museum, devoted to Russian and Soviet paintings, where nineteenth-century genre pictures sustain great energy and give one a fresh understanding

of traditional Russian novelists. I would be glad to go through
the gallery at a slower pace.

We returned to Moscow from Leningrad on the midnight
train, the Red Arrow, a magnificent all-sleeper, arriving at six
thirty in the morning, as Moscow began to go back to work. In
our comfortable hotel a Russian friend asked us anxiously, 'And
nobody hurt you? Nobody harmed you?' No, nobody hurt us,
nobody harmed us.

The idea of the cultural exchange originated between Charles
Osborne and Yevgeni Yevtoshenko. Yevtoshenko greeted us at
the airport on our arrival and gave us a dinner that evening in
the Moscow Writers' Club. On our lasting evening, before flying
home, we met him again, a large talkative man very conscious of
the magic of his name, a star in his own right. He made a long
rambling speech about better understanding and the continued
existence of Czarist cockroaches; by way of return, Jon read a
bottle-shaped poem. I preferred the poem.

The days of the tour were crowded, apart from the sogginess
in Borzomi. One of my most vivid memories is of the morning
when we were due to fly back from Georgia to Leningrad. I
woke at five a.m. and padded on to my balcony. The air was
warm, with a suspicion of dawn in the sky. Tbilisi lay in the bowl
of its hills, bisected by its muddy river. Hundreds of dim lights
burned in its anonymous dwellings. A cock was crowing. I
might have been in Macedonia.

Lugging my case, I went down, receiving on the way the
memorial address to John Galsworthy from the floor-lady. The
great marble floor was deserted. Stallworthy appeared. We were
ready, for once, before the cars. He and I took a walk along the
back streets of Tbilisi. The houses slept, the trees blossomed.
Cats stretched on wood balconies. A comfortable permanent
shabbiness prevailed. Turning back, we saw the bulk of the
Iveria looming.

The Chaikas arrived as we reached the hotel steps. We
climbed in, we were off. The driver switched on his radio as we
moved through the suburbs, where bent old women swept streets
and pavements. Radio Georgia was just opening up; the
national anthem was played. It was six a.m. One more of the
world's stack of days was getting into gear.

A Swim in Sumatra

'We are about to land at Polonia Airport,' the nice Singapore Airlines hostess told us. 'Please fasten your safety belts and try not to smoke.'

Standing in the muggy heat waiting for Immigration, passport in hand, I looked about and decided that Polonia Airport at least had changed very little. This was the very building through which I had passed to climb aboard a Dakota for home over three weeks ago. I had never expected to see Sumatra again; yet here I was, and really in no worse nick than the old building.

Change showed as soon as we left the airport gates. The city of Medan was all around us, its inhabitants calling for taxis excitedly as if those vehicles had been invented that very day. Once the airport had stood out in the wild countryside, and monkeys had sported among the rusting Zero fighters beside its single runway.

Sumatra is the fourth largest island on the globe, and the most interesting. It is over a thousand miles long, nearly as big as Spain, and spitted neatly through its centre by the equator like a *satay* on a stick. It has somehow managed to sink below British consciousness entirely, perhaps lost under the haze of an abstraction labelled Indonesia. Sumatra, like Burma, found new owners a generation ago, since when both countries have scarcely been heard of again.

The British were better informed regarding the East when we went about it as conquerors and travellers and explorers, rather than as infrequent tourists. We commanded much of the trade of Sumatra's west coast during the eighteenth century while, in the Napoleonic Wars, the entire island passed briefly into our hands. The great early history of Sumatra is written by an Englishman, William Marsden. Following World War II, also,

the island was taken over by the British. I was one of that occupying force, and spent a year there.

Thirty-one years later, I found a chance to return. By one of
those concatenations of circumstance which we find mysterious,
the opportunity arose immediately after my publishers,
Weidenfeld and Nicolson, accepted a novel which is my
fictionalised version of that period. Returning to England from
Sumatra all those years ago, I nursed the determination to set
down what I had experienced. That determination shaped the
novelist in me, although much time and many abandoned
manuscript drafts lay between my return home and what was
eventually published as *A Rude Awakening*.

Happy and amazed to be going back, I joined in Singapore a
small package tour consisting entirely of Singaporeans —
Chinese, Malay, and Tamils.

Singapore, that glittering twenty-first century sewing-
machine, the computer with an oriental heart, the tropical
paradise of commerce, the gourmet's, the photographer's, the
voluptuary's, the trader's, the scholar's mechanised Mecca, that
hellish Eden where the succulent travel poster brag 'Never Below Thirty Degrees'. Singapore: sweet-smelling, autocratic,
clean, clear as crystal, sharp as a kris! And only an hour's flight
from Singapore is that other city, Medan, Sumatra's capital.

After the war, after Dutch rule, after the Japanese invasion,
during British occupation, Medan was a shadowy place were
men in vests and sarongs stood against pillars and looked across
deserted streets to a better future. Such wheeled traffic as there
was consisted of delapidated army vehicles. Traders traded in
old things. Everything was worn, used, or travelled over and
over, as in a vast prisoner-of-war camp, where no item is renew-
able.

Progress has arrived in Medan. The city has boiled over,
become vastly more populous. I have never been in a more noisy
city, not even in Italy in the cacophonous dawn of transistors
and Hondas. Medan houses 1.8 million inhabitants now, and
every one of them rides a vicious two- or three-wheeled item of
traffic whose accelerator is linked electronically to the hooter.
The climate is hot and muggy, with flavoursome lead and
carbon monoxide additives. Agitation and stupefaction mate.

Every country has its Great Good Place, its needful dream of
a better spot almost within reach. As British shopkeepers dream
of the Costa Brava, Swedes of Copenhagen, or the clerks in
Brazilian cities of Bahia's beaches, so the dwellers in Medan
dream of Lake Toba.

It was the power of that dream which took me back to
Sumatra. I did not so much wish to re-visit the places I had
known as to see unknown Toba, of which I had so often been
told by Dutch and Chinese friends in the old days.

As one drives into the mountains from the plains about
Medan, the world becomes tremendous again. Jungle returns,
savage and restful, and, at a picturesque spot called Gundaling,
there you can photograph the great volcanoes which form part
of the Barisan chain, still fuming sulphurous breath, preparing
the visitor for Toba itself.

Gundaling came by its name in a way which re-creates much
of Europe's and the East's unrecorded experience of one
another, through love. The European fell in love with the native
girl from Brastagi. They used to meet in secret on this hill. But
he was recalled to Europe, never to return to her despite his
promises. And the only English words she could say were 'Gone
darling, gone.' Hence 'Gundaling'. Lies sometimes enshine truth,
and this was the lie our guide told us as we climbed towards
Lake Toba.

First sight of the lake was all that could be hoped for. Sunlight
rose in columns from its forsaken shores and hillsides.

'There's the Lost World!' we said. Only to the imagination
was that gigantic scale familiar. Even our guide, Anthony
Pardede, was excited.

The tour drove into Parapat, a small town of five thousand
people, built at the one place on the lake where the cliffs are not
impossibly steep. Nine of us – the whole tour – stood by the
water's edge, looking across that liquid shield. Toba is an inland
sea, fifty-five miles long, six times the size of Lake Maggiore. Its
sides are steep and tall. It forms the carcass of a gigantic
volcano which erupted about a million years ago, throwing out
debris which may be seen today in the form of tuffs, dotting
Malaysia, over two hundred miles away. As the cauldron
cooled, it filled with water.

When Toba blew its top, the effect must have been more devastating even than Krakatoa in 1883. Krakatoa is on the same fault line, in the Sunda Strait between Sumatra and Java. When Krakatoa erupted, sound waves travelled three thousand miles, while the oceanic disturbances reached Cape Horn, almost nine thousand miles away. Doubtless, the sound and fury of Toba travelled farther, and Neanderthal men and women looked at each other in their caves and muttered, 'It's all this new-fangled fire they're using nowadays – I said it would bring trouble.'

A tall-sided island stands in the middle of Toba, mysterious Samosir – Samosir, a flat-topped volcanic plug which, at 324 square miles, is considerably larger than the Isle of Wight (147 square miles) or Singapore Island (224 square miles), not to mention being more remote than either. Sumatra is the Africa of South-East Asia, Toba its eye. Samosir is the pupil.

My Singapore friends were a bit put out. 'These people have done nothing to Toba,' they said. 'They should hand this place over to the Singaporeans. With Singapore capital and know-how, we could get this place going – build first-class inter-national, hotels on the cliffs with superb views in all directions, piers into the lake, water-skiing – that surface is perfect – a fleet of cruisers with bars to take tourists over to the island. You could get your investment back in five years. The local people really need employment. It would do them a favour. In ten years, there would be schools here, then a university, and the whole economy revived. Poor devils, they have nothing at present. Nothing.'

And so on. But after our evening meal at the Hotel Atsari, by the lakeside, they were more relaxed. They smoked their cigarettes and said, 'Well, anyhow, it's nice to be out of the rat-race for a few days, isn't it?'

There was music, singing and dancing for us. Batak songs are tuneful with something like yodelling in them. The effect of living in mountains, I suppose. Close harmony and humour feature strongly, and the costumes are bright.

'These chaps could make their fortune in the night-clubs in Singapore,' said the Singaporeans in admiration.

The Bataks are fine people, the women beautiful, the men

handsome. Most of them wear the same bright colours you can buy in the tourist bazaar in Parapat. The manager of the hotel, who doubled as a PRO, told us that he earned 20,000 Rupiah per month, which is about £25 sterling. He worked from nine in the morning until ten or twelve at night. He was full of fun, with good English and Malay, as well as smatterings of Dutch and Mandarin. When we caught the little steamer across to Samosir, the PRO man came too, sitting in the bows with Anthony, singing and accompanying himself on the guitar.

We put in three times along the coast of Samosir. This is the white man's tropical dream, the snare that caught Gauguin, with palm trees leaning out over their still reflections, high-prowed huts among the palms about to set sail over the water, sandy beaches, water-buffaloes, naked kids, statuesque natives, leprosy, and the clock stopped always at some mysterious teatime in the late Stone Age.

At Tomok, we walked along a path where stalls had been set up to catch the once-a-week tourists. Our Chinese bank manager commented with delight on the poor selection of souvenirs. Who needs a complex Batak calendar? Not even the Bataks, apparently. Behind the stalls stands a village of massive carved Batak houses, all in neat lines, their tremendous curved roofs like the sails of a fleet waiting for a tide. All is not as it was. Many of the palm fibre roofs have been replaced with corrugated iron; they gleam in the sun like silver when new, become red as embers when old. Only a prejudiced eye could fail to see beauty in the new material.

Close to the village is a grove of trees, the trunks of which have flowed like petrified lava. The trees include a hariara, or sacred oak, which protects the sarcophagus of King Sidabutar. We sat about on gnarled roots while Anthony, our guide, held forth about King Sidabutar.

My conviction is that those complex Batak calendars are tokens of the way in which time travels differently through the consciousnesses contained in Batak, Chinese, and Western heads. It is as hard to translate time as to translate language; I believe that I am only approximately right (or approximately wrong) in stating that the Batak tribes who occupy the highlands of Sumatra arrived there about five thousand years ago; having been driven south from what is now Burma and Thailand; and the first tribe to reach Toba was led by Sidabutar in the fourth century AD (there goes the Christian calendar). He did well for his people. It is magnificent to lie as he does under the tall unfolding trees.

I swam in the lake a mile or so from where the king sleeps. Old ambitions were assuaged. As I swam, I knew. This was what I had left England for, had returned to Sumatra for, after thirty years; this is why I had gone to all that trouble and expense. I wanted a swim in Lake Toba. I swam in the sun, quietly, slowly, in a state of bliss. It was worth everything.

Only a few yards out from shore, you dive down, down as far as you can go before your lungs erupt. Nothing. No sign of bottom. It's gone. Toba has no bed, only bowels. Soundings have recorded depths of 450 metres, then the equipment gave out. Surprisingly, no plesiosaurs live in the lake, not even poisonous snakes or fish. Perfectly safe, just bottomless as a childhood dream.

You can stay on Samosir; for instance at the agreeable Tuk Tuk Hotel for about £6 per day, or right by the wharf in Ambarita village, at a place called Rokhandy's Accommodation. Rokhandy's costs about seventy pence per night, and European and Australian hippies lounge there on the balcony like guanas, smoking *ganja* and gazing at motes in the middle distance.

Back at Parapat next morning, I strolled forth early to look at Samosir, distant, blue, across the silvered water. My Chinese friend Tan already stood there, singing to himself. 'Morning has broken, like the first morning . . .' We both had the ambition to get back when humanly possible. More time, more saving, more planning, more hope, more visas . . .

Of course the area will all be developed. A spectacular lake, lying on the equator, three thousand feet above sea level? The very prospect makes cement-mixers purr in their sleep. The Western view that believes such places can be preserved (for them) is patronising or, if not patronising, too abstemious for the present stage of human development. Give us another million years and then try again. The Chinese, fortified by their tremendous success story in Singapore, are right — or, if not right, bound to win.

Population pressures alone demand the engorgement of any likely refuges from crowded cities – and Toba is only a lunch-break away from three million hard-working Singaporeans. But just at present, for a few more years, a few more hesitations, the trampling hooves of South-East Asia tourists cut their tracks across Bali, rather than Sumatra and Lake Toba. King Sidabutar still sleeps secure under his enfolding tree.

Index